The Basics of IT Audit

The Basics of IT Audit
Purposes, Processes, and Practical Information

Stephen D. Gantz

Technical Editor
Steve Maske

ELSEVIER

AMSTERDAM • BOSTON • HEIDELBERG • LONDON
NEW YORK • OXFORD • PARIS • SAN DIEGO
SAN FRANCISCO • SINGAPORE • SYDNEY • TOKYO
Syngress is an imprint of Elsevier

SYNGRESS.

Acquiring Editor: *Steve Elliot*
Editorial Project Manager: *Benjamin Rearick*
Project Manager: *Malathi Samayan*
Designer: *Matthew Limbert*

Syngress is an imprint of Elsevier
225 Wyman Street, Waltham, MA 02451, USA

Library of Congress Cataloging-in-Publication Data
Gantz, Stephen D.
  The basics of IT audit: purposes, processes, and practical information / Stephen D. Gantz.
    pages cm
  Includes bibliographical references and index.
  ISBN 978-0-12-417159-6 (pbk.)
  1. Information technology—Auditing. 2. Computer security.
3. Computer networks--Security measures. I. Title.
  T58.5.G37 2013
  004.068'1--dc23

                                                                        2013036148

British Library Cataloguing-in-Publication Data
A catalogue record for this book is available from the British Library

For information on all Syngress publications,
visit our website at store.elsevier.com/Syngress

ISBN: 978-0-12-417159-6

Dedicated to my wife Reneé, my son Henry, and my daughters Claire and Gillian, without whose support and forbearance I would not have been able to devote the necessary time and energy into this project.

Contents

Acknowledgments

I would like to acknowledge the very capable support provided by members of the Syngress/Elsevier team in bringing this project to completion, particularly including Steve Elliot and Ben Rearick. Thanks also go to Steven Maske for his helpful feedback, comments, and technical edits on this book. I am also grateful for the guidance and constructive criticism on my writing provided by Dr. Thomas Mierzwa, who served as my dissertation adviser as I completed my doctorate in management shortly before beginning work on this book.

Work in information technology (IT) characterizes my entire career—as a consultant, as a software and security architect, and as an educator and author. I appreciate the many professional opportunities I have received during that time, including my initial exposure to fraud detection and forensic investigation from Malcolm Sparrow more than 15 years ago and subsequent experience in IT auditing and information security since that time. I have been fortunate to work for many managers and executives who have encouraged my continued career development and self-directed projects and writing initiatives. I am especially grateful for the leadership and support of my current management team, including Michele Kang, Davis Foster, Aaron Daniels, Tom Stepka, and Sean Gallagher, who collectively helped in providing a dynamic and engaging work environment and the opportunity to challenge myself on many types of internal and client-facing projects.

About the Author

Dr Stephen D. Gantz (CISSP-ISSAP, CEH, CGEIT, CRISC, CIPP/G, C|CISO) is an information security and information technology (IT) consultant with over 20 years of experience in security and privacy management, enterprise architecture, systems development and integration, and strategic planning. He currently holds an executive position with a health information technology services firm primarily serving federal and state government customers. He is also an associate professor of Information Assurance in the Graduate School at University of Maryland University College (UMUC) and an adjunct lecturer in the Health Information Technology program of the Catholic University of America's School of Library and Information Science. He maintains a security-focused web site and blog at http://www.securityarchitecture.com.

His security and privacy expertise spans program management, security architecture, policy development and enforcement, risk assessment, and regulatory compliance with major legislation such as FISMA, HIPAA, and the Privacy Act. His industry experience includes health, financial services, higher education, consumer products, and manufacturing, but since 2000 his work has focused on security and other information resources management functions in state and federal government agencies and in private sector industries responsible for critical infrastructure. He holds a Doctor of Management degree from UMUC, where his dissertation focused on trust and distrust in inter-organizational networks, alliances, and other cooperative relationships. He also earned a master's degree in public policy from the Kennedy School of Government at Harvard University and a bachelor's degree from Harvard. He currently resides in Arlington, Virginia with his wife Reneé and children Henry, Claire, and Gillian.

About the Technical Editor

Steven Maske (CISA, CISSP) is an information security professional with over 12 years in the information technology (IT) industry. As the lead security engineer for a Fortune 1000 company he designs, develops, and tests information security solutions and establishes policies, procedures, and controls to ensure regulatory compliance. He is responsible for identifying and managing risks and overseeing IT projects and strategic initiatives. He has previous experience as a consultant where he performed over 150 vulnerability assessments, penetration tests, and IT audits.

He is an active member of the security community and can be found on Twitter as @ITSecurity or via his blog, http://SecurityRamblings.com.

Trademarks

Institute of Internal Auditors trademarks: Certified Internal Auditor (CIA®), Certified Government Auditing Professional (CGAP®), Certified Financial Services Auditor (CFSA®), Certification in Control Self-Assessment (CCSA®), Certification in Risk Management Assurance (CRMA®), International Professional Practices Framework (IPPF®)

International Council of Electronic Commerce Consultants EC-Council trademarks: Certified Ethical Hacker (C|EH™), Certified Hacking Forensic Investigator (C|HFI™)

International Information Systems Security Certification Consortium certifications: Certified Information Systems Security Professional (CISSP®), Systems Security Certified Professional (SSCP®), Certified Accreditation Professional (CAP®), Certified Secure Software Lifecycle Professional (CSSLP®)

ISACA® trademarks: Certified Information Systems Auditor (CISA®), Certified Information Security Manager (CISM®), Certified in Risk and Information Systems Control (CRISC®), Certified in the Governance of Enterprise Information Technology (CGEIT®), Control Objectives for Information and Related Technology (COBIT®)

Other trademarks:

American Society for Quality (ASQ®)

Certified Computer Examiner (CCE®)

International Organization for Standardization (ISO®)

Information Technology Infrastructure Library (ITIL®)

Projects in Controlled Environments, version 2 (PRINCE2®)

Project Management Institute (PMI®)

Project Management Body of Knowledge (PMBOK®)

Introduction

INFORMATION IN THIS CHAPTER:

- Introduction to IT auditing
- Purpose and rationale for this book
- Intended use
- Key audiences
- Structure and content of the book
- Summary descriptions of each chapter

Introduction to IT auditing

An audit is a systematic, objective examination of one or more aspects of an organization that compares what the organization does to a defined set of criteria or requirements. Information technology (IT) auditing examines processes, IT assets, and controls at multiple levels within an organization to determine the extent to which the organization adheres to applicable standards or requirements. Virtually, all organizations use IT to support their operations and the achievement of their mission and business objectives. This gives organizations a vested interest in ensuring that their use of IT is effective, that IT systems and processes operate as intended, and that IT assets and other resources are efficiently allocated and appropriately protected. IT auditing helps organizations understand, assess, and improve their use of controls to safeguard IT, measure and correct performance, and achieve objectives and intended outcomes. IT auditing consists of the use of formal audit methodologies to examine IT-specific processes, capabilities, and assets and their role in enabling an organization's business processes. IT auditing also addresses IT components or capabilities that support other domains subject to auditing, such as financial management and accounting, operational performance, quality assurance, and governance, risk management, and compliance (GRC).

IT audits are performed both by internal auditors working for the organization subject to audit and external auditors hired by the organization. The processes and procedures followed in internal and external auditing are often quite similar, but the roles of the audited organization and its personnel are markedly different. The audit criteria—the standards or requirements against which an organization is compared during an audit—also vary between internal and external audits and for audits of different types or conducted for different purposes. Organizations often engage in IT audits to satisfy legal or regulatory requirements, assess the operational effectiveness of business processes, achieve certification against specific standards, demonstrate compliance with policies, rules, or standards, and identify opportunities for improvement in the quality of business processes, products, and services. Organizations have different sources of motivation for each type of audit and different goals, objectives, and expected outcomes. This book explains all of these aspects of IT auditing, describes the establishment of organizational audit programs and the process of conducting audits, and identifies the most relevant standards, methodologies, frameworks, and sources of guidance for IT auditing.

Purpose and rationale

The use of IT auditing is increasingly common in many organizations, to validate the effective use of controls to protect IT assets and information or as an element of GRC programs. IT auditing is a specialized discipline not only in its own right, with corresponding standards, methodologies, and professional certifications and experience requirements, but it also intersects significantly with other IT management and operational practices. The subject matter overlap between IT auditing and network monitoring, systems administration, service management, technical support, and information security makes familiarity with IT audit policies, practices, and standards essential for IT personnel and managers of IT operations and the business areas that IT supports. This book provides information about many aspects of IT audits in order to give readers a solid foundation in auditing concepts to help develop an understanding of the important role IT auditing plays in contributing to the achievement of organizational objectives. Many organizations undergo a variety of IT audits, performed by both internal and external auditors, and each often accompanied by different procedures, methods, and criteria. This book tries to highlight the commonalities among audit types while identifying the IT perspectives and characteristics that distinguish financial, operational, compliance, certification, and quality audits.

Intended use

This book describes the practice of IT auditing, including why organizations conduct or are subject to IT audits, different types of audits commonly performed in different organizations, and ways internal and external auditors approach IT audits. It explains many fundamental characteristics of IT audits, the auditors who perform them, and the standards, methodologies, frameworks, and sources of guidance that inform the practice of auditing. This is *not* a handbook for conducting IT audits nor does it provide detailed instructions for performing any of the audit activities mentioned in the book. Auditors or other readers seeking prescriptive guidance on auditing will find references to many useful sources in this book, but should look elsewhere—potentially including the sources referenced below—for audit checklists, protocols, or procedural guidance on different types of IT audits. This book is intended to give organizations and their employees an understanding of what to expect when undergoing IT audits and to explain some key points to consider that help ensure their audit engagements meet their objectives. By covering all major types of IT auditing and describing the primary drivers and contexts for IT audits in most organizations, this book complements more detailed but narrowly focused texts intended to guide or instruct auditors in the step-by-step procedural execution of audits. The following are among recently published books especially relevant to IT auditing:

- *IT Auditing: Using Controls to Protect Information Assets* (2nd edition) by Chris Davis and Mike Schiller emphasizes auditing practices applicable to different types of technologies and system components.
- *Auditor's Guide to IT Auditing* (2nd edition) by Richard Cascarino provides broad coverage of IT audit concepts and practices applicable to information systems, organized and presented in the context of major IT management disciplines.
- *IT Audit, Control, and Security* by Robert Moeller highlights requirements, expectations, and considerations for auditors of IT systems stemming from prominent laws, frameworks, and standards.
- *Information Technology Control and Audit* (4th edition) by Sandra Senft, Frederick Gallegos, and Aleksandra Davis approaches IT auditing drawing largely on practice guidance and governance frameworks defined by ISACA, particularly including COBIT.
- *The Operational Auditing Handbook: Auditing Business and IT Processes* by Andrew Chambers and Graham Rand focuses on operational auditing and uses a process-based approach to describe auditing practices for different organizational functions.
- *The ASQ Auditing Handbook* (4th edition) edited by J.P. Russell offers prescriptive guidance for quality auditors, particularly those following the quality auditor body of knowledge defined by the American Society for Quality (ASQ) and its Certified Quality Auditor Certification Program.

Key audiences

This book provides a treatment of IT auditing that emphasizes breadth rather than depth. Audit professionals engaged in performing IT audits have a variety of standards, guidance, and prescriptive procedures for thoroughly and effectively conducting various types of IT audits. Auditors and other consulting or professional services practitioners who regularly conduct audits may find the information in this book useful as a point of reference, but will likely rely on more detailed, purpose-specific sources to assist them in their work. Auditors are important stakeholders in IT auditing, but only one of many groups involved in IT auditing or affected by how it is carried out. The material in this book is intended primarily to help develop an understanding of auditing purposes and practices to nonauditor groups such as operational and administrative personnel, managers, and IT program and project staff, all of whom may be required to furnish information to or otherwise support external or internal audits in their organizations. It also provides an explanation of IT auditing suitable for practitioners focused on other aspects of IT management or on the performance of functions supported by IT audits such as GRC, quality management, continuous improvement, or information assurance.

Structure and content

This book could not hope to provide, and is not intended to be, a substitute for formal standards, protocols, and practice guidance relevant to IT auditing. What it does offer is a thorough introduction to many aspects of IT auditing and the role of IT audits within the broader context of other major forms of audits. The book is structured in a way that should be equally helpful to readers looking for information on a specific audit-related subject or for those interested in developing a more general understanding of the IT audit discipline. The material in the early chapters focuses on describing why organizations undergo different types of audits and what characteristics distinguish those types of audits from each other. References provided in each chapter, in addition to the information in the last two chapters in the book, should help direct readers to authoritative sources of guidance on various aspects of auditing and to the major standards organizations and professional associations shaping the evolution of the field. This book does not recommend a particular approach or methodology, but instead highlights the similarities among many of the most prominent frameworks, methodologies, processes, and standards in the hope that readers will recognize the basic aspects of IT auditing in any real-world context.

A brief summary of each chapter follows.

Chapter 1: IT Audit Fundamentals

Chapter 1 establishes a foundation for the rest of the material in the book by defining auditing and related key terms and concepts and explaining the nature and rationale for IT auditing in different organizations, differentiating internal from external audits in terms of the reasons and requirements associated with each perspective. It also identifies organizations and contexts that serve as the subject of IT audit activities and describes the individuals and organizations that perform audits.

Chapter 2: Auditing in Context

Chapter 2 emphasizes the practical reality that IT auditing often occurs as a component of a wider-scope audit not limited to IT concerns alone, or a means to support other organizational processes or functions such as GRC, certification, and quality assurance. Audits performed in the context of these broader programs have different purposes and areas of focus than stand-alone IT-centric audits, and offer different benefits and expected outcomes to organizations.

Chapter 3: Internal Auditing

Chapter 3 focuses on internal IT auditing, meaning audits conducted under the direction of an organization's own audit program and typically using auditors who are employees of the organization under examination. This chapter highlights the primary reasons why organizations undergo internal audits, including drivers of mandatory and voluntary audit activities. It also describes some of the benefits and challenges associated with internal auditing and characterizes the role, experience, and career path of internal IT audit personnel.

Chapter 4: External Auditing

Chapter 4 provides a direct contrast to Chapter 3 by addressing external auditing, which bears many similarities to internal auditing but is, by definition, conducted by auditors and audit firms wholly separate from the organization being audited. This chapter identifies the key drivers for external audits, explains the role of internal staff in preparing for and supporting external audits, and describes benefits and challenges often encountered by organizations subject to such audits. Because audited organizations often have to choose their external auditors, the chapter also discusses the process of selecting an auditor, the registration requirements applicable to auditors in many countries, and key auditor qualifications.

Chapter 5: Types of Audits

Chapter 5 offers an overview of the major types of audits organizations undergo, including financial, operational, certification, compliance, and quality audits in addition to IT-specific audits. For each type of audit, the chapter explains characteristics such as audit rationale, areas of focus, suitability for internal and external auditing approaches, applicable standards and guidance, and anticipated outcomes.

Chapter 6: IT Audit Components

The IT domain is too broad to easily address as a whole, whether the topic is auditing, governance, operations, or any other key functions that organizations manage about their IT resources. Chapter 6 breaks down IT and associated controls into different categories—reflecting decomposition approaches commonly used in IT audit methodologies and standards—to differentiate among IT audit activities focused on different IT components. The material in this chapter addresses technical as well as nontechnical categories, describing different technologies and architectural layers, key processes and functions, and aspects of IT programs and projects that are also often subject to audits.

Chapter 7: IT Audit Drivers

Chapter 7 describes key types of external and internal drivers influencing organizations' approaches to IT auditing, including major legal and regulatory requirements as well as motivating factors such as certification, quality assurance, and operational effectiveness. This chapter summarizes the audit-related provisions of major U.S. and international laws governing publicly traded firms and organizations in regulated industries such as financial services, health care, energy, and the public sector. It also explains the motivation provided by internally developed strategies, management objectives, and initiatives on the ways organizations structure their internal audit programs and external audit activities.

Chapter 8: IT Audit Process

The IT audit process description provided in Chapter 8 explains in detail the steps organizations and auditors follow when performing audits. Although there is no single accepted standard process applicable in all contexts, most methodologies, frameworks, standards, and authoritative guidance on auditing share many common activities and process attributes, often traceable to the familiar plan-do-check-act (PDCA) model originally developed for quality improvement purposes. Chapter 8 focuses on the activities falling within the generic process areas of audit planning, audit evidence collection and review, analysis and reporting of findings, and responding to findings by taking corrective action or capitalizing on opportunities for improvement.

Chapter 9: Methodologies and Frameworks

Although the high-level process of auditing is very similar across organizations, industries, audit purposes, and geographies, there is a wide variety of methodologies and control and process frameworks available for organizations and individual auditors to apply when performing audits. Almost all external auditors follow one or more of these approaches and many organizations choose to adopt established methodologies and frameworks as an alternative to developing their own. Chapter 9 presents the best-known and most widely adopted methodologies and frameworks, including those focused explicitly on auditing as well as those intended to support IT governance, IT management, information security, and control assessment.

Chapter 10: Audit-Related Organizations, Standards, and Certifications

There are many standards development bodies and other types of organizations that produce and promote standards relevant to IT auditing and that offer professional certifications for individuals engaged in auditing or related disciplines. Chapter 10 identifies the most prominent organizations and summarizes their contributions to available standards and certifications.

IT Audit Fundamentals

Dependence on information technology (IT) is a characteristic common to virtually all modern organizations. Organizations rely on information and the processes and enabling technology needed to use and effectively manage information. This reliance characterizes public and private sector organizations, regardless of mission, industry, geographic location, or organization type. IT is critical to organizational success, operating efficiency, competitiveness, and even survival, making imperative the need for organizations to ensure the correct and effective use of IT. In this context, it is important that resources are efficiently allocated, that IT functions at a sufficient level of performance and quality to effectively support the business, and that information assets are adequately secured consistent with the risk tolerance of the organization. Such assets must also be governed effectively, meaning that they operate as intended, work correctly, and function in a way that complies with applicable regulations and standards. IT auditing can help organizations achieve all of these objectives.

Auditing IT differs in significant ways from auditing financial records, general operations, or business processes. Each of these auditing disciplines, however, shares a common foundation of auditing principles, standards of practice, and high-level processes and activities. IT auditing is also a component of other major types of auditing, as illustrated conceptually in Figure 1.1. To the extent that financial and accounting practices in audited organizations use IT, financial audits must address technology-based controls and their contribution to effectively supporting internal financial controls. Operational audits examine the effectiveness of one or more business processes or organizational functions and the efficient use of resources in support of organizational goals and objectives. Information systems and other technology represent key resources often included in the scope of operational audits. Quality audits apply to many aspects of organizations, including business processes or other operational focus areas, IT management, and information security

FIGURE 1.1

IT auditing has much in common with other types of audit and overlaps in many respects with financial, operational, and quality audit practices.

programs and practices. A common set of auditing standards, principles, and practices informs these types of auditing, centered as they are on an organization's internal controls. IT auditing, however, exhibits a greater breadth and variety than financial, operational, or quality auditing alone in the sense that it not only represents an element of other major types of audits but also comprises many different approaches, subject matter areas, and perspectives corresponding to the nature of an organization's IT environment, governance model, and audit objectives.

What is IT auditing?

An *audit* is often defined as an independent examination, inspection, or review. While the term applies to evaluations of many different subjects, the most frequent usage is with respect to examining an organization's financial statements or accounts. In contrast to conventional dictionary definitions and sources focused on the accounting connotation of audit, definitions used by broad-scope audit standards bodies and in IT auditing contexts neither constrain nor presume the subject to which an audit applies. For example, the International Organization for Standardization (ISO) guidelines on auditing use the term *audit* to mean a "systematic, independent and documented process for obtaining audit evidence and evaluating it objectively to determine the extent to which the audit criteria are fulfilled" [1] and the Information Technology Infrastructure Library (ITIL) glossary defines *audit* as "formal inspection and verification to check whether a standard or set of guidelines is being followed, that records are accurate, or that efficiency and effectiveness targets are being met [2]." Such general interpretations are well suited to IT auditing, which comprises a wide range of standards, requirements, and other audit criteria corresponding to processes, systems, technologies, or entire organizations subject to IT audits.

> It is important to use "IT" to qualify *IT audit* and distinguish it from the more common financial connotation of the word *audit* used alone. Official definitions emphasizing the financial context appear in many standards and even in the text of the Sarbanes–Oxley Act, which defines audit to mean "the examination of financial statements of any issuer" of securities (i.e., a publicly traded company) [3]. The Act also uses both the terms *evaluation* and *assessment* when referring to required audits of companies' internal control structure and procedures. When developing IT audit plans and other materials that reference standards, principles, processes, or other prescriptive guidance for conducting IT audits, it helps to be specific, particularly if the audience for such documentation extends beyond IT auditors or other IT-focused personnel.

The definitions cited above also emphasize a characteristic that differentiates audits from other types of evaluations or assessments by referring to explicit criteria that provide the basis for comparison between what is expected or required in an organization and what is actually observed or demonstrated through evidence. Words like *assessment*, *evaluation*, and *review* are often used synonymously with the term *audit* and while it is certainly true that an audit is a type of evaluation, some specific characteristics of auditing distinguish it from concepts implied by the use of more general terms. An audit always has a baseline or standard of reference against which the subject of the audit is compared. An audit is not intended to check on the use of best practices or (with the possible exception of operational audits) to see if opportunities exist to improve or optimize processes or operational characteristics. Instead, there is a set standard providing a basis for comparison established prior to initiating the audit. Auditors compare the subjects of the audit—processes, systems, components, software, or organizations overall—explicitly to that predefined standard to determine if the subject satisfies the criteria. Audit determinations tend to be more binary than results of other types of assessments or evaluations, in the sense that a given item either meets or fails to meet applicable requirements—auditors often articulate audit findings in terms of controls' *conformity* or *nonconformity* to criteria [1]. Audit findings identify deficiencies where what the auditor observes or discovered through analysis of audit evidence differs from what was expected or required such that the audit subject cannot satisfy a requirement. In contrast, a typical assessment might have a quantitative (i.e., score) or qualitative scale of ratings (e.g., poor, fair, good, excellent) and produce findings and recommendations for improvement in areas observed to be operating effectively or those considered deficient. Because auditors work from an established standard or set of criteria, IT audits using comprehensive or well thought-out requirements may be less subjective and more reliable than other types of evaluations or assessments.

It is impossible to overstate the importance of the baseline to an effective audit. In both external and internal audits, an auditor's obligation is to fully understand the baseline and use that knowledge to accurately and objectively compare the subject of the audit to the criteria specified in the baseline. The use of formally specified audit criteria also means that an organization anticipating or undergoing an audit should not be surprised by the nature of the audit, what it covers, or what requirements the organization is expected to meet. External audits—especially those driven by regulatory mandates or certification standards—follow procedures and apply criteria that should be available and just as well known to organizations being audited as by the external auditors conducting the audits. Internal audits follow strategies, plans, and procedures dictated by the organization itself in its audit program, so internal auditors and the business units, system owners, project managers, operations staff, and personnel subject to or supporting audits should also be familiar with the audit criteria to be used.

Like other types of audits, IT audits compare actual organizational processes, practices, capabilities, or controls against a predefined baseline. For an external audit, the audit baseline is usually defined in rules or legal or regulatory requirements related to the purpose and objectives of the external audit. For internal audits, organizations often have some flexibility to define their own baseline or to adopt standards, frameworks, or requirements specified by other organizations, including those described in Chapters 9 and 10.

Internal controls

External and internal IT audits share a common focus: the internal controls implemented and maintained by the organization being audited. Controls are a central element of IT management, defined and referenced through standards, guidance, methodologies, and frameworks addressing business processes; service delivery and management; information systems design, implementation, and operation; information security; and IT governance. Leading sources of IT governance and IT auditing guidance distinguish between *internal control* and *internal controls*. The Committee of Sponsoring Organizations of the Treadway Commission (COSO) defines *internal control* as a process "designed to provide reasonable assurance regarding the achievement of objectives" including operational effectiveness and efficiency, reliable reporting, and legal and regulatory compliance. In this context, a *control* is "a policy or procedure that is part of internal control," the result of policies and procedures designed to effect control [4]. The IT Governance Institute offers a definition consistent with COSO: "policies, plans and procedures, and organizational structures designed to provide reasonable assurance that business objectives will be achieved and undesired events will be prevented or detected and corrected [5]." This makes for a somewhat circular and potentially confusing formulation in which internal controls are discrete elements applied within a management process of control in support of an organizational objective of establishing and maintaining control.

From the perspective of planning and performing IT audits, internal controls represent the substance of auditing activities, as the controls are the items that are examined, tested, analyzed, or otherwise evaluated. Organizations often implement large numbers of internal controls intended to achieve a wide variety of control objectives. Categorizing internal controls facilitates the documentation, tracking, and management of the diverse sets of controls present in many organizations. The prevalent control categorization schemes used in internal control frameworks, IT audit, and assessment guidance, and applicable legislation classify controls by purpose, by functional type, or both. Purpose-based categories include preventive, detective, and corrective controls, where organizations use preventive controls to try to keep unintended or undesirable events from occurring, detective controls to discover when such things have happened, and corrective controls to respond or recover after unwanted events occur. Controls are further separated by function into administrative, technical, and physical control types, as illustrated in Figure 1.2. Administrative controls include organizational policies, procedures, and plans that

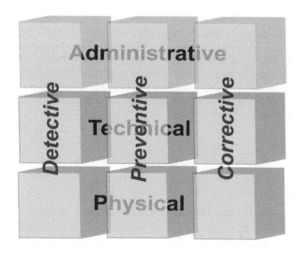

FIGURE 1.2

Internal and external IT audits focus primarily on internal controls, differentiated by purpose and type; different auditing methods apply when evaluating different kinds of controls.

Table 1.1 Examples of Internal Controls Categorized by Type and Purpose

	Preventive	Detective	Corrective
Administrative	Acceptable use policy; Security awareness training	Audit log review procedures; IT audit program	Disaster recovery plan; Plan of action and milestones
Technical	Application firewall; Logical access control	Network monitoring; Vulnerability scanning	Incident response center; Data and system backup
Physical	Locked doors and server cabinets; Biometric access control	Video surveillance; Burglar alarm	Alternate processing facility; Sprinkler system

specify what an organization intends to do to safeguard the integrity of its operations, information, and other assets. Technical controls are the mechanisms—including technologies, operational procedures, and resources—implemented and maintained by an organization to achieve its control objectives. Physical controls comprise the provisions an organization has in place to maintain, keep available, and restrict or monitor access to facilities, storage areas, equipment, and information assets. Table 1.1 provides example of internal controls for each combination of control type and purpose.

Some sources use different control categorizations, such as the management, operational, and technical control types defined by the U.S. National Institute of Standards and Technology (NIST) in its information security guidance for federal government agencies [6]. NIST uses *operational* to distinguish controls implemented and performed by people. In many auditing contexts, however, "operational controls" is used to mean "internal controls" so to avoid confusion auditors and organizations prefer the more prevalent administrative–technical–physical categorization.

What to audit

Just as financial, quality, and operational audits can be executed entity-wide or at different levels within an organization, IT audits can evaluate entire organizations, individual business units, mission functions and business processes, services, systems, infrastructure, or technology components. As described in detail in Chapter 5, different types of IT audits and the approaches used to conduct them may consider internal controls from multiple perspectives by focusing on the IT elements

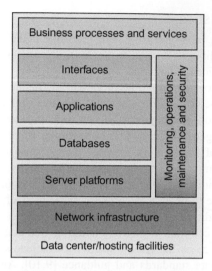

FIGURE 1.3

Whether performed from a technical, operational, business process, or organization-wide perspective, IT audits typically consider internal controls associated with different IT components or architectural layers and common processes supporting technologies across multiple layers.

to which the controls correspond or on controls implemented in the context of processes performed or services delivered by an organization. Irrespective of the overall IT auditing method employed, IT audits invariably address one or more technology-related subject areas, including controls related to the following:

- Data centers and other physical facilities
- Network infrastructure
- Telecommunications
- Operating systems
- Databases
- Storage
- Virtualized servers and environments
- Outsourced services and operations
- Web and application servers
- Software and packaged applications
- User and application interfaces
- Mobile devices

Internal IT control elements can be audited in isolation or together, although even when a given IT audit focuses narrowly on one aspect of IT, auditors need to consider the broader technical, operational, and environmental contexts, as reflected in Figure 1.3. IT audits also address internal control processes and functions, such as operations and maintenance procedures, business continuity and disaster recovery, incident response, network and security monitoring, configuration management, system development, and project management.

IT audit characteristics

Definitions, standards, methodologies, and guidance agree on key characteristics associated with IT audits and derived from Generally Accepted Auditing Standards (GAAS) and international standards and codes of practice. These characteristics include the need for auditors to be proficient in conducting the types of audits they perform; adherence by auditors and the organizations they represent to ethical and professional codes of conduct; and an insistence on auditor independence [7,8]. Proficiency in general principles, procedures, standards, and expectations cuts across all types of auditing and is equally applicable to IT auditing contexts. Depending on the complexity and the particular characteristics of the IT controls or the operating environment undergoing an audit, auditors may require specialized knowledge or expertise to be able to correctly and effectively examine the controls included in the IT audit scope. Codes of conduct, practice, and ethical behavior are, like proficiency, common across all auditing domains, emphasizing principles and objectives such as integrity, objectivity, competency, confidentiality, and adherence to appropriate standards and guidance [9,10]. Auditor independence—a principle applicable to both internal and external audits and auditors—means that the individuals who conduct audits and the organizations they represent have no financial interest in and are otherwise free from conflicts of interest regarding the organizations they audit so as to remain objective and impartial. While auditor independence is a central tenet in GAAS and international auditing standards, auditor independence provisions mandated in the Sarbanes–Oxley Act and enforced by the Securities and Exchange Commission (SEC) legally require independence for audits of publicly traded corporations.

Why audit?

Performing and supporting IT audits and managing an IT audit program are time-, effort-, and personnel-intensive activities, so in an age of cost-consciousness and competition for resources, it is reasonable to ask why organizations undertake IT auditing. The rationale for external audits is often clearer and easier to understand—publicly traded companies and organizations in many industries are subject to legal and regulatory requirements, compliance with which is often determined through an audit. Similarly, organizations seeking or having achieved various certifications for process or service quality, maturity, or control implementation and effectiveness typically must undergo certification audits by independent auditors. IT audits often provide information that helps organizations manage risk, confirm efficient allocation of IT-related resources, and achieve other IT and business objectives. Reasons used to justify internal IT audits may be more varied across organizations, but include:

- complying with securities exchange rules that companies have an internal audit function;
- evaluating the effectiveness of implemented controls;

- confirming adherence to internal policies, processes, and procedures;
- checking conformity to IT governance or control frameworks and standards;
- analyzing vulnerabilities and configuration settings to support continuous monitoring;
- identifying weaknesses and deficiencies as part of initial or ongoing risk management;
- measuring performance against quality benchmarks or service level agreements;
- verifying and validating systems engineering or IT project management practices; and
- self-assessing the organization against standards or criteria that will be used in anticipated external audits.

Further details on organizational motivation for conducting internal and external IT audits appear in Chapters 3 and 4, respectively. To generalize, internal IT auditing is often driven by organizational requirements for IT governance, risk management, or quality assurance, any of which may be used to determine what needs to be audited and how to prioritize IT audit activities. External IT auditing is more often driven by a need or desire to demonstrate compliance with externally imposed standards, regulations, or requirements applicable to the type of organization, industry, or operating environment.

Who gets audited?

Given the pervasive use of IT in organizations of all sizes and types, and the benefits accruing to organizations that successfully establish and maintain internal IT audit programs, almost any organization can find IT auditing valuable. With respect to external IT auditing, organizations may not be in a position to determine whether, how, or when to undergo IT audits, as many forms of external audits are legally mandated, not optional. To the extent that organizations seek certification or other external validation of their controls or operations they effectively choose to subject themselves to external IT audits. Other types of organizations are subject to specific legal and regulatory requirements based on the nature of their business operations or the industries in which they participate. As explained in detail in Chapter 7, legal and regulatory requirements are among the most prevalent IT audit drivers for organizations in some industries and sectors. Table 1.2 lists significant sources of external IT audit requirements for different types of organizations. More than one category or attribute may apply to a given organization, in which case the organization is likely subject to multiple IT audit regulations and requirements.

As noted above and emphasized in Chapter 2, beyond any intrinsic value to an organization it might provide, IT auditing is also a critical component of enterprise risk management, IT governance, and quality assurance programs and initiatives, in addition to supporting regulatory and standards compliance. This means that an organization that implements formal governance, risk, and compliance (GRC)

Table 1.2 Sources of External IT Audit Requirements

Sector, Industry, or Type	External IT Audit Drivers
Public corporations	SEC rules; Sarbanes–Oxley Act rules on internal controls (§404) [3] and the PCAOB the law created
Financial institutions	Federal Financial Institutions Examination Council IT Examination Handbook, Audit Booklet [11]
Health care organizations	Revisions to Health Insurance Portability and Accountability Act (HIPAA) Security Rule and Privacy Rule in the Health Information Technology for Economic and Clinical Health (HITECH) Act [12]
Nonprofit organizations	Federal and state audits of internal controls for various types of nonprofits, often tied to sources and amount of funding received
Government agencies	Government Auditing Standards (the "Yellow Book") [13]
Federal funding recipients	Single Audit Act of 1984 [14] and OMB Circular A-133, Audits of states, local governments, and nonprofit organizations [15]
Service providers	ISAE 3402: Assurance reports on controls at a service organization [16]

models or quality assurance standards also needs an effective IT auditing capability. For many organizations the decision to establish and maintain risk management or IT governance programs is a choice, not a requirement, but such approaches are commonly viewed as best practices. United States publicly traded companies listed on the New York Stock Exchange are required, by rules promulgated shortly after the passage of the Sarbanes–Oxley Act, to maintain an internal audit function. Rules in effect for firms subject to statutory audit in countries in the European Union also emphasize the importance of monitoring the effectiveness of internal audit functions, although they do not explicitly require organizations to maintain such a function [17]. Collectively, the combination of legal and regulatory requirements and business drivers give organizations a strong incentive to establish an internal IT audit capability if they do not already have one, and to make sure that the IT audit programs they put in place are properly structured, staffed, managed, and maintained.

Who does IT auditing?

Auditing internal IT controls requires broad IT knowledge, skills, and abilities and expertise in general and IT-specific audit principles, practices, and processes.

Organizations need to develop or acquire personnel with the specialized understanding of control objectives and experience in IT operations necessary to effectively conduct IT audits. This requirement is equally true for organizations whose IT audit programs focus on performing internal audits as it is for professional service firms that conduct external audits or provide auditors or expertise to support organizations' internal audit activities. The types of organizations and individuals that perform IT audits include:

- Internal auditors, comprising either employees of organizations that undertake internal IT auditing or contractors, consultants, or outsourced specialists hired by organizations to carry out internal audits;
- IT auditors working as independent contractors or as employees of professional service firms that provide external or internal IT auditing services;
- Auditing or accounting firms (or the audit or accounting divisions of firms offering a wider range of services);
- Certification organizations authorized to evaluate organizational practices and controls and confer certification to organizations whose internal processes, systems, services, or operational environments adhere to applicable standards or other certification criteria;
- Organizations with the authority to oversee the implementation of required controls or enforce regulations, such as the Government Accountability Office (GAO), SEC, Federal Deposit Insurance Corporation (FDIC), and Department of Health and Human Services (HHS) Office for Civil Rights (OCR) within the U.S. federal government; and
- Inspectors general, audit executives, or equivalent officials charged with the authority to provide independent review of many aspects of the organizations for which they work, including compliance with organizational policies, provision of adequate security, effective allocation of resources, and maintenance of fiduciary responsibility or other standards of care.

Various types of organizations and audit professionals conduct different types of IT audits, as the breadth of skills and experience required and the primary objectives depend substantially on the scope of the audits to be performed. Figure 1.4 depicts types of audits with increasing specificity ranging from organization-wide scope at the broadest level through audits of all internal controls, IT-specific controls, controls implemented for an individual information system, and information security controls. Technology vendors, service providers, and other types of organizations may conduct narrowly focused IT audits to monitor performance against service level agreements, check compliance with legal or contractual terms and conditions, enforce licensing agreements, or safeguard against fraud, waste, or abuse.

External auditors

External IT audits are, by definition, performed by auditors and entities outside the organization subject to the audits. Depending on the size of the organization

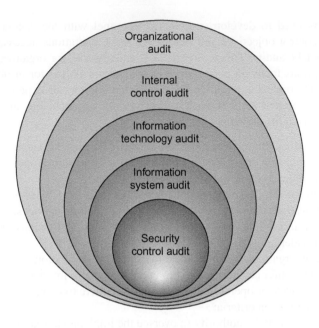

FIGURE 1.4

The scope of IT audit activities ranges from organization-wide to more narrowly defined subsets of internal controls, including those implemented for specific information systems or to achieve specific objectives such as information security.

and the scope and complexity of the IT audit, external audits may be performed by a single auditor or a team. In general, the relationship between an organization and its external auditors is typically established and managed at entity level—that is, organizations engage the services of outside firms or professional organizations that perform the type of IT audits needed or required. This type of relationship is required for publicly traded companies in the United States and many other countries, under rules that require firms that audit these corporations to be registered or licensed with government oversight bodies, such as the Public Company Accounting Oversight Board (PCAOB) in the United States and the members of the European Group of Auditors' Oversight Bodies (EGAOB) in countries in the European Union. Publicly traded companies are therefore constrained in their selection of external auditing firms, but by requiring that audits of such companies are performed only by qualified firms (and the qualified personnel working for them) the regulatory structure for statutory audits in many countries ensures that audits are conducted in a consistent manner that conforms to applicable principles, standards, and practices.

Auditor independence is important for both internal and external audits, but in the context of external auditing such independence is often not just required but legally enforced. Title II of the Sarbanes–Oxley Act [3] includes provisions mandating independence of both the firms that conduct audits and the employees of those firms that lead audit engagements at client organizations. Specifically, registered firms and their employees engaged to perform audits of a given organization cannot provide nonaudit services to that organization such as accounting, design and implementation of financial systems, actuarial services, outsourced internal audits, management functions, investment banking or advising, legal or expert services, or any other activity that the PCAOB determines cannot be performed at the same time as external auditing services [3]. In many organizations it is not uncommon to retain the same external auditor for many years, so regulations adopted by the SEC after Sarbanes–Oxley Act was enacted that required external audit firms to rotate lead personnel ("audit partners") at least every five years, a reduction from a maximum of seven years prior to the Act (European Community regulations similarly require audit partner rotation every seven years).

While firms providing external auditing services are subject to organization-level regulations and oversight, individual auditors performing external audits typically must demonstrate adequate knowledge and expertise and appropriate qualifications. Professional certifications provide one indicator of auditor qualification, particularly where specific certifications correspond to the type of external audit being conducted. Many certifications available to audit professionals have substantial higher education and prior work experience requirements in addition to the demonstration of subject matter expertise through formal examinations. Both audit firms and the organizations that engage such firms to perform external audits place a high value on certified personnel to help ensure sufficient competency, integrity, and domain-specific experience. Due to the close connection and overlapping subject matter between financial audits and IT audits in external auditing contexts, the Certified Public Accountant (CPA) certification—conferred by the American Institute of Certified Public Accountants (AICPA)—is often seen among experienced external auditors. Other common external IT auditor credentials include the ISACA's Certified Information Systems Auditor (CISA) and Certified in Risk and Information Systems Control (CRISC); the GIAC Systems and Network Auditor (GSNA) from the SANS Institute; and ISO/IEC 27001 Lead Auditor. These certifications and the organizations that manage them are described in Chapter 10.

Internal auditors

Auditing internal controls is a discipline in its own right, having much in common with external IT auditing but in many respects extending further in terms of the technical expertise, operational knowledge, and level of detail required to effectively conduct internal IT audits. Internal auditors often work as employees of the organizations they audit, which over time yields an understanding of organization-specific IT environments, controls, information systems, and operational characteristics that is difficult if not impossible to replicate in outsourced internal auditors or external auditors. In a well-structured internal IT audit program, internal auditors also possess knowledge of mission and business processes and organizational goals and objectives that provide a clear context for the IT resources and associated controls deployed in an organization. Due to the emphasis on auditor independence in internal as well as external auditing, the internal IT audit function is often organized in a way that facilitates objectivity and integrity, including a management and accountability structure that reports directly to an organization's board of directors or, for organizations lacking such oversight bodies, to a senior member of the executive management team. Although their skills often overlap to some degree with IT operations and information security personnel, technical project managers, and compliance officers, the need for independence means that internal IT auditors in most organizations do not have any operational job duties in addition to their audit responsibilities.

Because the scope of internal IT auditing is broad, internal auditors may represent many different knowledge areas, skills, and capabilities. Depending on the size of an organization and the scale and diversity of its IT operations, ensuring the internal audit program adequately covers the relevant functional areas and technical domains that may require a small team of relatively senior audit personnel with broad IT experience or a larger group of auditors with more specialized areas of expertise corresponding to the facilities, infrastructure, processes, systems, and technology components implemented by the organization. Internal IT auditors also need appropriate nontechnical skills and characteristics, including personal and professional integrity and ethical standards. Internal IT auditors may demonstrate qualifications that satisfy the combination of IT-related capabilities and individual professional traits by attaining relevant certifications, notably including the Institute of Internal Auditors' Certified Internal Auditor (CIA) credential and ISACA's CISA or Certified Information Systems Manager (CISM). The certifying organizations responsible for these and other internal control-related certifications require holders of these credentials to adopt explicit principles and standards for auditing and to adhere to codes of ethics and standards of professional practice. Details on these and a variety of more specialized technical certifications appear in Chapter 10.

IT auditor development paths

Like financial, operational, or quality auditing, IT auditing is a discrete profession that shares core principles and standards of practice applicable to auditing in general but that also requires specific knowledge, skills, and abilities. There is no single "standard" career development path for IT auditors; instead, successful IT auditors may come from a variety of backgrounds and follow many different career tracks, as illustrated in Figure 1.5. No matter where future IT auditors begin, an individual's career progression and the development of necessary knowledge, skills, and abilities typically combines:

- Formal education in one or more applicable subject areas, potentially including completion of degree or certificate programs in higher education institutions;

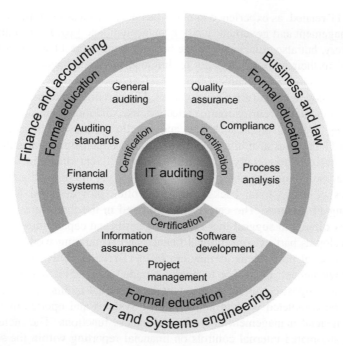

FIGURE 1.5

Individuals travel through many different career paths to develop the skills and expertise needed for IT auditing, coming from traditional finance and accounting, business and legal, or IT backgrounds.

- On-the-job training or assigned duties that provide exposure to IT projects and operations, business processes supported by IT resources, compliance initiatives, or audit-related activities;
- Employer-provided or self-directed professional training and skills development, continuing professional education, or study in pursuit of relevant certifications or other professional qualifications; and
- Acquired work experience directly or indirectly involving risk management, IT governance, quality management, information assurance, standards development or adoption, or controls assessment.

If the education and relevant professional experience prerequisites associated with many IT audit-related certifications are any indication, auditors need extensive training, domain knowledge, and practical experience before they can be effective in conducting audits. Even for IT audit specialists, relevant knowledge and abilities are not only IT-related, as experience in many facets of business operations, organizational management and governance, risk management, and process execution and service delivery, but also contributes to the body of knowledge IT auditors need to be successful in their work. This is not to diminish the significance of IT-specific experience, particularly for technical types of IT audits, addressing systems engineering and deployment, software development, IT operations and maintenance, IT project management, or security control selection, use, and monitoring.

IT auditing requires broad technical and functional knowledge and touches business and IT domains at multiple levels within an organization, meaning effective IT auditors can potentially come from many different disciplines or initial areas of expertise. Figure 1.5 highlights three discrete yet interrelated subject matter categories of professional backgrounds that often provide good foundations for developing IT auditors. The career paths implied in the figure are representative examples offered to suggest that IT auditing skills and capabilities are equally likely to develop as part of conventional finance and accounting work or business analytical and legal professions as they are from IT-related fields. In the modern regulatory environment applicable to publicly traded companies and many other types of organizations, comprehensive internal or external audits of internal controls cannot be completed without addressing IT systems and operations in place to support financial management and related business functions. The inclusion of manual and automated internal controls on financial reporting within the scope of audit requirements prescribed in the Sarbanes–Oxley Act in practice demands that firms performing audits—and the auditors they employ—be able to address IT controls. This experience offers a potential avenue for professional specialization in IT auditing for individuals with a background in finance or accounting. Many institutions of higher education offer undergraduate and graduate programs in these fields; completion of such a program offers a point of entry for careers in auditing. The CPA or CIA certifications often possessed by audit professionals following this sort of career direction provide a strong foundation for IT auditing from the standards, principles, and codes of conduct adopted by the AICPA and the IIA. These professional organizations also offer IT audit-specific guidance and specialized credentials, such as the IIA IT Auditing Certificate.

Organizations subject to legal, regulatory, or industry standards or that choose to pursue certification for quality management, information security management, service delivery, or other operational functions rely on personnel with knowledge of effective business and operational practices and of applicable standards and regulatory requirements. Many formal education programs concentrating in business, law, or other fields emphasizing research and analytical skills provide good preparation for this type of work. Positions in business process analysis, corporate compliance, and organizational legal departments offer individuals significant exposure to internal operations and practices that may be the subject of internal or external audits. Such experience may facilitate the development of the level of expertise in particular regulatory or compliance frameworks or standards and certification criteria to qualify individuals to conduct applicable types of external or internal IT audits.

This type of career path is characterized by specialization in areas such as quality assurance, industry-specific regulations, compliance with particular standards, and service or process maturity frameworks. Various organizations offer standards, guidance, and professional certification in these areas, as described in Chapter 10.

The preceding paragraphs described career paths for IT auditors originating from non-IT disciplines. Many IT audit professionals do of course come from backgrounds in IT. Working in areas such as systems design and implementation, software development, information assurance, IT operations and maintenance, or technical project management provides substantial opportunities to learn about implement, monitor, and assess IT controls. This experience is directly relevant to IT auditing and to the governance and risk management processes which the IT auditing supports. Organizations following formal IT governance or information security control frameworks and guidance typically perform control self-assessments to satisfy organizational policies and procedures or externally driven requirements. IT personnel responsible for implementing, configuring, operating, monitoring, or assessing IT controls often acquire sufficient knowledge and relevant skills to perform many types of IT audits. A seemingly unlimited number of IT certifications and professional credentials are available to help individuals attest to their qualifications in different technologies or processes. These include narrowly focused certifications in technical areas of specialization such as software engineering, quality, and programming; network hardware, device configuration and analysis; operating systems configuration and administration; penetration testing; intrusion analysis and incident handling; and computer forensics. Relatively few certifications focus explicitly on IT auditing and, with the exception of the CISA and GSNA credentials, those that do address specific IT domains such as information security.

Although multiple alternatives exist in higher education to prepare individuals for professional work in finance and accounting, business management, law, and IT disciplines such as software development and systems engineering, relatively few formal higher education programs focus on auditing beyond financial analysis and accounting contexts. This gap in institutional education options means that IT audit professionals must rely primarily on work experience and professional training and certification programs to develop the skills necessary to perform many types of IT auditing.

Relevant source material

The fundamental concepts and characteristics of IT auditing have a common foundation in general audit principles and practices, including GAAS [7] and the International Standards for the Professional Practice of Internal Auditing [8], as well as codes of practice and of professional ethics which many auditors and organizations follow. The most significant influences on the practice of external auditing of internal IT controls include major legislation and resulting regulations establishing various audit requirements for publicly traded, nonprofit, and government organizations and for entities in specific industry sectors such as financial services and health care. These requirements also affect internal IT audit practices, which are also driven by internal control frameworks, methodologies, standards, and guidance, including those described in Chapter 9. Exemplary sources of such guidance include COSO's Internal Control—Integrated Framework [4] and the Control Objectives for Information and Related Technology (COBIT) [5] offered by ISACA and the IT Governance Institute.

Summary

This chapter introduced key concepts relevant to understanding IT auditing and provided an overview of IT audit purposes and organizational rationale, described different subjects and areas of focus for various types of organizations subject to IT audits, and identified the individuals and organizations typically responsible for conducting different types of IT audits. It also highlights the significance of internal and external IT audits to different types of organizations, as its own discipline as a subordinate function to enterprise risk management, IT governance, quality assurance, and regulatory and standards compliance.

References

[1] ISO 19011:2011. Guidelines for auditing management systems.

[2] ITIL glossary and abbreviations. London (UK): Cabinet Office; 2011.

[3] Sarbanes–Oxley Act of 2002, Pub. L. No. 107-204, 116 Stat. 745.

[4] Committee of Sponsoring Organizations of the Treadway Commission. Internal control—Integrated framework. New York (NY): Committee of Sponsoring Organizations of the Treadway Commission; 2013.

[5] IT Governance Institute. COBIT 4.1. Rolling Meadows (IL): IT Governance Institute; 2007.

[6] Recommended security controls for federal information systems and organizations. Gaithersburg (MD): National Institute of Standards and Technology, Computer Security Division; 2009 August. Special Publication 800-53 revision 3.

[7] Generally accepted auditing standards. New York (NY): American Institute of Certified Public Accountants, Auditing Standards Board; 2001 December. Statement on Auditing Standards 95.

[8] International standards for the professional practice of internal auditing. Altamonte Springs (FL): Institute of Internal Auditors; 2012 October.

[9] Code of Ethics [Internet]; Altamonte Springs (FL): Institute of Internal Auditors; [cited 2013 May 4]. Available from: <https://na.theiia.org/standards-guidance/mandatory-guidance/Pages/Code-of-Ethics.aspx>.

[10] Code of Professional Ethics [Internet]; Rolling Meadows (IL): ISACA; [cited 2013 May 4]. Available from: < http://www.isaca.org/Certification/Code-of-Professional-Ethics/Pages/default.aspx > .

[11] IT examination handbook. Arlington (VA): Federal Financial Institutions Examination Council; 2012 April.

[12] Health Information Technology for Economic and Clinical Health Act of 2009, Pub. L. No. 111-5, 123 Stat. 226.

[13] Government auditing standards. Washington (DC): Government Accountability Office; 2011 December.

[14] Single Audit Act of 1984, Pub. L. No. 98-502, 98 Stat. 2327.

[15] Audits of states, local governments, and non-profit organizations. Washington (DC): Office of Management and Budget; 2007 June. OMB Circular A-133.

[16] Assurance reports on controls at a service organization. New York (NY): International Auditing and Assurance Standards Board; 2011. International Standards for Assurance Engagements 3402.

[17] Directive of the European Parliament and of the Council on statutory audits of annual accounts and consolidated accounts, Directive 2006/43/EC; 2006 May.

Auditing in Context

INFORMATION IN THIS CHAPTER:

- IT governance
- Risk management
- Legal and regulatory compliance
- Quality management and quality assurance
- Information security management

With the exception of organizations subject to external regulations or policies requiring them to maintain internal audit functions or conduct information technology (IT) auditing, the decision to establish an internal IT audit capability is typically driven by internally defined objectives. The primary impetus leading organizations to set up and operate IT audit programs is the need to provide support to enterprise management initiatives or programs that depend on IT. Effectively supporting such programs is also an important factor in realizing anticipated benefits or value from such programs, at least to the extent that their success is measured in terms of efficiency, effectiveness, and related performance metrics. Organizational functions reinforced or facilitated through internal IT audit programs include IT governance, enterprise risk management, standards compliance and certification, continuous improvement, and quality assurance, all of which sustain mission and business initiatives and help organizations attain strategic planning goals, objectives, and outcomes. This chapter describes these organizational initiatives and the role of IT audit in each of them. It summarizes the major structural elements, processes, and other characteristics of enterprise programs that IT auditing supports and describes the reciprocal relationship between IT auditing and governance, risk, compliance, and quality, as illustrated in Figure 2.1. Planning and executing the processes associated with these programs influences the design and implementation of the IT audit program and helps organizations identify and prioritize various aspects of their operations that constitute the subject of needed IT audits. Conversely, weaknesses or deficiencies in internal controls, gaps in meeting compliance requirements, or other potential IT audit findings influence organizational decisions made at the enterprise program level about allocation of resources, risk response, corrective action, or opportunities for process or control improvement.

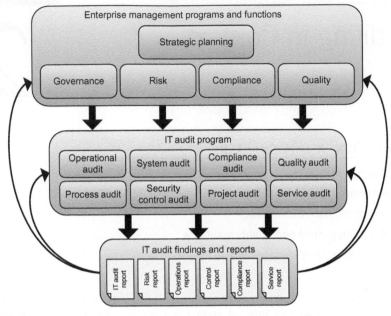

FIGURE 2.1

IT audit activities represent an integral part of several key enterprise management functions, which collectively contribute to the scope of the IT audit program and receive input from the output of audit processes.

IT governance

The term *governance* in business contexts refers generally to the set of policies, processes, and actions taken by management to define organizational strategy and operate the organization in a way intended to help realize its business goals and objectives. In contrast, *IT governance* refers to the structure and processes organizations use to try to ensure that their IT operations support the overall goals and objectives of the organization. According to the IT Governance Institute, governance objectives applicable to virtually any organization include aligning IT strategy with enterprise strategy, allocating IT resources efficiently to support the achievement of organizational objectives and realize the value anticipated from IT investments, and effectively managing IT-related risk [1]. With the addition of performance measurement to allow organizations to assess to what extent they are achieving their objectives, IT governance comprises the management functions as depicted in Figure 2.2.

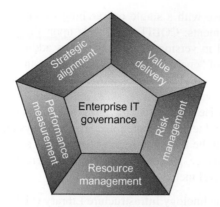

FIGURE 2.2

The scope of IT governance comprises five key focus areas, each supported by well-defined processes and sets of internal controls [2].

As implemented in practice, IT governance comprises a wide range of processes and controls for applications, systems, networks, infrastructure, personnel, and data centers and other facilities, including:

- IT-related policies;
- standard operating procedures;
- management plans;
- performance monitoring and management;
- supervisory or oversight functions;
- IT controls and control monitoring;
- system and software development processes; and
- operations and maintenance activities.

The IT governance function and its associated processes and activities can apply at multiple levels of an organization—to internal controls, business functions and processes, infrastructure, system operations and maintenance, or individual projects, as well as enterprise-wide. There are a variety of governance frameworks available for use, including those taking an organization-wide perspective such as Control Objectives for Information and Related Technology (COBIT) or ISO/IEC 38500. The ISO/IEC 38500 standard focuses on corporate IT governance, emphasizing high-level principles and recommendations that organizational executives or other leaders with responsibility for governance should consider. The enterprise perspective in ISO/IEC 38500 is consistent with COBIT 5—the most recent version of the framework, released in 2012—which is intended to offer a holistic approach to governance with a single overarching framework incorporating many formerly separate elements. COBIT 5 expands upon the prior, similarly process-centric approach used in version 4.1 and integrates additional guidance organized into seven categories of "enablers": principles, policies and frameworks; processes; organizational structures; culture, ethics and behavior; information; services, infrastructure and applications; and people, skills and competencies [3]. IT governance managed at the enterprise level covers the full scope of the IT audit universe—operating units, business and technical functions, processes, systems, controls, and other activities that represent the focus of different types of IT audits.

Sources of governance guidance focused on different organizational aspects below the enterprise level include:

- The Information Technology Infrastructure Library (ITIL) and ISO/IEC 20000 for service management;
- The Project Management Body of Knowledge (PMBOK) and Projects in Controlled Environments version 2 (PRINCE2) for project management;
- Capability Maturity Model Integration (CMMI) and ISO/IEC 15504 for software development processes; and
- The ISO/IEC 27000 series and National Institute of Standards and Technology (NIST) risk management framework for information security management.

External sources of guidance on governance processes, requirements, or best practices typically offer organizations models of governance that can be adopted as published or adapted to suit an organization's particular needs. For example, the COBIT 5 framework describes a total of 37 IT-related processes in five categories—evaluate, direct, and monitor; align, plan, and organize; build, acquire, and implement; deliver, service, and support; and monitor, evaluate, and assess—and specifies numerous IT controls in each category. Organizations adopting COBIT are neither required to implement all the controls nor constrained to use only the controls in the COBIT framework. Instead, the framework provides a structured overarching governance model, that accommodates whatever governance functions and controls an organization chooses, including controls specified in other standards and frameworks [3].

The role of IT audit in governance

Organizations do not need to follow a formally defined framework to practice effective governance. For organizations that do, the framework and its associated standards and procedures provide the foundational elements of IT audit baselines used in the areas covered by the governance framework. Organizations that develop their own governance methodologies also need to define corresponding sets of audit criteria. Organizations also need to support governance with an effective IT audit function that allows them to validate that their processes are working as intended; that their systems are implemented, configured, and operated correctly and effectively; and that the resources they allocate to their IT initiatives are properly aligned to their organizational business objectives.

The variety of ways in which IT auditing contributes to the successful practice of IT governance activities reflects the broad scope of processes and functions IT governance comprises. IT governance typically comprises management processes and activities and the documented policies, procedures, standards, and guidelines the organization specifies to guide the execution of management processes and provide effective oversight of operations. Policies and procedures prescribed by the organization typically represent guidance intended to ensure that IT is used effectively and efficiently and that established performance objectives are achieved. Conducting IT audits of internal operations is one way to confirm that processes and activities actually executed by the organization conform to policies and procedures and to identify any areas of disagreement. If an organization tracks cost or other IT resource allocations and has consistent performance measurement in place, the results of IT audits may be correlated with cost and performance data to provide some insight about IT operations' contribution to achieving business objectives and desired outcomes. Beyond providing information to management about IT operations, IT audits of this type can also offer evidence to demonstrate that the organization's implemented processes indicate a level of maturity or conform to externally defined criteria such as those in the Software Engineering Institute's CMMI or the Six Sigma process improvement methodology. IT auditing can confirm achievement of (or failure to achieve) organizational objectives relating to each of the functions as shown in Figure 2.2.

Defining an organization's audit universe—the set of things at all levels of the organization that may be the subject of an IT audit—is one of many responsibilities often assigned to the IT audit program. Organizations with established IT governance or formal risk management programs should have available functional decompositions, asset inventories, and enterprise architecture artifacts that substantially describe the IT management, operations, and technical scope of the organization and thus provide a good basis for establishing the IT audit universe.

Risk management

All organizations have some exposure to risk—the potential for loss, damage, injury, or other undesirable outcome resulting from decisions, actions, or events. Risk exists because the future cannot be predicted with certainty; organizational plans or strategies regarding future events reflect assumptions, calculations, or estimates about what will occur, but there is always a chance that events will unfold differently than anticipated, potentially with results less favorable than what the organization planned. The International Organization for Standardization (ISO) defines *risk* simply as the "effect of uncertainty on objectives,"[4] but most sources of guidance on risk management characterize risk as a function of threats and vulnerabilities applicable to an organization, where the magnitude of risk is expressed in terms of the impact that could occur should a potential threat materialize and the likelihood of that occurrence. The scope of enterprise risk management covers all organizational aspects for which adverse events have the potential to affect the achievement of objectives and intended outcomes. The presence of risk makes it essential for organizations to develop the capabilities and procedures necessary for managing risk. Regardless of the types of risk involved, the core processes specified in different risk management frameworks and methodologies tend to be similar and include risk strategy (or planning), risk identification, risk assessment, risk monitoring, and risk response [5].

Enterprise risk management in many organizations comprises not only the scope of IT auditing but also includes many types of risk not ordinarily addressed through the IT audit program. Organizations often choose to adopt risk management practices, limited in scope to IT or information security, rather than embracing enterprise risk management more broadly. Focusing risk management on information systems or security controls is the norm in many smaller organizations and in public sector organizations of any size where truly enterprise-wide or integrated risk management comprising technical and nontechnical sources of risk is rare. For instance, the risk management framework published by the U.S. NIST for use in federal government agencies addresses only information security risk [6]. When the Government Accountability Office (GAO) recommended in 2005 that agencies executing homeland security missions adopt risk management practices, it then noted the widespread use of risk management in commercial sectors and the relative lack of maturity of similar processes in government organizations [7]. In these organizations, the limited sphere of risk management operations may be more closely aligned to IT auditing practices, although organizations should be aware that IT audit findings may correspond to types of risk beyond IT and information security risk. Such narrowly focused risk management programs are in stark contrast to those seen in many commercial organizations, particularly in regulated industries or among publicly traded companies where the scope of risk management covers IT and information security risk as well as financial, operational, strategic, market, supply chain, reputation, legal, or other types of business risk [8].

Enterprise risk management frameworks such as those produced by the Committee on Sponsoring Organizations of the Treadway Commission (COSO) and the ISO adopt an integrated risk management perspective spanning all types of risk, all levels of an organization, and multiple types of organizational objectives. Such models typically do not enumerate specific types of risk, recognizing that organizations of different types or in different sectors may use specific risk categorization schemes and associated risk management techniques. Some risk management approaches address enterprise perspectives and more narrowly focused risk management practices with separate guidance or standards. For example, the ISO/IEC 31000 and ISO/IEC 27005 risk management standards share the same general risk management concepts and prescribed processes, but ISO/IEC 31000 addresses all sources of risk and all organizational activities involving risk [5], while ISO/IEC 27005 applies only to information security risk [9].

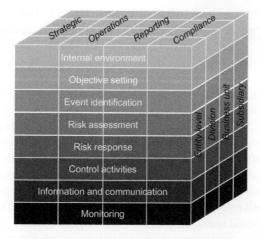

FIGURE 2.3

The COSO's enterprise risk management framework[10] is among the most comprehensive approaches to risk management due to its coverage of all levels of an organization and broad focus well beyond IT.

Source: Enterprise Risk Management—Integrated Framework, Committee of Sponsoring Organizations of the Treadway Commission, ©2004. All rights reserved. Used by permission.

Risk management addresses strategic and operational objectives and, for organizations in sectors subject to oversight or regulatory requirements, also supports reporting and compliance objectives. Many organizational governance approaches incorporate risk management as an integral component, including the COBIT 5 framework described earlier in this chapter that integrates risk management processes from ISACA's Risk IT model [3]. Different types of risk can impact operational, tactical, and strategic aspects of individual business units or entire organizations. Effective risk management often requires visibility into multiple parts of the organization and coordination of many different resources. The specific set of functions, personnel, and other resources allocated to enterprise risk management varies depending on the size and complexity of an organization and the maturity of its risk management approach. Comprehensive risk management models incorporate management, structural, and process perspectives to enable organizations to address all types of risk and the different elements to which that risk applies. As illustrated in Figure 2.3, organizational components integrated in COSO's framework for enterprise risk management include [10]:

- Description of the internal environment, which comprises the organizational culture and risk management perspective for the organization, influencing both risk management strategy and risk tolerance;
- Establishment of strategic goals and objectives, which must be stated clearly in order for organizations to identify potential events affecting their achievement;

- Identification of internal and external threat sources or events with the potential to positively or negatively impact the achievement of an organization's objectives;
- Assessment of risk, considering likelihood and impact, to support selection of appropriate risk responses or other approaches to managing risk;
- Selection of risk responses—avoidance, acceptance, mitigation, sharing, or transference, alone or in combination—and development of a course of action consistent with the nature of the risk and with the organizational risk tolerance;
- Creation and implementation of policies and procedures and other control mechanisms sufficient to ensure that risk responses are executed as planned;
- Information sharing and communication at all levels of the organization to enable all risk management stakeholders to carry out their responsibilities; and
- Monitoring of all relevant types and sources of organizational risk through ongoing operational management activities, purpose-specific evaluations, automated monitoring and reporting capabilities, or other means preferred by the organization.

Risk management components

Regardless of the scope of activities or organizational levels risk management addresses, most risk management approaches share the same core concepts and processes, although different organizations implement these common elements in different ways. Much of the variation in risk management across organizations—especially in terms of risk prioritization and resources allocated to risk management and mitigation—is attributable to differences in risk tolerance. An organization's risk tolerance (also sometimes called risk appetite or risk propensity) is the level of risk it is willing to accept before it takes action to mitigate or otherwise respond to risk. An organization that is relatively more risk averse is more likely to invest resources in reducing risk or to refrain from some types of activities, and may be inclined to evaluate risk more frequently to ensure that the risk the organization faces remains at or below acceptable levels. Organizations manage their risk by developing and executing a risk plan or risk strategy that reflects an organization-specific perspective on the types of risk it faces and how it intends to manage that risk. The strategy specifies strategic planning assumptions, constraints, decision-making criteria, and other factors influencing risk management in the organization, including the use of risk identification and evaluation procedures such as those associated with IT audit functions. Once defined, organizations implement their risk management plans using an iterative cycle of processes and procedures, typically including risk identification, evaluation, response, monitoring, and review.

The information security risk management life cycle defined in NIST Special Publication 800-39 and recommended for use in federal government agencies is structurally very similar to ISO/IEC 27005, ISACA's Risk IT, and other risk management frameworks and processes developed to support enterprise risk management in public and private sector organizations. The core activities in the NIST risk

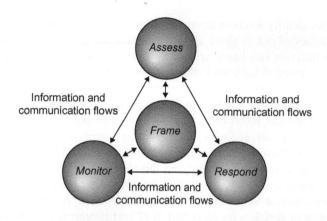

FIGURE 2.4

NIST's risk management framework is a representative example of processes and methodologies that address specific types of risk, such as risk associated with operating information systems [6].

management process, as illustrated in Figure 2.4, include risk framing, risk assessment, risk response, and risk monitoring, all supported by information flows and communication across all levels of an organization and among all risk management processes. Similar to risk planning or risk strategy, risk framing establishes the scope of risk management activities, which in the case of the NIST framework is limited to information security risk associated with information systems and their operating environments. Risk assessment entails the identification of threats and other sources of risk and the determination of the relative magnitude of risk from each source. Risk response addresses what an organization chooses to do about risk it faces; alternative responses typically include accepting, mitigating, avoiding, or transferring risk. Risk monitoring involves periodic or continuous action to validate currently known risk sources, identify new risk sources (whether due to external threats or internal environmental changes), and verifying the implementation or validating the effectiveness of courses of action chosen as part of risk response.

The role of IT audit in risk management

IT auditing has both dependent and supporting roles within risk management. The results of risk management activities influence the way the IT audit program plans and conducts audits, and the findings and recommendations from IT audits represent important inputs into ongoing risk planning, assessment, and response. In most organizations, time, money, personnel, and other resource constraints make it impractical or infeasible to audit everything included in the audit universe, so it is important to prioritize the aspects of the organization where audit program resources should be focused. The risk assessment processes in risk management methodologies identify assets in an organization and identify and evaluate the threats and other sources of risk to those assets. Organizations may choose to prioritize IT audits using different risk-based criteria, such as focusing first on IT processes or components assessed to have the highest risk or on those considered to be of greatest value to the organization. IT audit programs almost certainly operate under other drivers and constraints in addition to risk management guidance, but considering asset valuation and risk levels helps the organization ensure that it allocates IT audit resources in a manner aligned with strategic business goals and objectives.

Another area of overlap between risk management and IT auditing is in threat and vulnerability assessment. Identifying threats and vulnerabilities is a key part of risk assessment and a set of activities informed by both external and internal sources of information about threat sources and types of vulnerabilities. Some of the weaknesses or deficiencies identified in IT audits represent vulnerabilities that must be evaluated to determine what level of risk they expose for the organization. Along with routine vulnerability scanning and other functions typically performed as part of continuous monitoring of IT systems and infrastructure, IT audits are an important internal source of vulnerability information. When combined with external information available to organizations on threats and vulnerabilities, IT audit findings help give risk assessors a more complete view of the range of threats and vulnerabilities applicable to the organization. Popular sources of vulnerability information include the Common Vulnerabilities and Exposures (CVE) database [11], the Computer Emergency Response Team Coordination Center (CERT/CC) [12], and the U.S. Computer Emergency Response Team (US-CERT) [13]. In addition, publicly available information security risk management guidance often includes information on threats, such as the information included in International Standards of Supreme Audit Institutions (ISSAI) 5310 [14] and NIST Special Publication 800-30 [15]. IT auditors can use this information to analyze the vulnerabilities they find and help determine how significant a risk to the organization with those vulnerabilities may be.

In organizations with IT- or information security-focused risk management programs, IT auditors and risk managers alike need to be aware that some weaknesses potentially identified in IT audits correspond to types of risk beyond those related to IT. For example, deviations from certification or compliance criteria may be sources of legal, market, or reputation risk rather than (or in addition to) any IT or security risk attributed to gaps or weaknesses in controls.

Compliance and certification

Organizations operate under a variety of rules and requirements—some self-imposed, some derived from laws and regulations, and others stemming from standards or certification criteria that organizations follow. Compliance activities consider all requirements applicable to an organization and assess the extent to which the organization meets those requirements, identifying any gaps or failures to satisfy requirements that may exist. The rationale for engaging in compliance activities often includes external drivers such as regulatory requirements, but in organizations with formal governance in place, achieving and demonstrating compliance with internal policies, procedures, and standards may be equally important reasons. Compliance is one dimension of governance used to measure progress or organizational maturity in terms of implementing and consistently executing specified processes and standards. Some professional service and product vendors refer collectively to governance, risk management, and compliance (GRC) as an integrated management discipline. Compliance programs also stand on their own, providing support to governance and risk management but positioned separately within the organization, particularly when their activities focus on adherence to legal requirements.

Certification is a special type of compliance. To achieve certification, organizations typically adopt standard processes or methodologies in a specifically prescribed manner and then have their compliance with the chosen standards evaluated by an external entity explicitly authorized to grant certification. Compared to general compliance activities that may focus on internal or external drivers and evaluations, formal certification almost always involves examination by an external party. Organizations typically know the criteria that must be satisfied to achieve certification, so internal self-assessments may be used to help organizations prepare for certification or to validate ongoing compliance with required criteria after certification. Certifications are available in many different operational areas, as summarized in Table 2.1, including quality management, information security management, service management, and process adoption, execution, and improvement. Certifications for some organizational capabilities such as software development, IT security, service delivery, and operations control denote a maturity level the organization has attained. Examples of standards used in external certification and attestation engagements include CMMI and ISO/IEC 15504, which assess capabilities and maturity levels for IT-related processes, and Statements on Standards for Attestation Engagements (SSAE), International Standards for Assurance Engagements (ISAE), and Service Organization Control (SOC) Reports used to certify controls implemented by service providers. More narrowly focused certifications apply to specific tools, technologies, processes, or other products developed by organizations, where certification is an indication that the product meets or exceeds specific functional and technical standards or other criteria. These certifications include Federal Information Processing Standards (FIPS) specified by NIST, the Communications-Electronics Security Group (CESG) Assisted Product Scheme, and the protection profiles and associated assurance levels specified under the common criteria framework.

Managing compliance and certification

Managing compliance and certification is an ongoing process, punctuated by externally driven deadlines or required examination frequencies, in organizations subject

Table 2.1 Types of Organizational Certifications and Standards

Certification Focus	Certifications
Quality management	• ISO 9001 • ISO 14001
Information security management	• ISO/IEC 27001 • Cybertrust
Service management	• CMMI for services • ISO/IEC 20000
Service organization controls	• SSAE 16 • ISAE 3402 • SOC 2 and 3
Process improvement	• CMMI • ISO/IEC 15504 • Six Sigma
Products or technologies	• Common criteria • CESG assisted products scheme (United Kingdom) • FIPS (United States)

to regulatory requirements or certification criteria. Compliance and certification programs also typically perform self-assessments or internal evaluations scheduled to coincide with pending external audits or conducted on a periodic or ad hoc basis (such as when changes to operations, systems, or environments occur). Part of the process of seeking and achieving certification is ensuring that the controls, processes, or standards associated with the certification are actually implemented in the organization. For example, the maturity levels in the Software Engineering Institute's CMMI process improvement framework correspond to specific processes that an organization is expected to use in its internal operations in order to receive certification at each level.

Both compliance and certification are often the subject of external audits intended to enable an objective determination by an outside entity of adherence to regulatory or industry standards or certification criteria. For some organizations compliance with regulatory requirements is audited on an annual basis, as is the case with internal controls for publicly traded companies subject to the Sarbanes–Oxley Act. Chapter 7 describes many industry-specific legislative and regulatory audit requirements, including those applicable to organizations in education, financial services, health care, and government. There are also standards and criteria applicable to organizations in different industries or lines of business for which compliance reporting occurs largely through self-attestation rather than external audit. Until recently, this self-attestation model applied to many aspects of compliance in the health care industry including regulatory requirements under Health Insurance Portability and Accountability Act (HIPAA) and qualification for incentive funding programs in the American Recovery and Reinvestment Act of 2009. Recent changes in federal oversight of these programs brought about through provisions in the Health Information Technology for Economic and Clinical Health (HITECH) Act introduced external compliance audits conducted by the government [16]. For other legal and regulatory requirements organizations are subject to selection for external audits, but actual audits are performed on a small percentage of organizations in a given industry or geographic area.

Organizations need their own internal processes to assess certification and compliance, whether or not they expect to be audited by external parties, to help ensure on an ongoing basis that they conform to applicable requirements and can demonstrate evidence of their compliance if and when they need to. Part of the focus of an externally administered certification or compliance audit is satisfactorily demonstrating to auditors that the organization follows its own policies and procedures and that those are implemented in practice and not just written in official documentation. Performing regular internal audits of the extent to which an organization actually does the things specified in such documentation is an important part of being ready for external certification audits and of helping to ensure that the organization realizes the benefits of the standards or methodologies against which it is certified.

Much like IT auditing in general, certification against specific standards is typically evaluated and conferred against criteria representing a particular version or publication date of the standard in question. For example, the formal designation of most ISO standards and corresponding certifications includes the year in which the most recent version of the standard was officially released. Standards development organizations and the standards they produce are not static, however, so organizations conducting internal audits against such certification criteria need to be aware when updates or other changes occur to standards that alter the criteria they need to satisfy to remain certified under new versions. Repeatedly performing internal audits to validate certification against a fixed set of criteria is of little value in helping the organization pass external audits if the internal audit uses an out-of-date or deprecated version of the standard that has been superseded by a new version.

The role of IT audit in compliance and certification

The central role of IT auditing in organizational compliance and certification is readily apparent from the nature of compliance activities—internal and external compliance evaluations alike compare organizational behavior or operational characteristics to explicit sets of requirements. This procedural feature is a defining characteristic of auditing. Internal compliance audits support management and operational oversight functions performed as part of governance, while external compliance audits help organizations satisfy legal, regulatory, or industry requirements. Even in the absence of external mandates, validating compliance using internal audits provides important information about many aspects of program or organizational effectiveness. Similarly, successfully completing an external audit is often a prerequisite to achieving or maintaining certification, which in turn enables organizations to leverage certifications for a variety of purposes, including differentiating their operations from peer organizations that have not achieved certification. Organizations with strategic business or IT objectives that include compliance with external requirements can use formal internal IT auditing procedures to prepare for external audits, and reduce uncertainty regarding the results and improve the likelihood of passing such audits. The American Institute of Certified Public Accountants (AICPA) provides guidance on compliance audits in its Statement on Auditing Standards 117 [17].

Quality management and quality assurance

Quality *assurance* refers to the processes associated with achieving and maintaining a desired level of quality in a product or service. The closely related concept of quality *control* focuses on maintaining consistent quality over time, such as meeting a specific standard or producing a product with characteristics satisfying prescribed criteria or falling within a specified tolerance level. The more general term quality *management* comprises all coordinated activities related to quality including quality planning, quality assurance, quality control, and quality improvement [18]. Like governance and risk management, quality assurance methods and practices apply across different levels of an organization. While many organizations cite quality explicitly as a business goal and make decisions to adopt quality initiatives at an enterprise level, in practice quality assurance is most often implemented at the business function or process level. Many commonly implemented quality management standards and approaches—such as ISO 9001, Total Quality Management (TQM), and Six Sigma—address quality management principles and practices throughout an organization, but certifications against such standards are conferred on specific processes, projects, or operating units. Other methodologies and standards apply quality assurance to specific business domains, such as the Software Engineering Institute's IDEAL (initiating, diagnosing, establishing, acting, and learning) model and Institute of Electrical and Electronics Engineers (IEEE) Standard 730 for software quality assurance [19], or to operational aspects such as service quality measured with performance frameworks like SERVQUAL [20].

Quality management as specified in leading standards and methodologies is an iterative set of processes intended to help organizations deliver products, services, and other process outputs that meet applicable requirements, whether those requirements are driven by laws and regulations, customers, or internal business

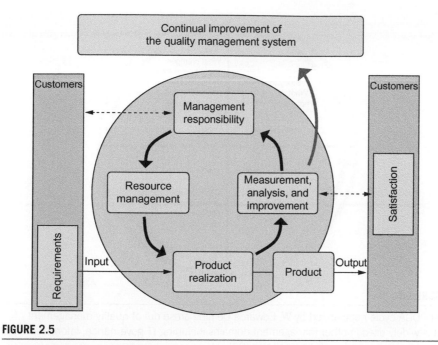

FIGURE 2.5

The process defined in ISO 9001 uses an iterative approach and emphasizes the continuous improvement characteristic of quality management systems [21].

objectives. These quality models typically emphasize continuous improvement of organizational processes, an aspect of quality management that organizations must demonstrate explicitly in order to achieve certification against standards such as ISO 9001 [21]. Quality is measured using multiple dimensions and criteria, potentially including internally defined specifications, customer requirements, industry standards, or government regulations. Effective, accurate, and consistent measurement is an integral component of quality management, as illustrated in Figure 2.5, to be able to set and adjust the quality baseline against which improvements in product or process quality can be compared. The collective set of policies, processes, resources, and tools used in quality-related activities constitutes a quality management system (sometimes termed as quality management program) that can be implemented at an organization-wide level or with a scope of control more narrowly defined to lines of business, functional domains, or discrete product or service offerings.

The contributions of quality management on the field of IT auditing go far beyond the use of audit procedures in quality assurance activities, as the processes specified in many governance, risk management, service management, and auditing methodologies share a common foundation in the plan-do-check-act

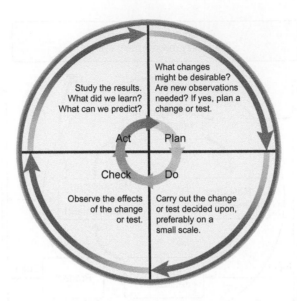

FIGURE 2.6

The PDCA cycle popularized by W. Edwards Deming arose out of quality management but is widely used in other management domains including IT governance, information security, risk management, and auditing [23].

(PDCA) cyclical model generally attributed to W. Edwards Deming (the "Deming cycle"). Originally developed as a statistical process control and continuous quality improvement model for product manufacturing, the four-phase Deming cycle shown in Figure 2.6 appears explicitly in or significantly influences COBIT, ITIL, multiple ISO standards, and U.S. government frameworks for risk management and information systems auditing. The Deming cycle provided the foundation for several quality control and process improvement approaches developed in Japan beginning in the 1950s and adopted in U.S. companies beginning in the 1980s notably including TQM. It also features prominently in quality management and quality audit procedures and guidelines from standards organizations such as the ISO and the American Society for Quality (ASQ) [22].

Deming himself credited the cycle most often attributed to him to Walter Shewhart [23], but after the rapid adoption of the quality improvement cycle in Japan in the 1950s using the name "Deming cycle," subsequent references in business literature almost invariably refer to the PDCA model as the Deming cycle.

The role of IT audit in quality management

IT auditing supports organizational quality management functions by confirming that operational processes produce the intended result and that the outputs of those processes satisfy quality-related criteria. Quality management systems are also subject to periodic audit to determine if the system as implemented meets applicable requirements (including those necessary for certification) and is properly operated and maintained. This means that an organization often conducts quality assurance of its internal auditing program (including IT auditing) and performs internal audits of its quality management system and associated processes. Several types of IT audits may be used in quality management or quality assurance activities, including audits of IT-related products or services, processes, or control systems [22]. Such audits may be conducted as part of internal or external audit programs, depending on the source of the requirements or quality criteria the organization needs to meet, the purpose for the audit, and whether the organization has or is seeking certification for its quality management capabilities. The results of IT audits performed in support of quality assurance can either confirm adherence to quality criteria and achievement of quality objectives or identify deviations from product specifications or service levels that become targets for corrective action. Because IT audits emphasize compliance with quality standards and criteria, they are not particularly well-suited to identifying opportunities for improvement for processes or systems that satisfy current requirements. Available quality-centric methodologies used for process improvement include business process reengineering, TQM, CMMI, and Six Sigma.

Information security management

Information security is often considered a subordinate function to IT governance, risk management, or both, and in that respect differs from the other management functions described in this chapter. The current emphasis in information security management on continuous monitoring, threat and vulnerability assessment, and evaluation of the implementation and effectiveness of security controls overlaps with IT auditing practices to such a significant extent that information security warrants separate consideration. Security controls—administrative, technical, and physical—are the primary focus of information security management and of the IT auditing or assessment activities performed in support of information security programs. Information security management entails the selection, implementation, configuration, operation, and monitoring of security controls sufficient to protect the confidentiality, integrity, and availability of information systems and the data they contain. Information security management is risk-based, in the sense that decisions to deploy security mechanisms or allocate resources to protect organizational assets must balance the cost of providing security with the level of risk to the organization, if threats it faces remain unaddressed. In simple economic terms, it does not make sense for an organization to invest more in security than the value of the assets under protection or the magnitude of or harm that would occur if those assets were lost, stolen, damaged, or compromised.

Organizations in the public sector and in many industries are subject to legal and regulatory requirements that mandate minimum security safeguards or protective measures. Such regulations rarely specify security products, tools, or explicit methods (partly in order to avoid favoring individual security vendors) and instead prescribe requirements, standards, or intended outcomes for security, leaving the choice of what specific controls to implement up to each complying organization. Government regulators often recommend or require organizations to adhere to separately developed standards. For example, Securities and Exchange Commission rules on the implementation of the Sarbanes–Oxley Act explicitly mention control frameworks and standards from the COSO and the AICPA [24] and in its Directive on statutory audits, the Council of the European Union specifies International Standards on Auditing (ISA) adopted by the International Accounting Standards Board (IASB) [25]. With the exception of U.S. federal government agencies—which under the authority of the Federal Information Security Management Act (FISMA) must comply with FIPS and associated security guidance issued by NIST—security regulations typically do not prescribe specific security control standards. To achieve the security objectives in such regulations, however, many organizations voluntarily choose to adopt formal security control frameworks such as ISO/IEC 27002, and to seek certification against these standards.

The term *certification* has two different meanings within the information security management context. In government sector environments and commercial sector organizations that require structured, formal procedures and approvals before putting an information system into production, certification refers to the self-evaluation and affirmation of the extent to which the security controls implemented for a system meet the system's security requirements. Beyond the scope of giving formal approval (in U.S. federal government parlance, "authorizing to operate") to information systems, certification typically indicates compliance with a specific standard or set of criteria. For instance, many organizations seek certification to demonstrate conformance with requirements and standards for information security management systems, such as ISO/IEC 27001. Such certifications are granted by accredited registrars or other organizations explicitly approved to serve as certification bodies. To avoid potential confusion over word meanings, it is important to clearly specify the context when referring to security certification activities, including security-focused IT audits.

In current practice, information security management emphasizes strategies such as continuous monitoring of security controls and independent security control assessments to gauge the effectiveness of the controls organizations implement and maintain. Available standards on information security management, such as ISO/IEC 27001, specify the same sort of iterative, cyclical set of processes seen in quality management, risk management, and governance disciplines, as illustrated in Figure 2.7. The scope of information security management includes IT

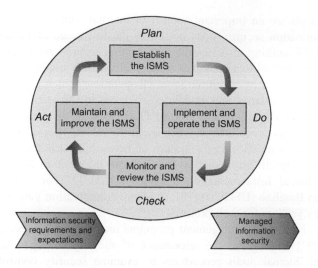

FIGURE 2.7

The ISMS process defined in ISO/IEC 27001 applies the familiar PDCA model to information security management [26].

audit activities—particularly audits of security controls—but also comprises many other types of evaluations intended to validate proper function and configuration of security controls, ensure the adequacy of implemented controls to satisfy security requirements, or determine whether those responsible for operating, maintaining, and securing IT do so in a way that achieves the organization's goals and objectives. Security controls assessments typically rely on assessors' expertise to judge whether the security controls implemented are effective. Such judgments rely on reviews of evidence and examination and testing by assessors, but effectiveness is an inherently subjective determination influenced by accepted security best practices as well as various organization-specific factors. Some security control assessments do use control frameworks or standards as points of reference for the set of security controls that should be implemented in a given organizational environment, but such assessments are still not the same as audits. Security control selection is a risk-based process, so the actual controls in place may differ from organization to organization due to variations in mission and business objectives, industry, threat profile, risk tolerance, or other characteristics. Internal IT audit criteria may be defined in a way that is organization-specific but audits against requirements specified in external standards should use the same set of audit criteria across organizations.

The role of IT audit in information security management

Information security management supports IT auditing by taking responsibility for implementing and correctly configuring internal controls related to security.

Security controls are an important subject of internal controls, but still a subset, meaning information security does not cover the full range of IT controls in an organization. IT auditing also supports information security management, by providing detailed, critical examinations of internal controls implemented to achieve security objectives and by confirming that IT operations match organizational policies, procedures, standards, and guidelines. As noted in Chapter 6, security criteria apply in audits of virtually every type of IT component that might be subject to an IT audit. IT audit procedures are also useful for some types of narrowly scoped examinations, such as checking a system or network device for proper configuration against a specification such as the Defense Information Systems Agency's Security Technical Implementation Guides (STIGs) [27] or U.S. Government Configuration Baseline (USGCB) [28], or secure configuration guidelines provided by technology vendors for their products.

Information security management programs are also the subject of IT audits. ISO/IEC 27001 emphasizes the importance of auditing an organization's ISMS using formal internal audit procedures to examine security control objectives, implemented controls, and processes and procedures for operating, maintaining, and improving the ISMS [26]. Information security programs may be subject to formal review, inspection, or audit, depending on the industry and the nature of oversight to which an organization is subject. Examination of security controls is also an element of many types of internal and external audits of internal controls including those focused on control of financial accounting and reporting systems in publicly traded companies.

Relevant source material

Each of the organizational functions addressed in this chapter represent business disciplines that are the subject of abundant business and management literature and the focus of multiple professional associations, standards bodies, and other organizations. Key sources of additional information include:

- IT governance
  - Control Objectives for Information and Related Technology (COBIT) [3]
  - COSO's *Internal Control—Integrated Framework* [29]
  - ISO/IEC 38500:2008, *Corporate Governance of Information Technology* [30]
  - Web sites and online resources of the IT Governance Institute (http://www.itgi.org) and ISACA (http://www.isaca.org)
- Risk management
  - COSO's *Enterprise Risk Management—Integrated Framework* [10]
  - ISO/IEC 31000:2009, *Risk Management—Principles and Guidelines* [5]
  - NIST Special Publication 800-39, *Managing Information Security Risk: Organization, Mission, and Information System View* [6]
- Compliance and certification
  - Statement on Auditing Standards 117, *Compliance Audits* [17]

- ISO online guidance on certification [31] and standards and guidance from the ISO Committee on Conformity Assessment (CASCO)
- Quality management
  - *The ASQ Auditing Handbook* [22]
  - ISO 9001:2008, *Quality Management Systems—Requirements* [21]
  - IAASB *Handbook of International Quality Control, Auditing Review, Other Assurance, and Related Services Pronouncements*[32]
- Information security management
  - ISO/IEC 27001:2005, *Information—Security Techniques—Information Security Management Systems—Requirements*[26]
  - ISO/IEC 27002:2005, *Information Technology—Security Techniques—Code of Practice for Information Security Management*[33]
  - NIST Special Publication 800-53 Revision 4, *Security and Privacy Controls for Federal Information Systems and Organizations*[34]

Summary

This chapter identified major organizational management functions that influence and are supported by IT auditing, including GRC and certification, and quality management. Each of these functions has a reciprocal relationship with organizations IT audit programs, helping to identify and prioritize target areas for auditing and using the findings produced in IT audits as inputs. The information in this chapter was intended to place IT auditing in the proper context and to explain the nature and intent of IT audits performed in support of different management disciplines. This information also highlights some of the key differences between internal and external audit programs and activities which will be expanded upon in the next two chapters.

References

[1] IT Governance Institute Board briefing on IT governance, 2nd ed Rolling Meadows (IL): IT Governance Institute; 2003.

[2] IT Governance Institute CobiT 4.1. Rolling Meadows (IL): IT Governance Institute; 2007.

[3] ISACA COBIT 5: a business framework for the governance and management of enterprise IT. Rolling Meadows (IL): ISACA; 2012.

[4] ISO Guide 73:2009. Risk management—Vocabulary.

[5] ISO/IEC 31000:2009. Risk management—Principles and guidelines.

[6] National Institute of Standards and Technology Managing information security risk: Organization, mission, and information system view. Gaithersburg (MD): National Institute of Standards and Technology, Computer Security Division; 2011 March. [special publication 800-39].

[7] Wrightson MT, Caldwell SL. Further refinements needed to assess risks and prioritize protective measures at ports and other critical infrastructure. Report to Congressional

Requesters. Washington (DC): Government Accountability Office; 2005 December. [GAO Report 06-91. The GAO risk management framework is defined in Appendix A].

[8] Crouhy M, Galai D, Mark R. The essentials of risk management. New York (NY): McGraw-Hill; 2006.

[9] ISO/IEC 27005:2011. Information technology—Security techniques—Information security risk management.

[10] Committee of Sponsoring Organizations of the Treadway Commission Enterprise risk management—Integrated framework. New York (NY): Committee of Sponsoring Organizations of the Treadway Commission; 2004.

[11] Common Vulnerabilities and Exposures [Internet]. McLean (VA): The MITRE Corporation [updated 2013 May 16; cited 2013 June 4]. Available from: <http://cve.mitre.org>.

[12] CERT Coordination Center [Internet]. Pittsburgh (PA): Software Engineering Institute [cited 2013 June 4]. Available from: <http://www.cert.org/certcc.html>.

[13] US-CERT—United States Computer Emergency Readiness Team [Internet]. Washington (DC): Department of Homeland Security [cited 2012 January 15]. Available from: <http://www.us-cert.gov>.

[14] International Organisation of Supreme Audit Institutions Information system security review methodology. Copenhagen (DK): INTOSAI Professional Standards Committee; 1995. [ISSAI 5310. Appendix H].

[15] Guide for conducting risk assessments. Gaithersburg (MD): National Institute of Standards and Technology, Computer Security Division; 2012 September. Special Publication 800-30 revision 1. Threat sources, events, and vulnerabilities appear in Appendices D, E, and F, respectively.

[16] Health Information Technology for Economic and Clinical Health Act of 2009, Pub. L. No. 111-5, 123 Stat. 226 § 13411.

[17] Compliance audits. New York (NY): American Institute of Certified Public Accountants, Auditing Standards Board; 2009 December. Statement on Auditing Standards 117.

[18] ISO 9000:2005. Quality management—Fundamentals and vocabulary.

[19] IEEE P730-2002 Standard for software quality assurance processes. New York (NY): Institute of Electrical and Electronics Engineers; 2002.

[20] Parasuraman A, Zeithaml VA, Barry LL. SERVQUAL: a multiple-item scale for measuring consumer perceptions of service quality. J Retailing 1988;64(1):12–40.

[21] ISO 9001:2008. Quality management systems—Requirements.

[22] Russell JP, editor. The ASQ auditing handbook (4th ed.). Milwaukee (WI): ASQ Quality Press; 2013.

[23] Deming WE. Out of the crisis. Cambridge (MA): MIT Center for Advanced Educational Services; 1986. p. 88–89.

[24] Securities and Exchange Commission. Management's report on internal control over financial reporting and certification of disclosure in Exchange Act periodic reports; final rule. 68 Fed. Reg. 36636; 2003.

[25] Directive of the European Parliament and of the Council on Statutory Audits of Annual Accounts and Consolidated Accounts, Directive 2006/43/EC; 2006 May.

[26] ISO/IEC 27001:2005. Information—Security techniques—Information security management systems—Requirements.

[27] Security Technical Implementation Guides [Internet]. Defense Information Systems Agency, Information Assurance Support Environment [updated 2013 June 7; cited 2013 June 7]. Available from: <http://iase.disa.mil/stigs/index.html>.

[28] U.S. Government Configuration Baseline (USGCB) [Internet]. Gaithersburg (MD): National Institute of Standards and Technology, Information Technology Laboratory [created 2010 February 19; updated 2013 June 3; cited 2013 June 7]. Available from: <http://usgcb.nist.gov>.

[29] Committee of Sponsoring Organizations of the Treadway Commission Internal control—Integrated framework. New York (NY): Committee of Sponsoring Organizations of the Treadway Commission; 2013.

[30] ISO/IEC 38500:2008. Corporate governance of information technology.

[31] Certification—ISO [Internet]. Geneva: International Organization for Standardization [cited 2013 June 7]. Available from: <http://www.iso.org/iso/home/standards/certification.htm>.

[32] International Auditing and Assurance Standards Board. Handbook of international quality control, auditing review, other assurance, and related services pronouncements. New York (NY): International Auditing and Assurance Standards Board; 2012 June.

[33] ISO/IEC 27002:2005. Information technology—Security techniques—Code of practice for information security management.

[34] Security and privacy controls for federal information systems and organizations. Gaithersburg (MD): National Institute of Standards and Technology, Computer Security Division; 2013 April. Special Publication 800-53 revision 4.

Internal Auditing

INFORMATION IN THIS CHAPTER:

- Internal audit as an organizational capability
- Internal IT audit drivers and rationale
- Benefits of internal auditing
- Internal audit challenges
- Internal auditors

The purpose and scope of IT audits, and the procedures used to perform them, differ significantly for internal audits compared to external audits. The Institute for Internal Auditors includes a formal definition of internal auditing as part of its International Professional Practices Framework (IPPF): "Internal auditing is an independent, objective assurance and consulting activity designed to add value and improve an organization's operations. It helps an organization accomplish its objectives by bringing a systematic, disciplined approach to evaluate and improve the effectiveness of risk management, control, and governance processes" [1]. External auditing also features a formally defined disciplined approach and informs risk management, determinations of control effectiveness, and organizational governance, but internal audits are performed by employees of the organization (or contractors hired to work on the organization's behalf) subject to the audits, following plans, procedures, and criteria chosen by the organization. In contrast, external audits are performed by auditors representing firms wholly separate from the organization being audited, typically applying regulatory or industry standards, or other criteria developed outside the organization.

The differences between internal and external auditing go well beyond the organizations and their auditors responsible for conducting audits, as a wider variety of motivations often drives internal auditing. Many of the same standards and sources of guidance influence internal and external IT auditing, but as illustrated in Figure 3.1 internal auditing reflects organizational policy and program perspectives on what to audit and how different types of audits are conducted, as well as subject matter knowledge applicable to each organization and the kinds of IT audits it performs. Broadly defined auditing standards and practices—such as Generally Accepted Auditing Standards (GAAS) and International Standards on Auditing (ISA)—are just as applicable to IT auditing as they are to financial or

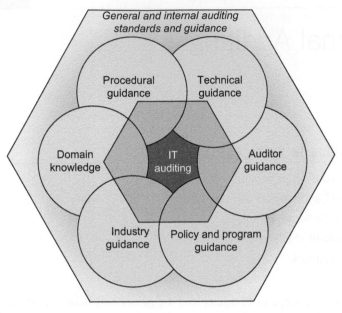

FIGURE 3.1

Internal IT auditing draws upon many sources of guidance informing audit program structure, audit procedures and protocols, areas of audit focus, and auditor practices and qualifications.

more general operational audits. These standards establish a basic set of principles and audit program requirements to which organizations add industry or domain-specific guidance as well as any internally developed procedures and criteria. This chapter describes the structural and operational characteristics of internal IT audit programs, the expectations and obligations for the organizations that maintain such programs, and the knowledge and skills needed by the auditors who conduct internal audits. It also explains common drivers and sources of motivation for internal auditing and highlights some of the primary anticipated benefits and potential challenges associated with internal IT auditing.

Internal audit as an organizational capability

Both external and internal IT audit practices depend on formally defined procedures executed by capable auditors with sufficient organizational knowledge and domain expertise to effectively carry out the different types of audits an organization needs. The key structural difference with respect to internal auditing is the need for an organizational component or function—typically called the internal audit program—responsible for conducting audits within the organization. Depending on the size and management structure of the organization, the industry in which it participates, and factors such as whether the organization is publicly traded, the internal audit program may be a large unit within the organization with resources dedicated only to auditing or it may be a functional capability drawing resources as needed from many parts of the organization. Irrespective of the specific structural features or the number of staff or other resources associated with it, an internal audit program needs proper authority to conduct audits, an audit strategy or plan to guide the program's management and operations, and personnel qualified to perform the full range of audits applicable to the organization. The audit program must also establish and continually demonstrate independence and objectivity, for the program overall, the managers and executives responsible for the program, and the auditors who perform the audits.

Independence and objectivity

Independence is the freedom from bias, outside control, or authority that, in an internal auditing context, ensures that the audit program is neither responsible for nor beholden to the parts of the organization it audits and, similarly, that individual auditors do not work for projects, operational functions, or business units that they audit. Objectivity in audit practices connotes more than independence—an objective auditor makes judgments based on evidence, is free from conflicts of interest with the subjects of auditing activities, and is able to act with impartiality. Because employees of an organization acting as internal auditors cannot be fully independent from the organization (due among other things to the fact that they presumably earn a salary from the organization) in a way that external auditors can, standards and practices intended explicitly for internal auditors tend to emphasize auditor objectivity rather than independence [2,3]. Independence is a central tenet of most auditing standards, practice guidance, and codes of ethics specified by major audit-related professional associations and standards development organizations. No matter which standards and sources of auditing guidance an organization chooses to adopt, independence needs to be considered. Notable examples include:

- The second general standard in the GAAS, dictates that "In all matters relating to the assignment, an independence in mental attitude is to be maintained by the auditor or auditors" [4].
- The ISA issued by the International Auditing and Assurance Standards Board (IAASB) emphasize the importance of maintaining both an attitude and the appearance of independence, as auditor independence "safeguards the auditor's ability to form an audit opinion without being affected by influences that might compromise that opinion" [5].
- Attribute standard 1110 in the Institute of Internal Auditors (IIA) International Standards for the Professional Practice of Auditing stipulates that, "The internal audit activity must be independent, and internal auditors must be objective in performing their work" [2].

- Independence is one of the principles of auditing in ISO 19011: "Auditors should be independent of the activity being audited wherever practicable, and should in all cases act in a manner that is free from bias and conflict of interest" [6].
- The International Federation of Accountants (IFAC) Code of Ethics requires both objectivity and independence for professionals engaged in assurance engagements, including independence of mind "that permits the expression of a conclusion without being affected by influences that compromise professional judgment, allowing an individual to act with integrity, and exercise objectivity and professional skepticism" [7].
- ISACA's Code of Professional Ethics requires members and holders of ISACA certifications to "Perform their duties with objectivity, due diligence and professional care, in accordance with professional standards" [3].

In practice, the prominence across so many audit standards and sources of guidance means that many organizations and their auditors are obligated to ensure that internal audit programs reflect appropriate structural independence and levels of objectivity. This can be challenging for smaller organizations or organizations of any size that lack the resources to dedicate to auditing; the emphasis in these organizations should be on demonstrating independence by making sure that no shared responsibility exists between audit program personnel and what they audit.

Establishing the IT audit program

The audit program is the formally defined department, business unit, or function within an organization responsible for planning, performing, and reporting the results of all internal audit activities. The scope of operations for an internal audit program typically comprises all types of audits the organization conducts, including financial and non-IT operational audits as well as audits of IT controls, procedures, environments, and capabilities. Large organizations or organizations of any size that specialize in IT-intensive operations or that provide IT services may have dedicated IT audit programs. In many cases, however, IT auditing is a specialized function within a more broadly focused internal audit program. As shown in Figure 3.2, the internal audit program operates under the supervision of a Chief Audit Executive (CAE) and reports through the CAE to the audit committee of the organization's Board of Directors. The existence and exact composition of the audit committee depends on the type of organization, but audit committee members typically must not be part of the management team to ensure the committee's independence. The audit committee in many large organizations is responsible for overseeing both external and internal audit activities, regardless of how many different business units or functions have responsibility for performing or supporting various types of auditing. The CAE (or equivalent role designated with an alternate title) is responsible for the internal audit program, which typically comprises multiple audit managers and groups of auditors with specialized expertise suited to conducting the different types of internal audits needed by the organization.

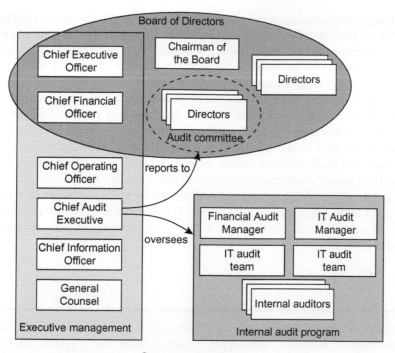

Board of Directors

Chief Executive Officer

Chairman of the Board

Directors

Chief Financial Officer

Directors

Audit committee

Chief Operating Officer

reports to

Chief Audit Executive

oversees

Financial Audit Manager

IT Audit Manager

Chief Information Officer

IT audit team

IT audit team

General Counsel

Internal auditors

Executive management

Internal audit program

Corporate governance

FIGURE 3.2

An internal audit program works under the supervision of an audit executive or comparable member of the senior management team and reports to the audit committee of the organization's Board of Directors.

> Smaller organizations may not have boards of directors or dedicated executive oversight for auditing, but organizations of any size with a formal internal audit program need a member of the executive team with responsibility for the program and a full understanding of the key audiences and stakeholders for internal audits.

The general characterization of an internal audit program and its reporting structure comes primarily from the context of publicly traded companies (or, to be more specific, issuers of securities as these companies are referred in United States or European Community regulations), as current U.S. regulations applicable to such organizations require, as a condition of listing on a regulated exchange, the existence of an audit committee within boards of directors and mandate external and internal examination of internal controls with results reported to the audit committee [8,9]. While public sector organizations often do not have individual boards of directors, in government agencies in the United States and many other countries the position of Inspector General is functionally equivalent to the CAE in a commercial organization, and offices of inspectors general serve as internal audit programs. Not all organizations recognizing the need for or value of internal auditing have the same formal management and oversight, although boards of directors are typically in place in many privately held commercial firms and nonprofit organizations. Even without formal organization structure and reporting relationships, the functional roles and responsibilities for internal auditing summarized in Table 3.1 are similar across most organizations. More variation exists regarding the presence of a dedicated IT audit function—some organizations maintain IT auditing capabilities only to satisfy requirements associated with financial, operational, or compliance audits, often relying on internal auditors whose skills and experience include IT subject areas. Organizations with formal IT governance, IT-centric risk management, or control certification programs may be more likely to have dedicated IT audit programs.

With respect to IT auditing, the word *program* is often used to refer to the department or functional unit within an organization that performs audits. In some published reference books and available online sources of guidance from professional associations, however, the term connotes a set of explicit procedures for completing particular types of IT audits. This second usage of audit *program* has the same meaning as *protocol*, *checklist*, or *guide* in referring to step-by-step instructions and examination methods used in IT auditing. Internal IT auditors need to be aware of the correct organization-specific connotation of these terms, and when incorporating externally developed guidelines and materials should both recognize and seek to avoid the potential for confusion from different usage or interpretation of these terms by different sources.

Internal audit program charter

The audit program charter describes the purpose of the internal audit program, including external and internal needs the program is intended to address and, in particular, the relationship between the audit program and governance, risk management, compliance, and other enterprise management functions. No matter where the internal audit program is positioned within the structure of the organization, its existence, purpose, and authority needs to be formally documented and communicated throughout the organization to help ensure that internal auditing activities are viewed in the proper context. Organizations that do not communicate this type of information about their internal audit programs are likely to encounter

Table 3.1 Internal Audit Roles and Responsibilities

Role	Responsibilities
CEA (alternately called Chief Auditor, Director of Audit, Lead Auditor, or equivalent title)	• Oversees the internal audit function with the organization • Reports directly to the audit committee
Audit committee	• Subset of the Board of Directors, typically comprising only independent directors • Provides oversight of internal and external auditing • Required for public company boards of directors under the Sarbanes–Oxley Act
Management team	• Key members of the management team, such as the CEO, COO, and CFO, typically in consultation with the full Board of Directors, approve budgets and resource allocations for the internal audit program
Board of Directors	• Considers audit reports and recommendations and makes decisions regarding actions to take in response to audit findings
Audit Manager	• Responsible for ensuring the proper conduct of specific types of audits (financial, operational, IT) within the audit program • Supervises one or more teams of internal auditors
Auditor	• Performs audits, working alone or as part of a team depending on the type and scope of audit activities needed • Develops and maintains knowledge and subject matter expertise relevant to the types of audits performed • Reports to the Audit Manager and/or the CAE
Operations Manager	• Ensures access is afforded to auditors when components or processes under the Manager's responsibility are audited • Furnishes or assigns resources as needed to support audits and, as applicable, provide information to auditors
Operations staff	• Supports or facilitates audits of components or processes operated by staff • May be observed, interviewed, asked to demonstrate controls, or otherwise provide evidence to auditors

FIGURE 3.3

The internal IT audit program's responsibilities include defining strategic and operational planning, selecting auditing tools, procedures and resources, conducting audits and reporting their results, and ensuring audit program quality.

misperceptions or fear about internal audits and may find operations personnel hesitant or resistant to cooperate with auditors. Audit program charter templates and associated guidance on creating charters are publicly available from professional associations such as the IIA [10] or ISACA [11]. Recommended contents for an audit program charter include clear statements of purpose, authority, and commitment to independence and objectivity; descriptions of roles and responsibilities including reporting relationships within the organization; delineation of scope of audit program activities; explanation of basic operating structure; and any standards, frameworks, or guidelines explicitly adopted or adhered to by the audit program. The charter also specifies the types of activities to be conducted by the audit program, including developing and maintaining organizational audit strategy and audit plans, as well as structuring and performing audits and reporting their results. The audit charter typically describes the roles and responsibilities for functions or personnel outside the audit program, including establishing points of contact for program communications to management and to the departments, or business units responsible for aspects of the organization that will be audited. In summary, the audit charter touches on all of the areas for which the audit program is responsible, including those illustrated in Figure 3.3.

Internal IT auditing has its own domain-specific principles, practices, assumptions, and vocabulary, all of which may be well understood by personnel working within the audit program but less familiar to others in the organization who interact with auditors. Clarity of purpose, intent, and terminology can be just as important for operations staff and managers responsible for parts of the organization subject to internal audit as they are for auditors. The internal audit program can facilitate such an understanding by making audit plans and procedures available to those in the organization who will undergo audits or will provide support to audit activities.

Internal audit program responsibilities

As the organizational function that manage and conducts IT and other types of audits, the responsibilities of the internal audit program include creating and executing the overall audit strategy for the organization and, potentially, domain-specific strategies or plans for IT, operational, and compliance and other types of internal audits. The audit strategy declares goals and objectives that the internal audit program seeks to achieve and specifies outcomes or performance metrics against which to measure the success of the program in meeting its objectives. The internal audit program executes the strategy using one or more audit plans that define what will be audited, by whom, at what frequency, and with what protocols, standards, or criteria. Both the audit strategy and audit plans typically refer to a formally documented audit universe—an inventory of all assets, business processes, programs, functions, and components within the organization that may be subject to audit. The audit strategy may explain the process and criteria by which organizational decisions are made about what to audit and when. Audit plans reflect the application of prioritization criteria to establish the set of audit activities that will be undertaken during the period the plan covers. Organizations often update or revise their audit strategies when significant changes occur in mission focus, operating environment, regulatory requirements, or market conditions. Audit plans typically span a shorter time horizon than strategies reflecting annual or quarterly budgeting and investment cycles or schedules associated with major projects or organizational initiatives. Regardless of intended duration, audit program managers need to align audit plans with known or anticipated audit needs and the availability of program funding, auditors, or other resources.

The audit program (or different units with the program where an organization maintains separate audit teams to address different domains or types of audits) develops or selects the audit methodologies, procedures, and protocols to be used in each type of audit the organization needs to perform. The breadth of processes, operating environments, technologies, and controls potentially subject to IT auditing can present many challenges, from specifying the right set of audit criteria to apply to ensuring the reliability and validity of audit procedures conducted by different teams or individuals. Defining standard audit protocols is one way to help ensure the quality and consistency of internal IT audits, especially for types of audits an organization needs to perform more than once. It can be equally important for auditors to have explicit instructions when conducting a particular type of audit for the first time, to make sure the audit covers the subject matter at an appropriate depth and level of rigor. While organization-specific characteristics may justify the use of internally developed audit protocols, for a large proportion of IT audits there are available checklists, technical configuration specification, and sources of procedural guidance that organizations can use as-is or adapt to suit different IT audit needs. External guidance is often available addressing IT audits in particular industries, such as the *IT Examination Handbook* [12] from the Federal Financial Institutions Examination Council (FFIEC) or the American Institute of Certified Public Accountants' (AICPA) guide, *Reporting on Controls at a Service Organization* [13]. In addition to purpose-specific audit protocols, an audit program also typically defines policies and standards addressing how auditors should perform their examinations, preferred testing methods for different kinds of controls, types of evidence required to substantiate findings, and formats and templates to be used to produce reports and other audit documentation. Available management standards used to assess the quality of internal auditing, such as ISO 19011, can provide guidance to organizations regarding the policies, procedures, and other elements the audit program should have in place [6]. Organizations seeking to operate their internal audit programs in accordance with relevant international standards should plan to undertake periodic quality audits of the audit program itself, following standards such as ISO 19011 or the American Society for Quality's *Auditing Handbook* [14].

Internal IT auditors tasked with performing audits of specific technical components or IT-related processes or functions can often adapt or incorporate externally defined audit protocols or checklists. Where suitable for meeting internal objectives, using these sources saves time compared to developing such protocols from scratch, and also introduces a level of commonality or consistency across audits and auditors that can help ensure the reliability of audits performed by the internal audit program. Achieving audit process consistency also corresponds to a higher degree of maturity for the audit program through implementing well defined and proven program elements. For example, ISACA offers a variety of IT audit and assurance resources based on standards and guidelines in its IT assurance framework [15]

Perhaps the most obvious responsibility assigned to the internal audit program is performing audits. Operating from its position of independence within the organization structure, the audit program assigns auditors and other resources following the audit plans it has developed and approved. The set of audit activities conducted in a given time frame should reflect appropriate organizational priorities based on criteria such as business or asset value, assessed risk, internal policies, or regulations or other external drivers. These priorities affect IT audits as well as other types of audits, although the risk factors and other drivers typically differ for

IT audits compared to financial, quality, or operational audits. The performance of each IT audit should follow established audit protocols, leveraging available methodologies and tools as appropriate, and should result in the development and delivery of an audit report and associated supporting evidence. A thorough description of IT auditing appears in Chapter 8. One advantage to internal over external forms of auditing is the flexibility organizations often have to engage in informal or partial audits when resources or audit priorities constrain the ability of the audit program to address all desired areas. IT auditing by definition represents a formally structured process, but that does not mean that auditors or other personnel cannot conduct some types of tests or control examinations as needed, without committing to the full procedural and documentation requirements specified for formal audits. Informal auditing can be especially useful in situations where an organization is working to improve operational controls or remediate weaknesses found in previous audits—informal audits offer an opportunity to verify if corrective actions have been taken and to try to determine if those actions have properly addressed the weaknesses and mitigated corresponding risk.

The results of internal audits are typically documented in formal reports and communicated to the organizational executive in charge of the audit program and the audit committee. The CAE is responsible for providing status reports or updates on internal audit activity to the audit committee to facilitate the effective monitoring and oversight of the internal audit program by the committee. Where weaknesses and corresponding risks have been identified, the audit committee has an important role in reviewing and approving recommendations for corrective action. Members of the audit committee are typically independent directors and therefore may not have the familiarity with day-to-day operations needed to fully understand the implications of audit findings and recommendations. Determining the appropriate courses of action to respond to audit findings often requires collaboration among the audit program, operational personnel, organizational management, and the audit committee.

Most widely available internal audit standards and guidance approach auditing from a perspective that assumes certain organizational characteristics, which are common among large, publicly traded companies but not always present in smaller organizations or those in noncommercial sectors. Legislation and regulations influencing audit requirements—including internal auditing—in force in the United States, European Union countries, and many other industrialized nations also focus on the creation and enforcement of rules for large commercial enterprises, particularly those with public stockholders. This emphasis does not mean that prevailing audit standards and practices do not apply to other types of organizations. In such organizations, however, operating internal audit programs conforming to those sources of guidance may require greater adaptation or more flexible interpretation to achieve audit program objectives in a manner that fits with actual resources, governance, and management structure.

Benefits of internal IT auditing

In contrast to the compliance focus of many types of external audits, internal audits are driven in large part by an organization's desire to find operational weaknesses, discover any deviations from established policies or standards, assess effectiveness, and identify opportunities to improve operational processes and capabilities where possible. As emphasized in Chapter 2, IT audits differ from other types of assessments or analyses in that an audit compares what the organization does to an explicitly defined set of criteria, whether those criteria represent internal policies and procedures, externally defined standards or certification requirements, or legislated rules and regulations. Beyond mandatory internal audit requirements applicable to many publicly traded companies, the rationale for establishing and operating internal IT audit capabilities commonly includes objectives such as:

- supporting corporate IT governance, risk management, and compliance programs;
- verifying adherence to organizationally defined policies, procedures, and standards;
- satisfying requirements to achieve or maintain process maturity, quality management, or internal control certification;
- adding formality to or increasing the rigor of self-assessment processes and activities; and
- preparing for or "shadowing" anticipated external audits.

Although internal IT auditing often requires a substantial investment of resources, in many organizations the potential benefits to be realized from conducting effective, well managed IT audits justify the resource commitment. Establishing an internal audit program is required for some organizations, in which case the desire to comply with legal or regulatory requirements may provide sufficient motivation. Where internal IT auditing is discretionary rather than mandatory, organizations are more likely to realize the potential benefits from audit activities if they have committed to enterprise management functions such as IT governance or risk management, both of which make use of IT auditing and audit results to inform the selection and operation of internal controls. Maintaining an effective internal auditing program also helps organizations demonstrate adherence to the principle of due care by showing that they are acting in a competent and diligent manner with respect to operating and maintaining their internal controls. Providing evidence of due care offers information of potential importance to investors and business partners and may also offer legal protection in disputes over liability or business practices.

Compared to external auditing, organizations have more flexibility to structure their internal IT audit programs to suit the needs of the organization. In IT auditing contexts where both internal and external audits apply, some organizations may prefer to forego internal auditing and instead rely on the work of external auditors to provide information about their IT operations, controls, or compliance. Even where both types of auditing address the same subject matter, there are several potential advantages to using internal audits, in combination with or (where feasible) instead of external audits. These advantages include the ability to leverage auditors and other personnel who are familiar with the organization, its mission and business objectives, and its operations. External auditors—even those who conduct audits of an organization on a repeated basis—rarely develop an understanding of the organization's processes and controls that can match the knowledge and organization-specific experience of internal auditors. Another beneficial aspect is that internal auditing allows organizations to review audit results (positive or negative) and plan necessary responses without the outside scrutiny or publicity that might accompany external audits. Similarly, performing an internal IT audit to help prepare for an anticipated external audit often gives organizations the opportunity to implement corrective action to remedy weaknesses or deficiencies that would presumably have been identified by external auditors.

Internal audit challenges

Although many potential benefits accrue to organizations that establish effective internal IT audit capabilities, not all organizations have sufficient resources available to dedicate staff to auditing, or to do so in a way that covers all the areas within an organization that need auditing. For some organizations—notably including many publicly traded companies—internal auditing must be in place, forcing such organizations to find ways to overcome the challenge of limited resources. The cost associated with some types of mandatory internal auditing, such as the internal assessment of controls over financial reporting mandated by §404 of the Sarbanes–Oxley Act [8], is the source of a common objection to such requirements. Aside from the resource costs associated with internal IT auditing, other challenges include the significant skills and expertise needed by internal auditors and the perceived or actual lack of independence for internal audit activities, particularly in smaller organizations. The range of operational processes, technical components, and internal controls potentially subject to IT auditing is varied enough in many organizations, that it is unreasonable to expect that individual auditors would have sufficient breadth of knowledge and skills to address all of them. Even with detailed audit protocols in place, organizations often need to enlist the services of multiple auditors (possibly including outside contractors) to cover the scope of IT audits it wants to perform. Internal IT auditing performed by employees of the organization also raises potential questions regarding auditor independence and objectivity. With an obvious financial relationship between employer and employees, internal auditing standards and guidelines emphasize the importance for auditors to work outside the chain of management authority over the functions or operational aspects they audit [6]. Organizations can address matters of auditor objectivity by sponsoring or encouraging internal auditors to attend training or pursue certifications from organizations that prioritize objectivity and related professional practice principles among their members, such as the IIA, the American Society for Quality, and

ISACA. Organizations and their audit program staff should also be aware of and able to address common sources of unintended bias in making judgments. These include favoring easily obtained or frequently used information; mistakes in estimating chance, probability, samples, or rates of occurrence; and tendencies to seek information that confirms prior observations or expected results [16]. Auditors have the benefit of an explicit set of criteria against which to compare what is in place or what actually occurs in an organization; accurate audits depend on objective examinations of controls, behavior, and associated evidence.

Internal auditors

Chapter 1 provided a brief description of the varied educational and professional backgrounds and career development paths some IT auditors follow. Internal IT auditors often have substantial prior work in information technology, whether their experience includes broad IT knowledge spanning multiple domains or more specialized areas of expertise. It is certainly possible to begin in finance, accounting, or other business domains associated with conventional auditing and move towards a specialization in IT. IT-specific knowledge is required, however, to understand IT audit criteria and being able to compare them to the implementation, configuration, and operations and maintenance details of IT systems and technologies. Additional IT skills may be required to correctly execute test procedures or apply examination methodologies used in different types of IT auditing. Common subject matter topics with which internal IT auditors should be familiar include:

- business domains and associated processes supported by IT systems;
- data governance, data management processes, data backup and restoration, and storage technologies;
- IT policies and procedures;
- operations and maintenance processes;
- systems development life cycle process and activities;
- application, systems, and security architecture;
- computer operating systems;
- IT governance and risk management processes and frameworks;
- internal control types and applicability;
- IT process management or security management models; and
- IT-related standards and certification criteria.

IT auditing skills can often be developed on-the-job, particularly in organizations with internal audit programs having sufficient resources to assign teams of auditors with multiple levels of experience to specific audit tasks. External training and certification programs are also widely available to individuals seeking to specialize in internal auditing, including the Certified Internal Auditor (CIA) credential from the IIA and the Certified Information Systems Auditor (CISA) from ISACA. Many professional organizations and standards development bodies publish auditing guidance or other materials that can be used to help train or expand the skills of audit personnel. One challenge for IT audit personnel is that much of the available guidance on auditing standards, principles, and practices covers internal auditing overall without addressing considerations specific to IT auditing. For instance, the Statements on Auditing Standards (SAS) and Statements on Standards for Attestation Engagements (SSAE) published by the AICPA contain extensive guidance on conducting audits generally, but offer little explicit information about IT environments or IT-related internal controls. The same is true for the different sets of ISA issued by the IIA and the IAASB. All of these sources of audit guidance acknowledge the significance of IT in auditing engagements, but none distinguish areas of expertise or identify skills needed for conducting IT audits. Some guidance from organizations focused on IT governance or assurance is specifically applicable to IT auditing, such as ISACA's *COBIT 5 for Assurance*, published in 2013 [17].

Organizations without sufficient internal resources to staff their internal audit programs may find it more practical to engage the use of outside contractors than to recruit, hire, or train their own employees. For smaller organizations or those with limited IT auditing needs, outsourcing their internal auditors may be more cost effective as well, particularly if auditing activity demands less than full-time resources and internal-audit-focused employees cannot be assigned to other responsibilities. Despite the higher direct labor cost for contractors compared to employees, using auditors from outside sources may also enable an organization to ensure that the skills and experience of the contract auditors are appropriate for the type of IT audit to be conducted. While contractors—much like external auditors—are unlikely to know an organization's internal operating environment as well as employees, organizations can also specify qualifications, certifications, or domain expertise when enlisting the services of outside audit specialists such that hired contractors may be as well or more qualified as internally staffed and trained auditors would be. Organizations with recurring short-term internal IT audit requirements (such as annual preparation for an external compliance audit) can in some cases arrange for the same individual to perform the audit each time, building familiarity and continuity into the audit process in a way that provides some of the same benefits as using employees for auditing. Regardless of the staffing approach employed, organizations can help ensure the quality and consistency of its internal IT audits by assigning auditors with relevant experience and qualifications and by prescribing the use of formally defined audit protocols.

Relevant source material

Internal IT auditors rely on both general auditing standards and guidance and on IT-specific references appropriate to the subjects of the IT audits they perform and the approaches or organizational perspectives used by the IT audit program. GAAS and ISA provide principles and practices applicable to all types of auditing. Procedural guidance and standards specifically focused on internal auditing include:

- IIA's *International Standards for the Professional Practice of Internal Auditing* [2]
- ISACA's *Standards for IS Audit and Assurance* [11] and guidance on audit programs [14]

- FFIEC *IT Examination Handbook* [12]
- COBIT 5 for Assurance [16]
- ISO 19011, *Guidelines for Auditing Management Systems* [6]

Summary

This chapter focused on internal IT auditing, contrasting it with external auditing (the subject of the next chapter) and describing the structural and operational features of internal audit programs that include IT audits within their scope. It highlighted the purpose, objectives, and rationale for establishing and maintaining internal auditing capabilities and described some of the potential benefits organizations expect to realize from effectively managed internal audit programs. The material in this chapter explains the typical positioning of the internal audit function within the organization structure and its relation to governance bodies such as corporate boards of directors. It also described some of the characteristics of internal auditors and the relevant skills and experience auditors need to do their jobs effectively.

References

[1] Definition of Internal Auditing [Internet]. Altamonte Springs (FL): Institute of Internal Auditors [cited 2013 May 4]. Available from: <https://na.theiia.org/standards-guidance/mandatory-guidance/Pages/Definition-of-Internal-Auditing.aspx>.

[2] Institute of Internal Auditors International standards for the professional practice of internal auditing. Altamonte Springs (FL): Institute of Internal Auditors; 2012 October.

[3] Code of Professional Ethics [Internet]. Rolling Meadows (IL): ISACA [cited 2013 May 4]. Available from: <http://www.isaca.org/Certification/Code-of-Professional-Ethics/Pages/default.aspx>.

[4] American Institute of Certified Public Accountants Generally accepted auditing standards. New York (NY): American Institute of Certified Public Accountants, Auditing Standards Board; 2001 December. [statement on auditing standards 95].

[5] International Federation of Accountants Overall objectives of the independent auditor and the conduct of an audit in accordance with International Standards on Auditing. New York (NY): International Federation of Accountants; 2012. [International Standard on Auditing 200].

[6] ISO 19011:2011. Guidelines for auditing management systems.

[7] International Ethics Standards Board Code of ethics for professional accountants. New York (NY): International Ethics Standards Board; 2009 July.

[8] Sarbanes–Oxley Act of 2002, Pub. L. No. 107-204, 116 Stat. 745.

[9] Securities and Exchange Commission. Standards related to listed company audit committees [final rule]. 68 Fed. Reg. 18788 (2003).

[10] The Internal Audit Function [Internet]. Altamonte Springs (FL): Institute of Internal Auditors [cited 2013 June 14]. Available from: <https://na.theiia.org/standards-guidance/topics/pages/the-internal-audit-function.aspx>.

[11] Standards for IS Audit and Assurance [Internet]. Rolling Meadows (IL): ISACA [cited 2013 May 4]. Available from: <http://www.isaca.org/Knowledge-Center/Standards/Pages/Standards-for-IT-Audit-and-Assurance-English-.aspx>.

[12] Federal Financial Institutions Examination Council IT examination handbook. Arlington (VA): Federal Financial Institutions Examination Council; 2012 April.

[13] American Institute of Certified Public Accountants Reporting on controls at a service organization relevant to security, availability, processing integrity, confidentiality, or privacy. Durham (NC): American Institute of Certified Public Accountants; 2012 March.

[14] Russell JP, editor. The ASQ auditing handbook (4th ed.). Milwaukee (WI): ASQ Quality Press; 2013.

[15] ISACA ITAF: a professional practices framework for IS audit/assurance, 2nd ed. Rolling Meadows (IL): ISACA; 2013.

[16] Bazerman MH, Moore D. Judgment in managerial decision making. Hoboken (NJ): John Wiley & Sons; 2009.

[17] ISACA COBIT 5 for assurance. Rolling Meadows (IL): ISACA; 2013.

External Auditing

Two key characteristics distinguish external auditing from internal auditing: external audits are performed by outside auditors and auditing firms; and the standards, requirements, or other audit criteria used in external audits are defined outside the organization being audited. Some standards bodies and professional associations further divide external auditing into second-party and third-party audits, the former conducted by customers or suppliers or others with an interest in the operations of the subject organization and the latter conducted by independent organizations with no direct interest in the organization undergoing the audit [1,2]. Aside from the fundamental differences in who conducts external audits and establishes the basis for such audits, there are many other ways in which external audits stand in contrast to internal auditing as described in the previous chapter. The most prominent of these is the more limited set of reasons organizations undergo external IT audits, including legal and regulatory compliance, certification, quality assurance, or verification of self-reported or attested information the organization provides for various purposes. Organizations have the ability to choose their external auditors for many types of IT audits (subject to some regulatory requirements and restrictions), providing both an opportunity and an obligation to select external auditors with the appropriate qualifications and capacity to perform each needed audit.

The nature of an organization's participation in external IT audits is also quite different than for internal audits, as the primary responsibility of the organization and its personnel working in areas subject to external audit is to facilitate the work of the external auditors and support the accurate and efficient completion of the audit. External IT auditors typically require access to the organization's facilities, systems, personnel, and documentation and other types of evidence evaluated in the course of the audit. The audit criteria against which an organization will be evaluated in most external audits is available to the organization, so organizations may choose to allocate resources from their audit programs or assign operational personnel to review the aspects of the organization that will be audited in advance of the external audit itself. The audit processes, procedures, and methodologies employed by external auditors are also typically known to audit subjects and may be a factor in audit selection where organizations have the discretion to choose their external auditors. Organizations should consider requirements or expectations derived from external audit criteria when developing policies, procedures, plans, operational guidelines, and other types of documentation that constitute important sources of evidence examined by external auditors.

> The fundamental characteristics of external audits can be illustrated through an example familiar to many people—Internal Revenue Service (IRS) audits of individual or business tax returns. In an IRS audit, the government examines tax returns completed and submitted by a taxpaying entity (or tax preparer working on its behalf) to confirm that information on a tax return is correctly reported and accurate. The IRS establishes the basis for the audit (the audit criteria) using current tax laws, federal regulations, administrative rules and procedures, and judicial decisions addressing tax matters. The individual or organization subject to audit receives advance notice of the audit from the IRS with details regarding the taxpayer records to be examined, the examination methods to be used, and any expectations or obligations the taxpayer needs to satisfy as well as legal rights of appeal available to the taxpayer [3]. The use of externally developed audit criteria, formally specified procedures, and outside audit personnel unrelated to the audit subject are elements seen in virtually all types of external audits. The fact that the standards and requirements to which audit subjects are held are available to those subjects is also a common aspect of external audits for the purposes of legal or regulatory compliance or certification.

Operational aspects of external audits

Organizations undergo both mandatory and voluntary external IT audits, where mandatory audits are most commonly used to satisfy legal requirements or demonstrate regulatory compliance and voluntary audits include those associated with certification, quality assurance, or independent validation of internal controls, processes, or practices. Because external audits are conducted by firms and individual auditors from outside the organization, the nature of participation by organizational managers and staff is much different than in internal audits. In most cases, an organization being audited prepares materials and allocates resources intended to facilitate the completion of the external audit. Unlike internal audits—which are typically managed by a centrally organized audit program under the supervision of an audit executive—external audits involve different points of management, coordination, and support within an organization. In particular, different management executives and members of the board of directors (or comparable governance body) have responsibility for legal and regulatory audits than is typically the case for other types of IT audits. As shown in Figure 4.1, the audit committee of the board of directors selects the external auditors engaged to examine IT and other internal controls used to support financial reporting, while members of the internal

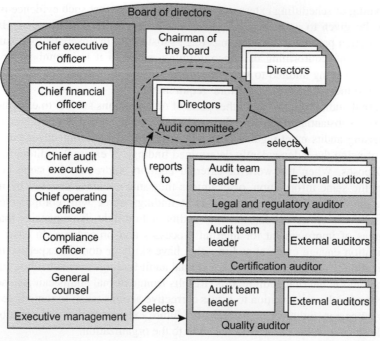

FIGURE 4.1

Organizational responsibility for external audits is typical divided between the independent audit committee of the board of directors and internal management personnel such as an audit executive, directory of quality assurance, or compliance officer.

management team choose external auditors to conduct certification, quality, or independent control audits. The specific positions with this responsibility vary across organizations, but often include executives such as the compliance officer, general counsel, director of quality, chief operating officer, or chief information officer.

One of the most important organizational responsibilities for external audits is to prepare for and effectively support audits. Many external IT audits involve examination of numerous types of documentation and other evidence maintained by the organization as well as audit procedures that may include direct observation, staff interviews, tests of system and procedural controls, and facility inspections. The internal audit program has an important role in this regard, the documented results of internal audits represent important sources of evidence that external auditors will likely need to review and potentially re-perform in order to validate, in addition to internal audit plans, procedures, and other artifacts used when conducting internal audits. Having an established and effectively operating internal audit program is itself a type of internal control required for many organizations. External auditors typically specify the nature and amount of evidence they need to examine in order to make appropriate findings and justify their determinations. Organizations anticipating or scheduling external audits need to ensure that such evidence is available to be given to auditors at the time when an external audit begins. External auditors often produce binary findings (e.g., satisfactory or unsatisfactory, sufficient or insufficient, conforming or nonconforming, etc.), so it is incumbent upon the organization being audited to furnish evidence of the right type, amount, and level of detail to meet the external auditors' requirements.

Internal audit programs and other parts of organizations subject to external audit can derive substantial value from the results of external audits, not only in the sense that passing audits meet regulatory requirements or business objectives but also in terms of using the independently determined findings of external auditors for internal purposes. When the work of external auditors addresses the same controls, gathers the same information, or examines the same evidence covered by internal audits, the extent to which external audit findings agree with comparable internal results can either validate internal audits or highlight discrepancies that indicate areas of improvement for internal processes and procedures. In cases where organization engage external auditors that have skills or domain expertise that the organization's internal auditors lack, external audit findings may substitute for or be incorporated in internal audit reports. Results from external audits can also serve as a baseline for the organization to assess corrective actions taken to remediate identified weaknesses, either in preparation for future external audits or to demonstrate the relevance or value of the external audit to the organization.

Roles and responsibilities for external auditing

Key roles and responsibilities in external auditing are divided among the organization, its board of directors or other governing body, and the external audit organizations and auditors that perform audits of the organization, as summarized in Table 4.1. Responsibilities for different actors within the external audit process depend largely on the type of audit involved and, in particular, whether there are regulatory requirements that specify roles and assign responsibilities. For instance, external IT auditing of internal controls associated with financial reporting and accounting systems falls under the same regulatory authority as financial auditing more generally, and statutory provisions applicable in many countries mandate many of the key roles and responsibilities. Under both the Sarbanes–Oxley Act and Council of the European Union's Directive 2006/43/EC require public corporations and other organizations subject to external financial audit to have formal audit committees within their boards of directors comprising independent board members as least one of which has expertise in finance and accounting [4,5]. The audit committee either directly selects external auditors for the organization or approves external auditors recommended by executive management. The audit committee is also the primary recipient of the external auditors' report, although the full board of directors and the organization's management team usually consider audit findings, recommendations, and potential corrective actions. For publicly traded companies in the United States, Sarbanes–Oxley also requires the Chief Executive Officer and Chief Financial Officer to formally certify external audit reports and other official regulatory filings submitted to the Securities and Exchange Commission (SEC).

Table 4.1 External Audit Roles and Responsibilities

Role	Responsibilities
Executive Management	• Key members of the management team typically sit on the board of directors and as such share responsibility for considering and responding to external audit findings • The CEO and CFO need to formally certify the accuracy of the external auditor's report in the case of financial or regulatory audits • The management team approves budgets and resource allocations for some types of external audits, including authorizing the organization to seek various kinds of certifications
Audit Committee	• Subset of the board of directors, typically comprising only independent directors • Provides oversight of external auditing, especially auditing required for regulatory compliance • Selects external auditors or approves selection recommendation from the management team • Required for public companies under the Sarbanes–Oxley Act and EU Directive 2006/43/EC
Board of Directors	• Considers audit reports and recommendations and makes decisions regarding actions to take in response to audit findings
Chief Audit Executive	• Aligns the internal audit function with external auditing needs • Reports directly to the audit committee
Compliance Officer	• Responsible for ensuring the achievement and maintenance of organizational compliance with applicable external standards or certifications
External Auditor	• Performs audits representing the selected auditing firm, typically as part of a team depending on the type and scope of audit activities needed • Develops and maintains knowledge and subject-matter expertise relevant to the types of audits performed • Reports to the lead auditor, audit partner, or other member of the external audit firm's management
Organizational Staff	• Facilitates conduct of external audits provisioning access to auditors as needed, participating in interviews, and preparing and furnishing documentation or other evidence

External auditing of internal controls, including IT controls, receives a great deal of attention among many organizations, auditors, and casual observers due to the significant legal and regulatory provisions in the Sarbanes–Oxley Act and subsequent SEC rules in the United States and similar actions in international environments. Many organizations engage in external audits driven by other regulatory requirements or by internally driven policies, strategies, and organizational objectives. In contexts such as quality assurance or certification, external audit roles and responsibilities are different than in audits intended to satisfy regulatory requirements. As Figure 4.1 indicates, not only are different types of audit firms and auditor personnel used for these other types of external audits, but executives within the organizational management team typically have responsibility for selecting external auditors and for receiving and acting upon the results of external audits. Organizations using external audits for multiple purposes often divide management responsibility based on the focus of each type of audit such as placing certification or voluntary compliance audits under the supervision of the organization's director of compliance, IT governance lead, or general counsel. There may be an opportunity in such organizations to coordinate external audit activities and analysis of results with the management and practices of the internal audit program and its designated chief audit executive (or equivalent position with another title). A key consideration for organizations is to ensure internal management or supervisory personnel have sufficient domain knowledge and relevant expertise to fully understand and effectively oversee external audit engagements.

Independence in external auditing

Auditor independence—meaning independence of both the firm engaged to perform external audits and the individual auditors who conduct the audits–is a central facet of external auditing. The previous chapter emphasized the importance of auditor independence and objectivity to internal auditing and noted the challenge to achieve true independence in internal auditing when the auditors are employees of the organization being audited. Aside from the contractual and financial relationship between an organization and its external auditors, maintaining the independence of external auditors is a strict requirement in most legal and regulatory forms of auditing, especially when the subject organization is a publicly traded entity. The lack of auditor independence in the accounting scandals and subsequent bankruptcy of major corporations including Enron and WorldCom, coupled with the subsequent dissolution of accounting firm Arthur Andersen, significantly influenced the inclusion of more stringent independence requirements in the Sarbanes–Oxley Act and subsequent rule-making by the SEC and the Public Company Accounting Oversight Board (PCAOB). The European Commission proposed and adopted similar rules in the wake of both major US corporate problems and similar scandals among European companies including Italian food producer Parmalat and Dutch retailer Ahold. The net result of these major corporate audit and accounting failures is a current regulatory environment in which auditor independence is considered absolutely essential.

The Enron scandal that came to light in 2001 involved audit failures at many levels by multiple parties, including several members of the executive management team at Enron and partners, auditors, and other employees at Arthur Andersen. Although the accounting fraud and collusion between Enron and its auditors was primarily financial, the case provides a clear example of the potential results when significant conflicts of interest exist between organizations and their auditors. It also illustrates much of the rationale behind provisions included in the Sarbanes–Oxley legislation enacted as a response to Enron and several other large-scale corporate accounting and auditing cases that the US Congress believed undermined confidence in American securities markets. Changes in many international legal and regulatory auditing requirements were similarly influenced by Enron and other American company scandals and the role of what was at the time one of the five largest external auditing and accounting firms.

Independence is not a recently introduced requirement; the Securities Exchange Act of 1934 explicitly mandates that members of the audit committee, comprising members from the board of directors, be independent and that the work of auditors (including the delivery of reports containing their findings) be submitted directly to the audit committee [6]. The Sarbanes–Oxley Act greatly expanded the definition of independence by specifying nine types of nonaudit activities that firms engaged to perform external audits are prohibited from performing while under contract to conduct audits. Prohibited activities comprise business and information technology services including:

1. "bookkeeping or other services related to the accounting records or financial statements of the audit client;
2. financial information systems design and implementation;
3. appraisal or valuation services, fairness opinions, or contribution-in-kind reports;
4. actuarial services;
5. internal audit outsourcing services;
6. management functions or human resources;
7. broker or dealer, investment adviser, or investment banking services;
8. legal services and expert services unrelated to the audit;
9. any other service that the Board determines, by regulation, is impermissible" [5].

The SEC issued new rules updating its auditor independent requirements in a manner consistent with provisions in the Sarbanes–Oxley Act, including prohibitions on nonaudit services; the need for audit committees to preapprove any nonaudit services or exemptions to prohibitions; mandatory rotation of the lead audit partner at least every 5 years; and additional conflict of interest protections that preclude audit firms from auditing organizations whose management team includes members previously employed by the audit firm [7]. The PCAOB, a governing body established by the Sarbanes–Oxley Act, also mandates ethics and independence rules for firms registered with the Board to conduct audits of public companies. Outside the United States, the European Commission Directive on statutory audits [5] and the International Standards on Auditing mandated for use in that Directive both require independence between auditors and audit firms and the listed entities they audit [8].

Auditor independence rules apply to organizations undergoing external audits and to the audit firms and auditors that perform external audits. Although the responsibility for ensuring independence is therefore shared by the organizations that choose their auditors and the auditors themselves, the negative consequences of using an external auditor with a conflict of interest or that otherwise violates independence are often more severe for the organization than for the auditor. While audit firms and individual auditors may face sanctions for violating independence rules, organizations, their executives, directors, and employees may be subject to criminal and civil penalties, in addition to decreases in shareholder value that typically accompany public disclosure of any type of accounting or securities regulatory violation. This makes it imperative that organizations thoroughly evaluate potential auditors before engaging their services.

Organizational participation in external audits

Although organizations subject to external auditing do not perform the audits, they participate in multiple processes and activities related to planning for, undergoing, approving, and responding to external audits. The representative activities shown in Figure 4.2 fall within three phases common to virtually all audit methodologies—planning the audit, conducting the audit, and reporting audit results. Whether mandatory or voluntary, external audits are often performed at the expense of the organization being audited. Even in cases where audits are funded by government or industry regulators, audited organizations still incur substantial costs in time and internal resources needed to facilitate external audit activities.

To ensure proper resource allocations for external auditing, organizations need first to determine their audit needs, considering any applicable legal or regulatory requirements as well as internally driven strategic or operational objectives. Different types of external audits correspond to audit criteria or other requirements for the organization and for the audit firm and auditors who will conduct the audits. By developing a thorough understanding of their audit requirements, organizations can choose auditors with the necessary qualifications, competence, independence, and experience for each type of external audit and prepare internal staff and evidentiary materials needed to support those audits. Once the external audits have been performed, the organization (or its audit committee or other governing body) receives the documented results and determines whether to accept the findings as presented or, if applicable, appeal the findings. For many types of regulatory audits,

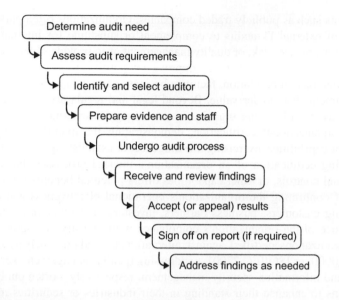

Determine audit need

Assess audit requirements

Identify and select auditor

Prepare evidence and staff

Undergo audit process

Receive and review findings

Accept (or appeal) results

Sign off on report (if required)

Address findings as needed

FIGURE 4.2

The external audit process requires significant advance planning and preparation to help ensure the successful completion of external audit activities.

one or more organizational executives need to sign off on the final audit report before it is submitted to regulators or other external audiences. After the external audit is completed, organizations respond to audit findings as necessary with corrective actions to remediate any weaknesses identified in audits. For types of audits repeated at regular intervals (such as annually or quarterly), the process of preparing, undergoing, reviewing, and responding represents continuous cycle in support of governance, risk management, quality, or compliance functions. Organizations may treat one-time audit or infrequently repeated audits as more discrete projects with clearly defined initiation and completion dates.

External IT audit drivers and rationale

The full scope of external IT audits conducted for organizations comprises both mandatory and voluntary types of audits, each of which correspond to different drivers, justifications, and sources of organizational motivation. Organizations are typically required to undergo external IT audits intended to establish and maintain legal and regulatory compliance, where passing an audit is a prerequisite to operating as a going concern or participating in some markets. The mandatory nature of these audits provides the primary rationale, along with the set of rules and enforcement mechanisms regulators or oversight bodies use to ensure compliance by organizations such as publicly traded companies. Organizations often pursue voluntary types of external IT audits to complement or substitute for internal audits in support of governance, risk, or quality management or to provide objective evidence of operational effectiveness that may improve competitive position within an industry, strengthen market reputation, facilitate business partnerships or other opportunities, or augment shareholder value. Beyond legal and regulatory compliance, other common reasons influencing organizations to engage in external IT audits include achieving organizational certification, demonstrating the maturity of operational processes or capabilities, exercising due diligence, or establishing safe harbor.

Achieving certification of an organization's internal processes, business practices, internal controls, or other capabilities offers potential benefits both internally in terms of confirming the organization's operational effectiveness and externally by providing customers, business partners, investors, and other interested parties with evidence of the organization's compliance with industry standards or frameworks. Organizations certified against international standards such as ISO 9001, ISO/IEC 20000, or ISO/IEC 27001—addressing quality management, service management, and information security management, respectively—often publicize their certifications to enhance their standing in their industries or securities markets, in addition to any operational benefits they receive from actually implementing and executing practices conforming to applicable standards. Similarly, an organization that achieves independent appraisal of processes or services such as the higher levels of the Software Engineering Institute's Capability Maturity Model Integration (CMMI) for development, services, or acquisition theoretically enjoys the benefits of formally defined, well-managed operational processes and procedures, and may also be more attractive to prospective customers seeking to outsource or contract for capabilities offered by the organization.

The term *due diligence* generally refers to any effort that seeks to examine or validate the accuracy of information about a person or an organization. The concept applies most often in finance, securities markets, and investment analysis, where due diligence involves a comprehensive investigation into any or all aspects of an organization that issues securities to investors or that is the target of a merger, sale, or acquisition. Many types of audits, including IT audits, may be used to support investigations for due diligence. The scope of such audits can include examination of operational or management practices, adherence to policies, compliance with applicable laws and regulations, and provision of adequate controls for information systems. Safe harbor is a legal principle incorporated in some laws and regulations which allows organizations that might not satisfy the requirements of the law or regulation to avoid being considered in violation if they comply with explicit standards and act in good faith. A notable example related to IT auditing is the safe harbor process negotiated between the United States and the European Commission regarding the Council's data protection directive. The directive, in effect since 1998, generally prohibits the transfer of personal data about Europeans to countries outside Europe (such as the United States) that do not have equivalent privacy protections [9]. The safe harbor provision allows US companies to attest to their voluntary compliance with a set of privacy principles that constitute adequate privacy protection. US organizations seeking safe harbor under this agreement either self-certify or engage a third-party auditor to assess their compliance with the required privacy principles.

Some types of external IT audits are conditional or represent random selection by regulators or external quality assurance bodies. Unlike other types of mandatory audits, organizations subject to these examinations usually have no say in which organizations get audited and are not able to choose their own auditors. For instance, under provisions in the Health Information Technology for Economic and Clinical Health Act, some health-care entities are subject to external audits to check regulatory compliance and to verify qualifications for government financial incentives. Specifically, the Office for Civil Rights within the US Department of Health and Human Services annually audits a small number of the thousands of entities subject to the security and privacy requirements of the Health Insurance Portability and Accountability Act. The Centers for Medicare and Medicaid Services (CMS) offers incentive payments used to purchase and implement electronic health record technology to eligible health-care providers, organizations, and other professionals. Eligible recipients must attest to their satisfaction of numerous criteria indicating their "meaningful use" of the technology to receive payments. CMS audits a small proportion (fewer than 10%) of incentive recipients, either before or after payment is made, to validate the accuracy of attestations and other eligibility criteria. In both of these health industry IT audit programs, the government organizations responsible for the programs engaged the services of external audit contractors to perform the audits on the government's behalf. Although these programs apply only to some organizations within the health-care sector, they reflect an approach common to audits where regulators examine a statistical sample or other subset of all organizations covered by specific regulations or participating in a government program.

External audit benefits

External audits are a cost of doing business in many industries and sectors, for IT and associated controls just as they are for financial reporting and accounting practices. From this perspective, undergoing and passing external audits provide value to audited organizations simply by successfully completing the audit process as required. In addition to help ensure organizational compliance with applicable laws, regulations, and standards, external auditing offers a variety of other benefits. External IT audits provide independent review and analysis of internal controls and operational processes that may be considered more credible than comparable internal audits, even when the same processes and audit criteria are used. This credibility extends to verification or validation of internal audit findings or self-attested results where external audits can examine the audit plans, procedures, and protocols the organization uses in its internal audit program as well as the satisfaction of audit criteria. Organizations voluntarily choosing to seek certification for some aspect of their business operations often perceive substantial benefits from certification, so external audits offer value to the extent that they help achieve or maintain certification. Similarly, external audits used in support of IT governance can help organization realize intended outcomes and objectives from adopting formal governance processes or frameworks. Objectives and anticipated benefits from effective governance include operational efficiencies that yield competitive advantages over organizations that lack such capabilities.

Advantages compared to internal audits

There are many types of IT audits—such as those intended to determine regulatory compliance or achieve certification—that cannot be performed as internal audits and therefore must use external auditors. Even where the requirement to engage external auditors does not exist, some organizations consider external auditing preferable to internal auditing due to presumed advantages about the level of organizational involvement required, internal resource demands, the reliability of audit findings and auditor skills, competence, or specialized expertise. External audits do not necessarily take less time to complete than internal audits, but the roles and responsibilities of the organization being audited are often substantially less than they would be in an internal audit of comparable scope. Organizations can also rely on external auditors to establish the set of requirements or audit criteria to be used or to be familiar with requirements associated with standards or certification criteria. Whether or not they establish their own internal audit programs, some organizations lack the resources and necessary subject-matter expertise to be able to perform all types of relevant IT audits. Choosing an external auditor can help ensure that the audit firm and the individuals assigned to conduct the audit have the necessary skills and experience (including applicable certifications) to perform the work accurately and effectively. The combination of external auditor qualifications, prior experience performing similar types of audits, and the use of standards-based or other formally defined audit criteria can also help ensure the reliability and validity of external audit findings.

External audit challenges

Neither external nor internal IT auditing has an inherent advantage in terms of cost or anticipated benefits. For different types of IT audits, external and internal auditing approaches may be equally costly, or each may offer cost savings over the other in different contexts where organizations have the flexibility to choose how the audit will be performed; they typically need to compare the total cost of external or internal auditing—including personnel and other resource costs, time to prepare and complete the audit, and any contract or service fees that must be paid to auditors—and the perceived value of each approach to the organization. Organizations should be fully aware of the costs and benefits associated even with mandatory types of external auditing that offer no discretion to organizations in the choice of audit approach. All types of external auditing present potential drawbacks to organizations, including substantial financial, time, resource costs; the need to open up the organization to outside entities; potentially less opportunity for in-process corrective action; and lower familiarity of external auditors with particulars of the organization subject to audit. External auditor expertise may be demonstrable through individual and firm qualifications or certifications, but even experienced auditors with appropriate competence and objectivity are susceptible to overconfidence, mischaracterization of related and independent events, or other forms of confirmation bias [10]. Organizations can, in some cases, mitigate potential misinterpretations by external auditors, but the emphasis on independence in external auditing means that organizations often must wait until findings are documented before raising objections or otherwise appealing the results.

Although organizations engaging external auditors delegate much of the potential complexity of structuring the audit, understanding audit criteria, and choosing appropriate protocols and procedures, in large organizations the scope of controls, processes, operational functions, facilities, and other aspects subject to audit can present a significant challenge to efficient external auditing. As illustrated in the notional example in Figure 4.3, the need to examine multiple control and

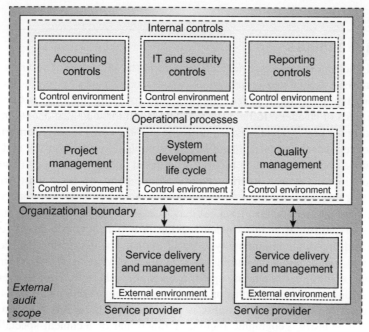

FIGURE 4.3

Depending on the size, operational complexity, and provision of controls characterizing an organization, the scope of an external audit can include processes and controls in multiple locations potentially operated by different entities and may involve more than one type of audit.

operational environments—including those associated with external service providers used by an organization, if any—limits the feasibility of finding and selecting a single external IT auditor that can address the full set of subject areas in scope for a comprehensive audit. The greater the variety of environments, processes, and systems maintained by an organization or the more specialized those organizational aspects are, the more likely it is that the organization will need to subdivide the audit scope along functional, technical, or geographic lines and engage the services of multiple external auditors to address each type of examination the organization needs. Even smaller and less operationally diverse organization may need to seek specialized external IT auditing support to adequately address emerging technologies or services such as cloud computing, large-scale data analytics, and the use of mobile devices. For instance, many commercial providers of cloud computing services undergo specialized attestation engagements using standards issued by the American Institute for Certified Public Accountants (AICPA) and resulting in Service Organization Control (SOC) reports that present an opinion on the effectiveness of the provider's controls related to security and privacy [11]. Service providers contract directly with qualified external auditors to conduct these engagements and issue SOC reports, while prospective and current customers of the service providers can leverage the information in SOC reports in their own IT audits.

External auditors

External auditing represents a distinct segment in the professional services market that comprises specialized organizations whose core business is providing audits of various types and more general services firms offering auditing as one among multiple lines of business. References to external auditors can also denote individuals working for professional services firms (or in some cases independently). In the context of regulatory audits, audits of large or complex organizations, or audits with significant scope attention often focuses on external audit firm, although audit laws and regulations in many countries impose requirements on both audit firms and the auditors that work for them. Organizations selecting external auditors typically evaluate candidates at the firm level but may assess the skills, experience, and qualifications of individual auditors when seeking providers for specialized forms of external auditing, including many types of IT audits. The distinction between individuals and organizations providing external audit services is also relevant when discussing auditor certifications, qualifications, or other prerequisites enabling external auditors to perform audits on behalf of client organizations.

Some organizations' core business is providing audits to clients, often within a particular industry, geographic region, or functional or technical specialization. It is also common to see larger or more diversified organizations that perform external audits in addition to a variety of other services. In heavily regulated business domains such as publicly traded companies, current laws do not significantly constraint the type of organizations that conducts audits—as long as they satisfy applicable rules and regulatory requirements—but do limit the ability of diversified firms to engage in nonaudit services for the same organization while they are serving as auditors. These laws address independence for both audit firms and individual auditors such as the Sarbanes–Oxley Act requirement instance that the position of lead partner on an external audit engagement rotate at least every 5 years [4]. Similar rules apply in many regulated industries, intended to prevent perceived or actual conflicts of interest between auditors and the organizations they audit. Organizations that do not perform public company audits but offer other types of external audit services may be less restricted in the specific activities they are allowed to perform for a client organization, but virtually all organizations providing certification, quality, information systems, and compliance audits follow formal codes of professional conduct, ethical standards, and conflict of interest mitigation procedures designed to maintain objectivity in external audits.

Many of the largest and best-known external audit firms provide multiple types of IT-related audit services, particularly including regulatory and information systems audits. Organizations providing certification, compliance, or quality audits typically must first be accredited to perform specific types of audits by the standards development organization or other authoritative body responsible for issuing and maintaining the basis for certification or compliance. Accreditation or oversight bodies essentially approve other organizations to conduct standards-based or other types of audits. For commonly sought certifications such as those associated with standards published by the International Organization for Standardization (ISO), accreditation of certifying organizations is performed by national or regional accreditation bodies, not by the standards development organizations. This results in a multiparty relationship, as shown in Figure 4.4, between external audit firms, the oversight bodies that give external auditors the authority to perform specific types of audits, and the organizations engaging the services of external auditors.

As is the case for internal auditors, there are multiple sources of education, expertise, and prior experience that provide appropriate backgrounds for individuals working as external auditors. Many external IT auditors gain experience performing multiple aspects of regulatory audits, which typically emphasize financial or operational controls and address IT controls within those broader contexts. For this reason, individual auditors working for external audit firms often seek Certified Public Accountant (CPA) certification (a credential many large audit firms require of their senior auditors and engagement partners). The AICPA specifies a broad set of competencies senior-level auditors should possess, including [12]:

- understanding the role of quality control and standards of professional conduct;
- Understanding the service to be performed including the performance, supervision, and reporting aspects of the engagement;
- technical proficiency in applicable professional and industry standards and the nature of the transactions or other business processes the client organization executes;
- familiarity with the industry in which a client operates;

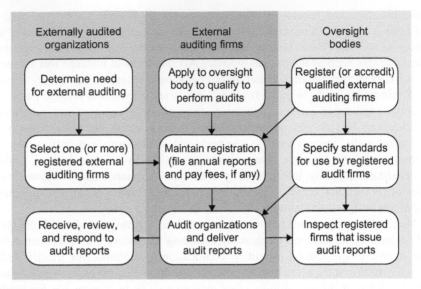

FIGURE 4.4

Organizations subject to audit often select their own auditors, in many cases, choosing external audit firms registered, accredited, or otherwise approved to perform specific types of audits.

- the ability to exercise professional judgment;
- understanding the organization's IT systems.

Many specialized certifications and associated training programs are available to external audit professionals seeking to bolster their qualifications to perform specific types of IT audits. Table 4.2 provides examples of the types of auditor and audit firm qualifications that organizations consider when selecting external auditors. Beyond most domain-specific certifications (e.g., quality, IT controls or information systems, and process maturity), there are numerous specializations for specific industries or types of controls.

Regulatory auditors

In many countries, external audit firms performing regulatory audits (also called statutory audits) on publicly traded companies must register with and be approved by a national-level governing and oversight body as a prerequisite to organizations engaging them as external auditors. Once registered, organizations seeking external auditor can use public registries to locate registered firms such as the registry maintained by the PCAOB in the United States [13] or the Register of Statutory Auditors in the United Kingdom [14]. As illustrated in Figure 4.4, external audit firms submit applications to the appropriate oversight body (or bodies, if they intend to perform audits in more than one country) and the oversight bodies evaluate whether applying firms meet applicable legal requirements to audit publicly traded companies.

Table 4.2 External Auditor Qualifications for Different Types of Audits

Audit Type	Qualifications	
	Audit Firm	**Individual Auditors**
Internal Financial Controls	Registration with auditor oversight body such as PCAOB or EGAOB members	Certification in applicable auditing standards and regulations such as CPA
Quality Assurance	Accreditation as certifying entity by national accreditation body or other authority	Certification in managing or auditing quality such as CQA
Certification	Accreditation as certifying entity for specific certifications by national accreditation body or other authority; adherence to ISO 17021	Certification-specific credentials such as certified Auditor or Lead Auditor; subject-matter certifications for certification standards
Process Maturity	Certification as an appraiser by SEI or other authority	Process improvement certification such as CMMI or SCAMPI Lead Appraiser
IT Controls	(Optionally) Registration with national oversight body or third-party accreditation for IT-related standards or services	Certification in information security or systems auditing such as CISA or GSNA
Government Organizations or Programs	Designation as national authorized audit institution; adherence to standards such as International Standards of Supreme Audit Institutions Standards (ISSAI)	Government-specific auditing certification such as CGAP

Oversight bodies typically operate under explicit legal authority with jurisdiction including the country or countries where registered firms will perform audits. For example, the PCAOB's authority comes from the Sarbanes–Oxley Act [4] while the recognized supervisory bodies in the United Kingdom and other European Union nations comes from Directive 2006/43/EC [5]. Public sector organizations or private sector entities receiving funding from or otherwise participating in government programs may be subject to audit, but in the government arena, organizations being audited typically do not have the discretion to choose their own auditors. Government agency or program audits may be performed by designated government audit organizations, such as members of the International Organization of Supreme Audit Institutions, or by third-party external auditors awarded contracts to conduct specific types of audits.

Certifying organizations

Organizations conducting external audits intended to grant or maintain certification for other organizations need, at a minimum, sufficient knowledge of the underlying standards or certification criteria to make an accurate determination that an organization merits certification. With few exceptions, standards development organizations or other organizations responsible for the creation and maintenance of certification standards do not directly perform audits of organizations seeking certification. Instead, certification audits are performed by third parties specifically authorized to conduct audits and grant certification to organizations that successfully meet certification requirements. Such authorization is either given to qualified organizations by official national accreditation bodies or by the organization responsible for the certification standard. For instance, national bodies accredit external auditors to certify organizations for various ISO standards, while the Software Engineering Institute designates its own partner organizations to conduct CMMI appraisals of organizations seeking certification at different CMMI maturity levels. Organizations seeking certification select their certification auditors, typically choosing from among auditors accredited for specific standards by the national accreditation body where the organization operates. The criteria used to accredit certification auditors vary to some extent and whether standards development organizations specify any minimum requirements. The ISO recommends that organizations seeking certification against its standards choose accredited auditors that implement ISO/IEC 17021, which specifies requirements for organizations that audit and certify management systems [15].

Organizations needing to find an external IT auditor, for regulatory, certification, or quality auditing or almost any other purpose, can typically leverage online registries of approved or accredited firms. The register maintained by the PCAOB [13], for example, includes over 1000 audit firms based in a large number of countries. With respect to certification auditors, the national accreditation bodies in many countries also provide public listings of accredited certifying organizations, often organized by specific standard or by the domain to which the standard applies.

Relevant source material

External IT auditors work from a foundation of general auditing standards and guidance, including procedures and guidelines used in conventional financial and operational audits. In addition to Generally Accepted Auditing Standards and International Standards on Auditing (ISA), guidance widely used in external auditing includes the Statements on Auditing Standards and Statements on Standards for Attestation Engagements issued by AICPA [16] and ISA and International Standards for Attest Engagements (ISAE) published by the International Federation of Accountants [17]. Procedural guidance and standards specifically focused on external auditing applicable to IT audits include:

- ISO 19011, *Guidelines for Auditing Management Systems* [1].
- Guidance from AICPA on *Reporting on Controls at a Service Organization* [18,19].
- ISAE 3402, *Assurance Reports on Controls at a Service Organization* [20].
- ISACA's *Standards for IS Auditing* [21].

Summary

External IT audits share many similarities with internal IT audits, but external auditing differs significantly in some structural and procedural aspects that require organizations to approach and support external auditing in ways quite distinct from the internal audit program operations described in the previous chapter. In many respects, organizations have less control and flexibility when it comes to external audits, although as noted in this chapter, many organizations voluntarily engage external auditors to help demonstrate compliance with quality standards or other certification criteria and thus support achievement of IT governance and operational goals and objectives. Organizations rarely have any ability to specify or influence the criteria used in external IT audits, but , in many cases, have some discretion in choosing outside firms to perform different types of audits. The explicit purposes for which most external audits are conducted typically result in formally defined and publicly available audit criteria that organizations can use to set expectations for audit requirements and to prepare adequately to produce needed evidence and otherwise support the external audit process. Organizations can use this knowledge—and any experience they have gained through the operation of their internal audit functions—to inform the selection of external auditors and ensure audits are performed with appropriate competence, independence, and objectivity.

References

[1] ISO 19011:2011. Guidelines for auditing management systems.
[2] Russell JP, editor. The ASQ auditing handbook (4th ed.). Milwaukee WI: ASQ Quality Press; 2013.
[3] Examination of returns, appeal rights, and claims for refund. Washington (DC): Internal Revenue Service; 2008 May. IRS Publication 556.
[4] Sarbanes–Oxley Act of 2002, Pub. L. No. 107-204, 116 Stat. 745.
[5] Directive of the European Parliament and of the Council on statutory audits of annual accounts and consolidated accounts, Directive 2006/43/EC; 2006 May.
[6] Securities Exchange Act of 1934, Pub. L. No. 73-291, 48 Stat. 881.
[7] Securities and Exchange Commission; Strengthening the Commission's requirements regarding auditor independence; final rule. 68 Fed. Reg. 6006 2003.

[8] Overall objectives of the independent auditor and the conduct of an audit in accordance with international standards on auditing. New York (NY): International Federation of Accountants; 2012. International Standard on Auditing 200.

[9] Directive of the European Parliament and of the Council on the protection of individuals with regard to the processing of personal data and on the free movement of such data, Directive 95/46/EC; 1995 October.

[10] Bazerman MH, Moore D. Judgment in managerial decision making. Hoboken NJ: John Wiley & Sons; 2009.

[11] Service Organization Control (SOC) Reports [Internet]. Durham (NC): American Institute of Certified Public Accountants [cited 2013 May 4]. Available from: <http://www.aicpa.org/InterestAreas/FRC/AssuranceAdvisoryServices/Pages/SORHome.aspx>.

[12] A firm's system of quality control. Durham (NC): American Institute of Certified Public Accountants; 2012. Statement on Quality Control Standards 8.

[13] Registered Firms [Internet]. Washington (DC): Public Company Accounting Oversight Board; [cited 2013 Jul 9]. Available from: http://pcaobus.org/Registration/Firms/Pages/RegisteredFirms.aspx.

[14] Register of Statutory Auditors [Internet]. Edinburgh (UK): Institute of Chartered Accountants of Scotland; [updated 2013 Jul 8; cited 2013 Jul 9]. Available from: <http://www.auditregister.org.uk/Forms/Default.aspx>.

[15] ISO/IEC 17021. Conformity assessment—Requirements for bodies providing audit and certification of management systems.

[16] Audit and Attest Standards, Including Clarified Standards [Internet]. Durham (NC): American Institute of Certified Public Accountants; [cited 2013 June 14]. Available from <http://www.aicpa.org/Research/Standards/AuditAttest/Pages/audit%20and%20attest%20standards.aspx>.

[17] Accounting Standards | Governance | Publications and Resources [Internet]. New York (NY): International Federation of Accountants; [cited 2013 May 4]. Available from: <http://www.ifac.org/publications-resources>.

[18] American Institute of Certified Public Accountants. Reporting on controls at a service organization relevant to security, availability, processing integrity, confidentiality, or privacy. Durham (NC): American Institute of Certified Public Accountants; 2012 March.

[19] American Institute of Certified Public Accountants Service organizations: reporting on controls at a service organization relevant to user entities' internal control over financial reporting. Durham NC: American Institute of Certified Public Accountants; 2013.

[20] Assurance reports on controls at a service organization. New York (NY): International Auditing and Assurance Standards Board; 2011. International Standards for Assurance Engagements 3402.

[21] Standards for IS Auditing [Internet]. Rolling Meadows (IL): ISACA [cited 2013 May 4]. Available from: <http://www.isaca.org/Knowledge-Center/Standards/Pages/Standards-for-IT-Audit-and-Assurance-English-.aspx>.

Types of Audits

INFORMATION IN THIS CHAPTER:

- Financial audits
- Operational audits
- Certification audits
- Compliance audits
- IT-specific audits

Information technology (IT) auditing is both a stand-alone activity and a core component of many other types of audits. Organizations performing IT auditing need to understand the full extent to which IT supports, drives, or otherwise contributes to different business and operational functions. Internal and external IT auditors must be aware of the organizational context to which a given type of audit applies and the set of IT-related internal controls or activities that need to be addressed when conducting audits that are not limited to IT. Among the major types of audits that typically include IT systems, processes, and associated controls are financial audits, operational audits, and certification, compliance and quality audits (which may represent a subset of operational, certification, or compliance activities) as illustrated in Figure 5.1. In these audit domains IT auditors may not have a leading role, but the pervasive use of IT across a wide range of organizational activities means that IT auditing skills and expertise are needed to fully address the scope of most internal and external audits. There are also many types of IT-specific audits, especially those intended to support IT governance, risk management, and standards certification and compliance. This chapter describes different types of IT audits commonly undertaken by private and public sector organizations. It emphasizes the role of IT auditing (whether leading or supporting) in each audit context and describes the primary objectives, participants, organizational responsibilities, and standards and guidance associated with different types of audits. Table 5.1 summarizes the primary areas of emphasis and objectives for each type of audit covered in this chapter.

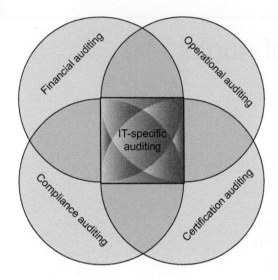

FIGURE 5.1

IT auditing has a role in financial, operational, certification, and compliance audits, but also constitutes a specific auditing domain on its own, focusing on IT-specific assets, processes, and controls.

Table 5.1 Emphasis and Objectives for Different Types of Audits

Type of Audit	Areas of Emphasis	Key Objectives	Performed by
Financial	Accounting practices, financial reporting	Confirm appropriate practices and internal control effectiveness	External auditors
Operational	Management practices, processes, and procedures	Review operational efficiency and effectiveness in meeting objectives	Internal or external auditors
Certification	Industry, quality, or management standards or other certification requirements	Judge satisfaction of certification criteria; grant (or deny) certification	External auditors (accredited to certify others)
Compliance	Legal, regulatory, or contractual requirements	Verify adherence to requirements and fulfillment of obligations	Internal or external auditors
IT/information systems	Controls for systems or IT development, operations and maintenance, security and privacy	Validate control, configuration, sufficiency, and effectiveness	Internal or external auditors

Financial audits

Financial auditing primarily addresses accounting practices and compliance with financial reporting requirements of many different types of organizations, particularly companies that issue securities to be exchanged in public markets and privately held or nonprofit organizations subject to legal or regulatory requirements about financial management. This type of auditing has long focused not only on what financial information organizations record and report, but also on how organizations maintain the completeness, accuracy, and integrity of that information [1]. The examination of internal controls in audits of finance and accounting practices predates the widespread use of technology, but since the advent of electronic data processing in the late 1950s and its application to accounting systems, IT has played a significant supporting role in accounting and financial reporting. In modern organizations, it is virtually impossible to audit internal financial controls without examining IT. The Sarbanes–Oxley Act increased the emphasis on including formal examinations of internal controls in audit reports. Section 404 of the law makes organizational management responsible for assessing and attesting to the effectiveness of its internal controls over financial reporting and requires external auditors to include the assessment of internal controls in their audit reports [2]. Financial management and accounting systems represent an important subset of internal controls, as they help automate, standardize, and secure organizational financial information, accounting processes, and transactions. IT auditing in conventional financial accounting focuses on the systems, software, security controls, and operational environments that organizations establish and maintain to use in financial recordkeeping and reporting.

Financial auditing in many organizations is part of both internal and external audit activity, but for publicly traded companies and other organizations in regulated industries financial audits performed by external auditors receive the most attention. Whether auditing is conducted by members of the internal audit team or by external auditors hired by the organization, primary responsibility rests with the organization to ensure that its financial management and accounting practices and internal controls over those functions are implemented, maintained, and effective. Financial auditors—including IT auditors examining systems, technologies, or technical procedures supporting accounting and financial reporting—are responsible for making an objective determination that the organization meets statutory requirements and applicable standards or for identifying and reporting weaknesses, deficiencies, or failures to meet requirements. Almost all aspects of financial audits in publicly traded organizations, government agencies, nonprofit organization, and many other entities—including reviews of IT-related controls and related processes—are driven by legislative and regulatory requirements. These requirements include the frequency required for financial audits and filings of audit results (such as annual or quarterly) and often specify an explicit time period covered by each audit (such as a fiscal year). Financial auditors follow professional practices, standards, procedures, and other guidance such as Generally Accepted Auditing

Standards (GAAS), International Standards on Auditing (ISA), and Standards for Attestation Engagements (SSAE).

Although organizations operating in different countries are bound by national laws and regulations, prevailing United States and international laws on financial audits of publicly traded companies (also called "statutory audits" or "audits in the public interest") have many common provisions. Auditors examining these organizations also adhere to substantially similar standards and audit guidance and often serve as members of the same professional associations and certifying organizations. The regulatory similarities and international audience for much of the information produced or sponsored by the American Institute of Certified Public Accountants (AICPA), International Federation of Accountants (IFAC), and Institute of Internal Auditors (IIA) results in remarkably consistent financial audit practices performed in many countries.

Cost accounting

In addition to statutory requirements for financial reporting, audits of accounting and financial management practices often examine the accounting methods adopted by different organizations, seeking to validate the appropriateness of the approaches used and to verify information such as asset valuation or cost allocation. Many financial practices involve cost estimation or the assignment of value to organizational assets, particularly including capital assets carried as expenses on balance sheets. Asset valuation is also a key step in quantitative risk assessment, as organizations need to know the value of the assets they hold—and the costs incurred to the organization if those assets are lost, stolen, or otherwise compromised—in order to determine what level of protective measures to implement. Financial assets of cost accounting provide an independent review of resource cost allocations and asset valuation, potentially including comparing an organization's costing approach to industry or market norms or authoritative third-party cost data. The primary intent of this type of financial audit is to ensure that asset values and assigned costs are accurate, consistent, and adequately supported by evidence. In some cases this type of audit overlaps with operational audits (described later in this chapter), at least to the extent that the functional decomposition of organizational activities incorporates cost allocation information. For example, organizations using activity-based costing in their approach to financial management and accounting first identify all activities the organization performs and then measure the use of resource associated with each activity used to determine its cost. The accuracy of such accounting methods relies on an organization's ability to correctly and consistently calculate direct and indirect costs of resources, including assets such as equipment, raw materials, and IT hardware, software, and infrastructure.

Organizations transitioning some or all of their internally managed IT operations to external service providers often need to modify their cost accounting methods to properly reflect processes and activities that use infrastructure, hardware, or other assets that the organization does not own. Organizations typically treat the costs associated with outsourced IT services such as cloud computing as operational expenses, with little or no capital expenditures or underlying asset valuation. Internal IT operations, in contrast, generally include significant capital investments and corresponding accounting procedures, presenting a challenge when making direct comparisons of IT costs. The use by an organization of alternative cost accounting methods, such as activity-based costing, can enable consistent allocation of resource costs between internally and externally provided IT services.

Programmatic audits

Another kind of financial auditing distinct from procedures used in audits driven by regulatory requirements is the examination of program or project financial information. Program-level financial audits typically focus on comparing proposed or budgeted spending to actual time, personnel, materials, and other resource costs. Organizations adopting program management approaches such as the Project Management Institute's (PMI), Project Management Body of Knowledge (PMBOK), or adhering to standards for earned value management (EVM) closely track program schedule and cost information. Audits of programs managed in this way examine— among other performance metrics—actual costs incurred as compared to planned or budgeted values and consider program outputs in terms of the resources allocated to produce them. Enabling this form of program management requires an accounting system capable of recording and tracking programmatic activities, associated direct and indirect costs, and performance measures [3]. IT-related elements of program audits therefore include technology supporting detailed program cost accounting and earned value analysis. This type of auditing emphasizes cost and schedule performance and in that respect is distinct from operational or IT-specific audits that focus on the effective execution of program or project management tasks.

Operational audits

Operational audits examine management practices and operational processes and procedures to determine how effectively or efficiently organizations are meeting their objectives. Such analysis presumes that organizations have explicitly stated business objectives, have developed an inventory of business processes and supporting

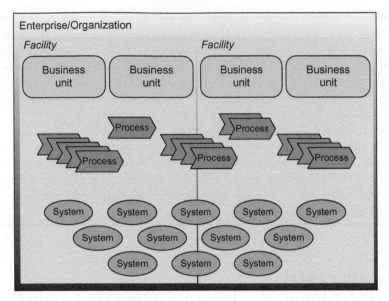

FIGURE 5.2

Different types of IT audit activities apply at multiple organizational levels, ranging from the broadest enterprise-wide perspectives to more audits with scope more narrowly focused on individual processes or systems.

administrative and technical functions, and have aligned their operational activities to the objectives they intend to achieve. As illustrated in Figure 5.2, the scope of operational IT audits may include the entire organization, one or more business units, organizational processes, and the systems that support those processes and organizational structures. In contrast to the retrospective perspective characterizing most financial audits, operational audits adopt a more future-oriented perspective by identifying operational strengths and weaknesses and using those findings to target opportunities for improvement. The IT perspective in operational audits considers the alignment of systems, infrastructure, and IT processes and procedures in supporting the achievement of organizational objectives. The range of objectives addressed in operational IT audits include IT-centric goals for IT governance, risk mitigation, certification, or compliance as well as mission and business objectives that IT capabilities are designed to enable or support. Like other types of audits, operational audits may address all activities performed by an organization, a subset of processes corresponding to a given business area, or a single administrative, technical, or business process. Operational audits may be performed by internal or external auditors, but in either case the accuracy and reliability of the audit results depend on auditors' thorough understanding of the organization's objectives in addition to relevant subject matter expertise in the operational areas being audited. The scope of an operational audit is typically defined in terms of the policies, processes, and procedures to be examined, whether those elements may be considered on their own, within the broader context of an organization's internal controls, or as applied to a specific business unit, program, or project.

Operational audits of internal controls

In an operational audit context, internal controls represent a focal point of both internal and external audits. The emphasis on internal controls is not unique to operational auditing, but operational audits consider internal controls from two distinct perspectives: first, to determine whether appropriate controls are in place to enable the efficient and effective execution of the business processes under examination and second, that the controls implemented by organizations function properly. The Committee of Sponsoring Organizations of the Treadway Commission (COSO) defines internal control as a process "designed to provide reasonable assurance regarding the achievement of objectives" related to operational efficiency and effectiveness, reliability of reporting, and legal and regulatory compliance [4]. Fully auditing an organization's internal control capabilities therefore involves operational, financial, and compliance auditing, respectively. As described in Chapter 9 (and as illustrated in Figure 9.1), the COSO's internal control framework comprises five key components: control environment, risk assessment, control activities, information and communication, and monitoring. With the sponsoring role the AICPA and IIA have in COSO and the references to the integrated control framework by the Securities and Exchange Commission (SEC) in rules and guidance implementing provisions of the Sarbanes–Oxley Act [5], COSO influences many external and internal auditors performing operational audits. The full scope of the COSO framework applies most directly to operational audits of corporate and IT governance activities, but both the control environment and control activities components emphasize factors consistent with the focus of operational auditing. Specifically, these two elements address the organizational policies, processes, procedures, and standards used to enable achievement of business objectives applicable throughout an organization and its business processes.

Audits of policies, processes, and procedures

Organizational policies, processes, and procedures are the core focus of operational auditing. To develop an appropriate organizational audit strategy and operational audit plans, organizations need to identify and categorize the set of operational activities they perform. This business process inventory provides the foundation for an operational audit universe of potential subject areas to be examined. Different organizations may choose to categorize their operational activities in different ways. The representative listing in Table 5.2 uses a functional classification according to mission and business areas, administrative domains, and technical capabilities typical of many large organizations. Not all of these activities are applicable to all organizations or relevant for the purposes of operational auditing. To conduct an operational audit focused on a given subject area, an organization needs to perform the activity in question and be able to align or correlate the activity to organizational objectives. Many organizations routinely conduct internal audits of many types of processes and activities, comparing their demonstrated performance to capabilities needed to achieve organizational objectives or benchmarking process execution against industry standards, competitors, or exemplary

Table 5.2 Categorization of Organizational Activities for Operational Audits[6,7]

Category	Activities
Mission and business	• Strategic and tactical planning • Corporate governance • Finance and accounting • Budgeting and investment • Sales and marketing • Research and development • Manufacturing, production, and distribution • Program management
Administration and support	• Customer support • Contracting • Asset management • Acquisition and procurement • Supply chain management • Service management • Quality management • Change management • Human resources
Technical	• IT governance • IT project management • Enterprise architecture • Risk management • Software development • Operations and maintenance • Technical support • Information security management

models established for each type of activity. With respect to IT processes, governance frameworks like the Control Objectives for Information and Related Technology (COBIT) [8] specify processes and corresponding controls for many aspects of organizational IT management. Such IT governance models focus not on business activities, but on the functional and technical processes that enable IT to effectively support the achievement of mission and business objectives.

Operational IT audits often focus on the policies, processes, and procedures associated with organizations' technical activities, but IT auditors may also have a role in audits of business or administrative functions because IT systems, infrastructure, and staff provide support for most of those functions. IT audits in this context focus on the extent to which IT-related capabilities operate as intended and therefore deliver the expected business value or contributed to other outcomes. Operational audits of some processes and procedures may overlap substantially with certification audits, particularly in the areas of quality management, service management, software development, technical support, and information security management.

Program or project-focused operational audits

Operational auditing can also be used to evaluate programs or projects established by an organization, examining management and operational characteristics in the context of meeting defined performance metrics, realizing program- or project-specific outcomes, and achieving business objectives or anticipated benefits consistent with expectations set at the time the programs or projects were initiated. A program or project audit generally has a more narrowly defined scope than other types of operational audits, in part, due to the tendency in many organizations to establish programs and projects for specific functional areas or to achieve a discrete purpose. Operational audits of programs and projects focused on deploying, managing, monitoring, or supporting IT capabilities have a clear IT audit need, but the same is true for less IT-centric initiatives that depend on program- or project-specific or enterprise-wide IT. Operational IT auditing activities in these contexts often focus on adherence to standard processes for software development, implementation, operations and maintenance, and other system development life cycle (SDLC) phases. The technical focus of audits addressing these IT-related processes is described in detail in Chapter 6. Depending on an organization's approach to IT governance and use of technical project management models or standards, points of reference for operational audits of IT programs or projects may include process or service frameworks such as COBIT or Information Technology Infrastructure Library (ITIL) and process standards from the International Organization for Standardization (ISO), the Institute for Electrical and Electronics Engineers (IEEE), and the Software Engineering Institute (SEI) at Carnegie Mellon University.

Certification audits

Certification audits are formal evaluations of one or more aspects of an organization's operational capabilities against explicit requirements associated with externally defined standards or methodologies. Achieving certification provides an external endorsement that an organization meets the criteria specified for a given standard. Successfully attaining certification is not an indication that an organization is performing in an optimal manner or in a way superior to other organizations; instead, certification represents an independent form of assurance that an organization satisfies at least a minimum set of requirements. Most certifications must be granted by authorized certifying bodies external to the organization seeking certification, meaning certification audits are typically performed by external auditors. Information on certification in Chapter 2 highlights some of the reasons why organizations pursue certification and describes the wide range of certification types available to organizations (see Table 2.1). Organizational responsibilities for achieving certification (and maintaining it once achieved) include making the management decision to pursue certification and to commit the internal resources necessary to bring the organization to conformance with certification criteria and to maintain conformance on an ongoing basis.

Organizations also must identify, select, and pay for the services of an authorized certifying body that performs the certification audit. As noted in Chapter 4, the responsibility for authorizing external audit firms to perform specific types of certification audits typically belongs to national accreditation bodies rather than standards development organizations. These national entities often give those seeking certification a consolidated source of information about available certifications and certifying bodies accredited to conduct certification audits and award certification to qualified organizations. Standards development organizations, industry associations, government agencies, and other entities responsible for the standards or methodologies on which certification is based typically make publicly available their certification criteria and expectations for organizations seeking certification, affording organizations an opportunity to become familiar with requirements and prepare for certification, potentially including conducting internal self-assessments against published criteria.

Organizations looking for appropriately qualified external auditors to perform certification audits can often find directories of certifying bodies through national accreditation authorities in the countries where the organization operates, such as the American National Accreditation Board (ANAB), Japan Accreditation Board (JAB), and United Kingdom Accreditation Service (UKAS). There are also online resources available through organizations such as standards.org, which maintains a searchable directory of certification bodies located throughout the world [9].

Service management

There is no single standard approach for structuring organization, business units, or operational capabilities. Different organizations establish management and governance structures according to their business functions and associated processes and activities, the market segments in which they participate, the products or services they create or sell, or the geographic regions in which they operate. Many organizations that have implemented service-oriented operating structures—particularly for IT-related services—pursue certification of their service management or delivery capabilities as an indicator of effectiveness or other quality measures and, in the case of services offered externally, to improve the marketability or attractiveness of their services to customers or business partners. There are many service management frameworks which the organizations often use as a basis for designing and operating service-based operations, including the ITIL, Microsoft's Operations Framework (MOF), and some aspects of COBIT 5, which includes services related to infrastructure and applications among its key enablers of IT governance [8]. Organizations implementing service management processes and capabilities cannot be certified in their use of these or other frameworks, but they can seek certification for satisfying the requirements of ISO/IEC 20000, a family of standards addressing requirements for planning, implementing, operating, monitoring, maintaining, and reviewing and improving formal IT service management systems in organizations

[10]. The scope of ISO/IEC 20000 certification can be limited to a discrete set of IT-related services (such as application management or technical support) or can encompass all services provided by an organization. The SEI has a service certification standard for organizations—the Capability Maturity Model Integration for Services (CMMI-SVC)—that aligns to ISO/IEC 20000 and many IT service management frameworks but which applies to all types of service providers and to service delivery in more general contexts in addition to IT services [11].

Security management

Organizations invest significant resources in security controls to safeguard the confidentiality, integrity, and availability of their enterprise assets including information systems and the information they contain. Although organizations in many sectors and industries are subject to legal and regulatory requirements for security and privacy, even organizations not legally bound by such obligations still have a strong interest in establishing and maintaining effective security protections, including security management capabilities. Government agencies and commercial organizations in specific regulated industries—such as financial services firms, health care entities, and providers of critical infrastructure—focus much of their security management attention on regulatory compliance, so may be less inclined to pursue explicit security certification. Among the most commonly sought certification is ISO/IEC 27001, a standard that specifies requirements for information security management systems and is typically implemented using the security control framework defined in the related security code of practice in ISO/IEC 27002. These standards address a broad set of information security management practices, objectives and controls; the ISO/IEC 27000 series of standards is described in detail in Chapter 9. Many more narrowly defined security standards and associated certifications apply to specific IT processes or types of systems. These include:

- The Common Criteria for Information Technology Security Evaluation (known formally as ISO/IEC 15408), [12] used to certify the relative security of different computer products, applications, or systems using protection profiles corresponding to levels of assurance requirements;
- The Computer Emergency Response Team (CERT) Resilience Management Model (RMM) [13], which provides the basis for appraisals of the maturity of organizations' processes for risk management, security, business continuity, and IT operations;
- The International Society for Automation (ISA) standard 62443 [14], which specifies security requirements for industrial automation and control systems;
- Service Organization Control (SOC) reports [15], issued as the result of specialized third-party attestation engagements that examine the controls implemented by service providers—SOC 2 reports are delivered to audited organizations for internal consumption only, while SOC 3 certification is a publicly available verification of the organization's successful completion of SOC 2 process.

As with other types of certification audits, organizations must first establish the business value or other justification for pursuing certification, implement the appropriate standards or methodologies in a way that satisfies certification requirements, and identify and engage the services of a certifying body authorized to conduct the certification audit.

Quality management

Quality certifications represent a somewhat broader category than certifications in other subject areas, because quality management is a domain in which organizations can be certified but the achievement of many process-centric certifications is also considered as an indicator of quality for the certified organization. Maturity models such as CMMI, service management certifications such as ISO/IEC 20000, and certification of compliance with standards for various types of management systems all provide evidence that organizations conduct their operations in ways conforming to established frameworks and processes explicitly designed to be effective or efficient when implemented properly. Similar to service management, organizations may seek to certify the quality of specific business functions or operational capabilities or to certify their overall approach to quality management. Organizations adopting quality management or quality improvement methodologies such as Total Quality Management (TQM) or Six Sigma can have individual employees attain various types of quality certifications, but there is no corresponding organizational-level certification. Organizations that seek certification to demonstrate their commitment to quality management practices capabilities typically do so with widely recognized standards-based certifications such as ISO 9001. Broad standards such as those collectively organized under ISO 9000 address many aspects of quality management, including requirements for quality management systems, recommendations for enhancing the efficiency and effectiveness of such systems, and guidance on conducting audits of quality management systems [16]. Many industry-specific standards for quality management systems also exist, such as ISO 13485 on the manufacture of medical devices [17], ISO Technical Specification 16949 on quality in automotive production [18], and ISO 29001 on quality in oil and gas production [19]. Audits for quality certification involve both accredited certifying bodies and, in many cases, individual external auditors holding quality-related certifications such as Certified Quality Auditor (CQA) or Certified Lead Auditor for any of the ISO standards related to quality management systems.

Compliance audits

Compliance audits comprise a wide range of externally and internally driven examinations of an organization's fulfillment of legal or regulatory requirements, industry standards, licensing terms, contractual commitments, or other formal obligations.

Compliance audits overlap conceptually with financial, operational, and certification audits in the sense that those types of audits often address standards, practices, or legal provisions that constitute mandatory requirements for organizations. As a category, compliance auditing applies more broadly than other types in terms of who performs such audits, the purpose for conducting compliance audits, and the organizational elements or subject areas that provide the scope for audits. Compliance audits driven by needs to demonstrate adherence to legal provisions or regulations (including those conducted as part of formal investigations) are most commonly performed by external auditors. Audits of organizational fulfillment of licensing terms, service level agreements, or other contractual obligations are usually conducted by the legal or contracting functions of one or both parties bound by the contract. Audits that verify compliance with organizationally specified policies, procedures, standards, and guidelines typically fall within the purview of internal auditing programs. The standards and methodologies used in compliance auditing vary according to the context of the audit and the organization or legal entity that has the responsibility to verify compliance. As is the case with many other types of external auditing, the audit criteria used to determine compliance with externally defined requirements are often available to organizations, facilitating their preparation for external audits and enabling organizations to conduct internal self-assessments if they choose to do so.

The organizational requirements underlying compliance audits come from many different external sources, in addition to internal policies and governance objectives. Organizations in many industries are subject to both government regulations and commercial standards, each corresponding to different sets of audit criteria. In the United States and many other countries, organizations that operate in regulated industries or that participate in government-sponsored programs must undergo compliance audits. Unlike the securities and financial management laws and regulations that apply to all publicly traded companies and result in all such organizations performing mandatory audits, other types of legal requirements obligate covered organizations to comply but may only formally audit compliance of a small proportion of organizations, selected at random or in response to suspicions, complaints, or prior noncompliant behavior. Examples include audits of small businesses, federal grant recipients, and health care providers. Similar approaches to compliance auditing apply to many industry and commercial requirements, including audits of IT and security standards for organizations in financial services, insurance, energy, and retail.

Compliance audits conducted on an ad hoc or one-time basis rather than as a routine or recurring process can sometimes identify serious deficiencies or systemic problems within an organization. For example, for its services acquisition program U.S. Department of Veterans Affairs (VA) has in place small business contracting rules that give preference to veteran-owned businesses. A 2010 audit by the VA's Office of Inspector General of the Department's small business programs found that as many as three-quarters of the small businesses registered with the VA for participation in the program were in fact ineligible, due to what the Inspector General cited as deficient oversight and verification practices [20]. The contracting rules favoring veteran-owned businesses implemented legislative previsions enacted in 2006 and first examined by the Government Accountability Office (GAO) in 2009, but the 2010 Inspector General audit was the first the Department conducted on its own veteran-preference contracting programs.

Legal compliance

Legislation and legislatively mandated rules and regulations are significant sources of compliance requirements. Organizations falling under the jurisdiction of various national, state or provincial, or local laws are obligated to comply with the mandatory provisions in the laws and may be subject to audit to verify their compliance. Many legal audit drivers and their corresponding requirements for subject organizations are described in Chapter 7. Not all laws include audits as a mechanism for checking compliance, but audit procedures are often found where legal provisions include penalties for noncompliance. Few laws and regulations apply to all organizations, so organizations in different industries, markets, and geographic areas need to be aware of what laws and regulations apply to them, which requirements may be subject to validation through compliance auditing, and what criteria need to be satisfied if and when the organization is audited. Compliance activities in many organizations extend beyond formal audits, as even in the absence of financial or other penalties for noncompliance some organizations need to perform self-assessments of compliance and report the results to external oversight bodies. Organizations also may focus internal audit program resources on maintaining and reviewing evidence of compliance that might need to be provided if the organization is chosen for a random audit or becomes the subject of civil or criminal litigation.

The need to maintain awareness of legal audit requirements applicable to each organization includes keeping abreast of changes in compliance or enforcement policies related to legal requirements. For instance, many U.S. organizations in the health care industry are subject to security and privacy provisions in the Health Insurance Portability and Accountability Act (HIPAA) [21]. For several years after those requirements went into effect, each covered organization was obligated to satisfy applicable security and privacy requirements but did not undergo auditing or any formal evaluation of its compliance unless someone filed a complaint with the government claiming the organization violated the law. The Health Information Technology for Economic and Clinical Health (HITECH) Act added an audit requirement to the regulations originally enacted in HIPAA, under which the government selects a small number of covered organizations to audit [22]. This change, coupled with a provision requiring organizations to self-report breaches of protected health information, gives covered organizations an added incentive to ensure their compliance with the law, in addition to any internal goals and objectives to operate in compliance with applicable rules and regulations.

Compliance with industry standards

Organizations operating in specific industries may be subject to standards developed, implemented, and maintained by government authorities, industry groups or associations, or standards development organizations. Organizations obligated to comply with these requirements often incorporate them in their internal policies, procedures, and standards and validate compliance through internal compliance audits, alone or in addition to external audits performed by appropriately qualified and authorized auditors. Organizations may also adopt voluntary technical standards developed with specific industry applicability in mind, such as HL7 for health care, point of sale (POS) standards in retail, or the industry-specific subsets of ANSI X12 standards. As with commercial standards, verifying or demonstrating compliance with voluntary industry standards may help organizations achieve greater levels of technical interoperability with peer organizations. In the United States, European Union member nations, and other countries, multiple government and industry oversight organizations have responsibility for standards applicable to financial services institutions. With the intent of ensuring consistency in regulatory compliance and oversight, the Federal Financial Institution Examination Council (FFIEC) issues standards—including IT audit standards—for use by different U.S. government entities with responsibility for supervising financial institutions. In many industries organizations are subject to multiple regulations administered and overseen by different types of organizations, potentially presenting a challenge in terms of evaluating compliance with all applicable requirements in a single audit. For instance, the North American Electricity Reliability Corporation (NERC) maintains reliability standards for energy companies operating in the United States, Canada, and Mexico. U.S. energy companies are also subject to regulations from the Federal Energy Regulatory Commission (FERC) and, in the case of companies producing electricity with nuclear power, to additional regulations and standards from the Nuclear Regulatory Commission (NRC).

Commercial standards

Distinct from industry-specific compliance requirements, commercial standards apply to many organizations based on the types of business functions or transactions they perform or the way in which they perform those functions. Organizations also often choose to implement voluntary standards, particularly in IT domains, to help ensure interoperability with customers or business partners or to enable use of different vendor products or technologies in their environments. Voluntary standards are typically not subject to required compliance audits, but organizations may perform their own compliance verification activities to be able to publicize their use of or support for standards. For instance, the Open Source Initiative encourages the adoption of open source technologies and facilitates interoperability among such technologies with two designated levels of compliance, one self-attested and the other based on a review of conformance to explicit open standards requirements [23]. A well-known example of mandatory commercial standards is the Payment Card Industry Data Security Standards (PCI DSS), which prescribe requirements for organizations that accept payment cards (such as credit, debit, or prepaid cards) and handle cardholder information in the course of doing business. The standards are sponsored by major commercial electronic payment processors including VISA, MasterCard, and American Express and are mandatory for all organizations that process, store, or transmit cardholder data [24]. Large merchants are subject to mandatory PCI compliance audits and can, in cases of repeated non-compliance, face significant fines and potentially lose their ability to process transactions using cards branded by the sponsors.

IT-specific audits

IT auditing has a significant role in each of the audit types described so far in this chapter, but there are additional audits that focus explicitly on various aspects of IT. Many IT audits are intended to achieve outcomes similar to those anticipated from other types of audits, including demonstrating compliance or achieving certification against specific standards. Chapter 6 provides a detailed breakdown of the technical components and organizational elements often addressed through IT auditing, while Chapter 2 established the broader organizational context for many kinds of IT audits. The information in this section briefly describes common IT-centric audits and the subject areas they address, in recognition of the differences in approach, sources of guidance, and necessary skill sets associated with IT-specific auditing.

IT process maturity

The effectiveness and efficiency with which organizations implement and execute IT processes is often expressed in terms of process *maturity*, a relative measure of how well processes are fully defined, documented, implemented, and optimized for use in an organization. Appraisals of an organization's process maturity examines the specific steps and activities the organization performs in a given business or technical domain and the extent to which the organization standardizes its processes to achieve more repeatable, predictable, and reliable results. The standards or normative references used to evaluate maturity specify process areas—categories of related practices and activities that collectively enable process improvement in a given domain—represent processes that organizations are expected to perform. To achieve specific maturity levels against these reference models, organizations must demonstrate that they have implemented and follow the processes included in each process area. Two of the most widely used process maturity models—the SEI's CMMI and the Object Management Group's Business Process Maturity Model (BPMM)—both define five-level maturity models with corresponding process areas at each level, as listed in Table 5.3. The number and type of processes specified in CMMI varies somewhat across the different versions of the model for acquisition,

Table 5.3 Levels of Process Maturity in Commonly Used Models

Level	CMMI [11,25,26]	No. of CMMI Processes (ACQ/DEV/SVC)			BPMM [27]	No. of BPMM Processes
One	Initial	0	0	0	Initial	0
Two	Managed	9	7	8	Managed	9
Three	Defined	9	11	12	Standardized	10
Four	Quantitatively managed	2	2	2	Predictable	5
Five	Optimized	2	2	2	Innovating	6

development, and services. All versions of the CMMI also include capability levels, where level zero means "incomplete" or not performed and levels one through three indicate "performed," "managed," and "defined" capabilities, respectively [25].

Models such as CMMI and BPMM apply broadly across many functional domains and sets of operational processes. Organizations wanting an objective determination of their process maturity can, under the CMMI appraisal program, pursue certification by an authorized third party. As part of improving internal processes and moving to higher levels of maturity, many organizations adopt standard processes or methodologies that prescribe accepted industry practices, such as the software life cycle processes defined in ISO/IEC 12207 [28]. Other relevant IT process standards include ISO/IEC 15504 on IT process assessment [29] and ISO/IEC 15026 on systems and software engineering and assurance [30].

Provision of IT services

Organizations that structure their IT operations to reflect the services they perform or offer to users—whether those users are service consumers internal or external to the organization that provides IT services—often conduct IT auditing to support the measurement and achievement of internal objectives related to governance or operational effectiveness. Such organization may also seek certification of their IT service management capabilities against standards such as ISO 20000 [10]. For purposes of implementing, operating, or improving IT services, many organizations rely on externally developed service management frameworks such as the ITIL or relevant aspects of COBIT. ISO/IEC 20000 certification requirements are consistent with the practices organizations adopt when they implement IT service management frameworks; while it is not required that organizations commit to an external service management models, following such frameworks can facilitate achieving certification. Auditing IT processes or services present some potential challenges compared to examinations of other types of IT controls, as it may be impractical for auditors to directly observe the full execution of processes executed or services delivered by an organization. Audits of IT processes and services are performed by both external and internal auditors whose qualifications may include general auditing credentials such as CPA or IIA in addition to IT domain certifications or specialized subject matter expertise.

> Organizations implementing IT services management certification such as ISO/IEC 20000 or acquiring services provided by such organizations should be aware that framework-specific certifications like ITIL and COBIT can only be attained by individuals (including IT auditors), not by organizations. Whether or not they adopt or publicize their adherence to formally specified service management frameworks like ITIL, only certifications like ISO/IEC 20000 or SOC designations are relevant organization-level qualifications for service providers.

In many organizations, IT operations comprise a wide range of IT processes and services performed on behalf of business units or process owners outside the IT function. Services delivered in this model commonly include application management and monitoring, systems operation and maintenance, and network, telecommunications, and infrastructure services. The technical capabilities, of personnel, and physical resources needed to deliver these and other IT services are typically consolidated in dedicated data center facilities or dedicated areas of more general-purpose facilities. The "customers" served by IT may include other parts of the same organization or service users in external organizations. With the advent of IT outsourcing, software-as-a-service delivery models, cloud computing, and other forms of externally hosted systems and infrastructure, the field of IT auditing increasingly needs to address IT services. Data center operators and cloud computing vendors are specialized types of IT service providers whose internal controls are audited using available SSAE and related guidance on preparing reports on service organization controls [31,32]. As illustrated in Figure 5.3, the control reports resulting from external audits of service providers are often directed both at internal and external audiences with an interest in the effectiveness of the service provider's controls. For example, SOC reports have different numerical designations indicating both the scope of the underlying audit and the intended use of the report, where SOC 2 reports are intended for internal use by service providers and SOC 3 reports are available to external audiences, including prospective users of the providers' services. The information in SOC 3 reports may be reviewed by an organization prior to using an external provider and by the user organization's auditor as part of examining the full set of controls applicable to the user organization.

Information systems controls

Organizations focus significant IT audit attention on information systems and the different types of controls implemented to help ensure the efficient, effective,

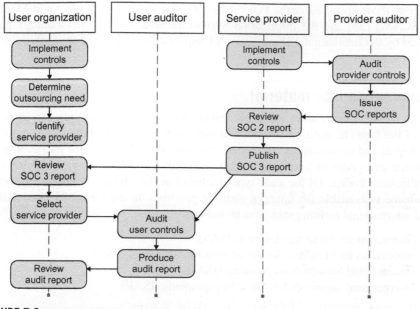

FIGURE 5.3

External providers of hosting or other outsourced IT services are subject to specialized IT control audits and reports used by both service providers and service consumers.

and secure operation of their systems. System-level audits are commonly performed as part of internal auditing, often in support of IT governance, risk management, or information security programs. The opposite is true in commercial organizations in some industries and public sector organizations such as government agencies, which are subject to external system audits by government oversight agencies. For instance, external IT audit guidance from the FFIEC applies to banks and other financial institutions under the supervisory authority of regulators such as the Federal Deposit Insurance Corporation (FDIC) or the Consumer Finance and Protection Bureau (CFPB). Many organizations in industries, not otherwise addressed by regulations on audits, may nonetheless face audits related to investigations by the U.S. Federal Trade Commission or European Commission. Government agencies are subject to laws and regulations that do not apply to nongovernment entities, including many that mandate IT management practices, information security provisions, and privacy protections. Maintaining compliance with these requirements drives substantial internal IT auditing activity in government agencies, in addition to external audits performed by authorized oversight bodies, such as the U.S. GAO. Public sector audits of information systems in the United States and many other countries follow specific procedures and methodologies such as those specified in the Federal Information System Controls Audit Manual (FISCAM) [33] and the Information System Security Review Methodology published by the International Organization of Supreme Audit Institutions [34].

Relevant source material

Much of the audit industry standards and guidance cited earlier applies to some or all of the types of auditing described in this chapter. In particular, GAAS and ISA principles and requirements are echoed or incorporated by reference into audit procedures and codes of conduct by most standards development organizations and certification bodies. Of the audit types included in this chapter, the most extensive guidance is available for financial auditing practices, in the form of United States and international auditing standards including:

- Statements on Auditing Standards (SAS);
- Statements on Standards for Attestation Engagements (SSAE);
- International Standards on Auditing (ISA);
- International Standards for Attest Engagements (ISAE).

Available frameworks on internal controls and IT governance provide substantial information relevant to operational auditing, notably including the COSO *Internal Control—Integrated Framework* [4] and ISACA's *COBIT 5: A Business Framework for the Governance and Management of Enterprise IT* [8]. Resources for certification and compliance auditing tend to be more narrowly focused on the standards, regulations, or other basis of examination. Generally applicable guidance for these types of auditing include ISO 19011, *Guidelines for Auditing Management Systems* [35] and the ISO 9000 and ISO/IEC 20000 families of standards on quality management and service management, respectively. Applicable sources of information and auditing guidance for IT-specific auditing also vary widely depending on the technical subject matter, but in general include:

- ISACA's *Standards for IS Audit and Assurance* [36].
- ISO/IEC 15504, *Information Technology—Process Assessment* [29].
- ISO/IEC 27007, *Information—Security Techniques—Guidelines for Information Security Management Systems Auditing* [37].
- Statement on Standards for Attestation Engagements (SSAE) No. 16, *Reporting on Controls at a Service Organization* [31].
- International Standards for Assurance Engagements (ISAE) 3402, *Assurance Reports on Controls at a Service Organization* [32].

Summary

This chapter differentiated among major types of auditing, highlighting the significant role of IT and IT auditing practices in financial, operational, certification, and compliance audits and describing common forms of IT-specific auditing.

Understanding the similarities and differences among various types of auditing clarifies the contexts in which IT auditing is often performed, and explains the tendencies of certain types of audits to be conducted by internal or external auditors. The areas of commonality or overlap described in this chapter should also help reinforce the idea that auditing in most organizations has multiple justifications, serves multiple purposes, and produces a variety of potential outcomes and benefits. The information in this chapter brings into alignment many of the topic areas addressed in the subsequent chapters, including the decomposition of IT audit subjects in Chapter 6, the key audit drivers presented in Chapter 7, the audit methodologies and frameworks described in Chapter 9, and many of the organizations, standards, and certifications listed in Chapter 10.

References

[1] Securities Exchange Act of 1934, Pub. L. No. 73-291, 48 Stat. 881.
[2] Sarbanes–Oxley Act of 2002, Pub. L. No. 107-204, 116 Stat. 745.
[3] Electronic Industries Alliance Earned value management systems. Arlington (VA): Electronic Industries Alliance; 1998. [ANSI/EIA 748].
[4] Committee of Sponsoring Organizations of the Treadway Commission Committee of Sponsoring Organizations of the Treadway Commission. Internal control—Integrated framework. New York (NY): Committee of Sponsoring Organizations of the Treadway Commission; 2013.
[5] Securities and Exchange Commission. Management's report on internal control over financial reporting and certification of disclosure in Exchange Act periodic reports. [final rule]. 68 Fed. Reg. 36636; 2003.
[6] Chambers A, Rand G. The operational auditing handbook: auditing business and it processes. West Sussex (UK): John Wiley & Sons; 2010.
[7] Senft S, Gallegos F, Davis A. Information technology control and audit, 4th ed. Boca Raton (FL): CRC Press; 2013.
[8] ISACA COBIT 5: a business framework for the governance and management of enterprise IT. Rolling Meadows (IL): ISACA; 2012.
[9] Certification Body Directory [Internet]. London: Standards.org [cited 2013 July 14]. Available from: <http://www.standards.org/certification_bodies/>.
[10] ISO/IEC 20000-1:2011. Information technology—Service management—Part 1: Service management system requirements.
[11] Software Engineering Institute CMMI for services, version 1.3. Pittsburgh (PA): Software Engineering Institute; 2010 November.
[12] ISO/IEC 15408: 2009. Information technology—Security techniques—Evaluation criteria for IT security.
[13] Software Engineering Institute CERT resilience management model, version 1.0. Pittsburgh (PA): Software Engineering Institute; 2010 May.
[14] International Society for Automation ISA 62443/IEC 62443-1. Security for industrial automation and control systems. Research Triangle Park (NC): International Society for Automation; 2007.
[15] Service Organization Control (SOC) Reports [Internet]. Durham (NC): American Institute of Certified Public Accountants [cited 2013 May 4]. Available from: <http://www.aicpa.org/InterestAreas/FRC/AssuranceAdvisoryServices/Pages/SORHome.aspx>.

[16]   ISO 9000:2005. Quality management—Fundamentals and vocabulary.

[17]   ISO 13485:2003. Medical devices—Quality management systems—Requirements for regulatory purposes.

[18]   ISO/TS 16949:2009. Quality management systems—Particular requirements for the application of ISO 9001:2008 for automotive production and relevant service part organizations.

[19]   ISO/TS 29001:2010. Petroleum, petrochemical and natural gas industries—Sector-specific quality management systems—Requirements for product and service supply organizations.

[20]   Department of Veterans Affairs VA Office of the Inspector General. Audit of veteran-owned and service-disabled veteran-owned small business programs. Washington (DC): Department of Veterans Affairs; 2011 July. [Available from: <http://www.va.gov/oig/52/reports/2011/VAOIG-10-02436-234.pdf]>.

[21]   Health Insurance Portability and Accountability Act of 1996, Pub. L. No. 104-191, 110 Stat. 1936.

[22]   Health Information Technology for Economic and Clinical Health Act of 2009, Pub. L. No. 111-5, 123 Stat. 226.

[23]   Open standards compliance [Internet]. Palo Alto (CA): Open Source Initiative [cited 2013 July 14]. Available from: <http://opensource.org/osr-compliance>.

[24]   PCI SSC Data Security Standards overview [Internet]. Wakefield (MA): PCI Security Standards Council [cited 2013 May 4]. Available from: <https://www.pcisecurity-standards.org/security_standards/index.php>.

[25]   Software Engineering Institute CMMI for acquisition, version 1.3. Pittsburgh (PA): Software Engineering Institute; 2010 November.

[26]   Software Engineering Institute CMMI for development, version 1.3. Pittsburgh (PA): Software Engineering Institute; 2010 November.

[27]   Object Management Group Business process maturity model, version 1.0. Needham (MA): Object Management Group; 2008 June.

[28]   ISO/IEC 12207:2008. Systems and software engineering—Software life cycle processes.

[29]   ISO/IEC 15504:2004. Information technology—Process assessment.

[30]   ISO/IEC 15026:2011. Systems and software engineering—Systems and software assurance.

[31]   American Institute of Certified Public Accountants Reporting on controls at a service organization. Durham (NC): American Institute of Certified Public Accountants; 2011. [Statement on Standards for Attestation Engagements No. 16].

[32]   International Auditing and Assurance Standards Board Assurance reports on controls at a service organization. New York (NY): International Auditing and Assurance Standards Board; 2011. [International Standards for Assurance Engagements 3402].

[33]   Government Accountability Office Federal information system controls audit manual (FISCAM). Washington (DC): Government Accountability Office; 2009 February.

[34]   INTOSAI Professional Standards Committee International Organization of Supreme Audit Institutions. Information system security review methodology. Copenhagen (DK): INTOSAI Professional Standards Committee; 1995. [ISSAI 5310].

[35]   ISO 19011:2011. Guidelines for auditing management systems.

[36]   Standards for IS Audit and Assurance [Internet]. Rolling Meadows (IL): ISACA [cited 2013 May 4]. Available from http://www.isaca.org/Knowledge-Center/Standards/Pages/Standards-for-IT-Audit-and-Assurance-English-.aspx.

[37]   ISO/IEC 27007:2011. Information—Security techniques—Guidelines for information security management systems auditing.

IT Audit Components

INFORMATION IN THIS CHAPTER

- Establishing the scope of IT audits
- Types of controls
- Auditing IT assets
- Auditing procedural controls or processes

Regardless of the type of IT audit performed or their underlying purpose, IT audits share a common attribute: the need to examine different IT components and the controls associated with them. The scope of IT auditing includes both technical and nontechnical components, requiring different auditor skill sets and involving different audit procedures and standards to effectively address administrative and physical as well as technical controls. The range of controls potentially in scope for a given IT audit covers a wide variety of technologies, processes, and procedures, organizational assets, operational capabilities, and management and oversight functions as illustrated in Figure 6.1. Previous chapters in this book have described different types of internal and external audits with an emphasis on the rationale and expected benefits or other outcomes. This chapter focuses specifically on the controls and other subject matter addressed across all types of IT audits and describes the areas of emphasis for auditors examining different IT components.

Establishing the scope of IT audits

The key prerequisites to an organizational audit program are determining what types of audits are needed and identifying what must be or could be audited. Developing an inventory of potential audit subjects—sometimes termed the *audit universe*—leverages business process decomposition, asset management, enterprise architecture, governance frameworks, or any other approach that helps identify the constituent elements of an organization. Organizations then conduct risk assessments on each item included in the audit universe to inform the prioritization of audit subjects, considering factors for each item such as the relative magnitude of risk (an estimate based on likelihood and impact), its importance to the organization, or the potential benefits to the organization from performing an audit. Audit

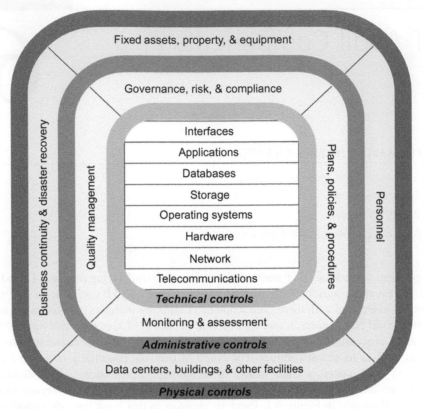

FIGURE 6.1

The range of potential IT audit subjects spans all types of physical, administrative, and technical controls implemented at any level of granularity within an organization.

prioritization reflects the practical reality that organizational resources available to support audit activities are not unlimited and helps ensure that the most significant auditable aspects of the organization are adequately addressed. Large or complex organizations may find it challenging to produce a comprehensive inventory covering all business units, operational functions, and assets unless they have also established formal governance or enterprise risk management functions. Both of these organizational domains emphasize asset identification and valuation as a basis for structuring management activities and allocating organizational resources. An alternative approach advocated by the Institute of Internal Auditors [1], among others, begins with the identification and analysis of enterprise risk and focuses resources—including audit and other control resources—on the organizational areas associated with the greatest sources of risk.

Developing and maintaining the audit universe

The structure of the audit universe in each organization typically reflects the way the organization itself is structured and managed. The audit universe may be arranged or categorized by business unit hierarchy, enterprise architecture, business process model, governance framework, service catalog, or any other functional decomposition that best matches the way organizations view their operations and assets. Regardless of how the organization describes the different structural, functional, or technical elements corresponding to items in the audit universe, there is almost always some level of common overarching entity-level controls subject to audit. As described later in this chapter, audits of entity-level controls often required the use of multiple audit approaches because they usually span many different types of internal controls. The broad scope of these audits and their applicability at all organizational levels also means that entity-level audit reports have a wider audience than those produced in other types of audits. In addition to enterprise-wide controls used throughout an organization, the inventory of controls and auditable items in the audit universe can also identify common controls shared across business units, facilities, operating environments, processes, or systems. Auditors performing audits at any level below the entire organization need to ensure that the scope of their audits includes entity-level and other shared controls as well as those implemented specifically for components the audit examines.

Most organizations have too many auditable elements to make it feasible to produce an audit universe as a simple list; instead, organizations need some sort of categorization or organizing scheme to align the audit universe with governance and risk management functions and facilitate the use of the information in audit planning and prioritization. In addition to categorizing auditable elements by business or technical function, location, control type, purpose, or other attributes, many source of guidance on internal controls also recommend distinguishing among the different levels within organizations at which controls apply. For instance, the *Internal Control—Integrated Framework* published by the Committee of Sponsoring Organizations of the Treadway Commission (COSO) categorizes internal control components by purpose (operational, reporting, or compliance) and by applicability (entity level, division, operating unit, or function) [2].Organizational elements typically included in the audit universe include:

- units of organizational structure such as business units, operating divisions, facilities, or subsidiaries;
- accounting structures such as cost centers, lines of business, or process areas;
- strategic goals, objectives, and outcomes, which are evaluated in part by auditing the resources allocated for their achievement;
- mission and business processes, services, and operational functions executed by the organization;
- assets—including IT assets—the organization owns, operates, manages, or controls;

- programs, projects, and investments to which the organization commits funding or other resources;
- internal and external controls implemented by the organization or on its behalf;
- management functions or programs such as governance, risk management, quality assurance, certification, and compliance as well as internal auditing.

Internal controls explicitly itemized in the audit universe or implicitly referenced through their implementation with other organizational elements may be further categorized by type and subject area in a manner conceptually similar to the decomposition shown in Figure 6.1. Organizations also try to align assets identified in the audit universe with similar asset inventories developed in support of risk management activities, since risk assessment results strongly influence the prioritization of elements the audit universe includes.

Governance, risk, and compliance drivers

IT auditing has a strong supporting role in organizational governance, risk management, and compliance functions, and in initiatives such as certification and quality assurance. To the extent that organizations establish and maintain formal programs in these areas, the need to assess their effectiveness and measure the achievement of program objectives influences the scope and frequency of IT audits and the procedures, standards, and criteria used in internal IT auditing. Governance, risk, and compliance (GRC) activities in particular help define and prioritize the audit universe, especially when organizations adopt formal management frameworks or enabling technologies that integrate the management and monitoring of these operational activities. Although governance and risk management frameworks and methodologies rarely specify a sufficiently broad set of elements to provide a full inventory of potential audit subjects, they offer a strong foundation, particular for IT-related components and controls in the audit universe. For instance, the widely used version 4.1 of the Control Objectives for Information and Related Technology (COBIT) includes 34 processes in four key governance domains and defines more than 200 control objectives associated with those processes [3]. COBIT 5 expanded the process reference model to 37 processes among five domains, replacing control objectives with recommended governance and management practices and basing audit criteria on seven enablers, similar to audit universe categories: principles, policies, and frameworks; processes; organizational structures; culture, ethics, and behavior; information; services, infrastructure, and applications; and people, skills, and competencies [4].

Enterprise risk management drives audit universe development and IT audit scope by identifying organizational assets at risk and specifying the types of risk applicable to different components or operational aspects of the organization. While the magnitude of risk associated with different audit subjects helps prioritize auditing resources, considering all applicable types of risk can affect the scope of IT audits, e.g., by highlighting ancillary processes or support functions that need to be addressed in addition to IT assets and controls. Compliance programs have a similar dual influence on IT auditing, where the need to meet compliance objectives or requirements (such as legal and regulatory mandates) is a key factor in prioritization and the criteria used as a basis for demonstrating compliance set the minimum scope for IT audits conducted to support compliance.

Audit strategy and prioritization

Chapter 3 emphasized the importance of the audit strategy to organizations and their internal audit programs. The audit strategy is a key driver determining the type, scope, and frequency of IT audits an organization conducts and defining the criteria organizations use to prioritize the items in the audit universe. Organizations follow procedures in the audit strategy to assign audit priorities and use those determinations to allocate internal auditing resources. In the hypothetical case where an organization had only voluntary internal audit drivers, resources available for auditing might be determined first, after which the organization would begin with the highest priority audits and continue until allocated resources were exhausted. In most organizations, however, the need to satisfy mandatory external and internal audit drivers means that the scope of the audit program must, at a minimum, include all required auditing activities. The corresponding audit plans specify the resources the organization must allocate to be able to comply with mandatory requirements and any additional discretionary audit objectives or requirements. Many organizations assign high-priority ratings to audit activities that support legal or regulatory compliance, such as the report on internal controls required of publicly traded companies under section 404 of the Sarbanes–Oxley Act [5]. Failure to comply with mandatory requirements is one of several types of risk organizations face that can result in adverse impacts measured directly in financial terms or indirectly from damage to reputation, negative publicity, legal sanctions, or other potential outcomes.

Types of controls

Among different elements subject to audit, business operations, IT assets, and supporting resources constitute the functional capabilities of an organization, while controls on those capabilities include management structures, processes and procedures, and technical measures that provide operational efficiency and effectiveness, compliance, reliability, and assurance. In a governance or risk management context, *controls* are any measures such as actions, policies, processes, procedures, practices, devices, or organizational structures—used to manage or mitigate risk. The set of individual controls (both internal and external) implemented by an organization stand in contrast to the governance process of internal control, which exists to help an organization achieve management objectives related to strategy, operations, legal or regulatory compliance, quality, security, or risk management [2]. Controls—especially internal controls—are the primary focus of many types of IT audits, whether performed by internal or external auditors. One or more types of controls typically apply to all the items in an organization's audit universe. As illustrated in Figure 6.1, the controls applicable to an organization's information technology include not only technical controls, but also the administrative controls used by the processes that leverage or support IT and the physical controls associated with people, facilities, equipment, and infrastructure. Organizations and IT auditors need a broad understanding of different types of controls and their intended purpose and applicability to be able to properly plan for and conduct audits of an organization's controls and to align the types of controls in use with their auditors' competencies, skills, and prior experience.

Control categorization

Organizations typically maintain a large number and wide variety of controls and select those controls from an equally broad or broader array of candidate controls considered for implementation. Just as the items in the audit universe can be arranged or categorized in multiple ways, many different control categorization approaches are used in available frameworks, methodologies, and guidance. Common organizing schemes for controls include those based on purpose, objective, function, nature of implementation, or level of applicability within the organization. Table 6.1 provides a list of representative control categorization approaches using different bases of categorization.

Control categorization is primarily intended to introduce consistency in the way controls are referenced and applied in different contexts and for different purposes. As Table 6.1 implies, there is no single accepted standard for categorizing controls, so organizations can select or adapt an approach specified in an external framework or methodology, develop their own categorization, or follow standards set in legal, regulatory, or policy requirements the organization must satisfy. The security regulations promulgated under the Health Insurance Portability and Accountability Act of 1996 (known collectively as the HIPAA Security Rule) for example, separate requirements into administrative, technical, and physical safeguards, so

Table 6.1 Control Categorization Approaches	
Basis	**Representative Categorizations**
Control purpose	• Preventive, detective, corrective
Control objective	• Operations, reporting, compliance • Governance, risk management, compliance
Control function	• Administrative, technical, physical • Management, operational, technical
Nature of implementation	• Centralized, shared, decentralized
Level of applicability	• Organization, division, business unit, function • Program, project, system, component

organizations covered by the law might find that using a similar categorization approach for internal controls facilitates compliance.

Control frameworks intended for use in specific domains often reflect one or more of the categorization approaches listed in Table 6.1, but they also further decompose sets of controls corresponding to the functions they support. Taking information security control frameworks as an example, the information security management code of practice in ISO/IEC 27002 identifies 39 control objectives and well over 100 controls grouped into 12 security domains [6]. The guidance for US federal government agencies in NIST Special Publication (SP) 800-53 describes over 400 controls, enhancements, and objectives organized into 18 control "families" that are further designated as belonging to management, operational, or technical control categories [7].

Organizational controls

Organizational controls are selected and implemented once with applicability across the entire enterprise. Entity-level controls are important as a focus area for internal and external audits because they provide the foundation for how organizations manage control-supported functions. Entity-level controls are also incorporated by reference into many types of audits performed at other levels of the organization, as business units, programs and projects, and technology assets all leverage different types of entity-level controls. Figure 6.2 shows different major categories of entity-level controls and the kinds of controls within each category

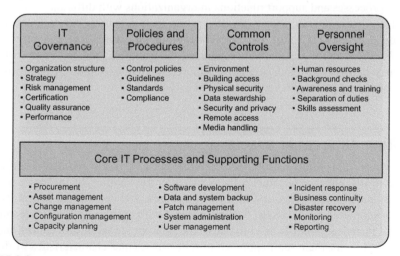

FIGURE 6.2

Entity-level controls include any policies, processes and procedures, standards, or measures specified for organization-wide use.

that may be implemented and subject to audit in different organizations. Audits of entity-level controls differ to some extent from examinations focused at more narrowly defined elements within organizations. The effectiveness of entity-level controls depends in part on the extent to which the organization establishes control authority and implements each control in a manner that pervades the entire organization. From this perspective, audits of entity-level controls essentially examine the organization's management and governance capabilities, including the structure of the organization, alignment of business and IT objectives, and existence and use of strategic and operational planning activities and artifacts. These control elements help ensure that the controls an organization specifies in policies are actually implemented and used to support the achievement of the organization's control objectives.

Prominent governance and risk management frameworks emphasize the importance of establishing entity-level controls and seem to assume that virtually all organizations recognize the value of implementing these types of controls [2,8,9]. Such assumptions stem in part from the large proportion of publicly traded companies or organizations in regulated industries or operating environments that make up the intended audience of guidance on governance, risk management, compliance, and auditing. Most organizations implement some controls at an enterprise-wide level, but the types of entity-level controls they implement vary substantially among different organizations, even within the same sector or industry. The categories of controls shown in the upper half of Figure 6.2—IT governance, policies and procedures, common controls, and personnel oversight—each reflect at least some functions or management activities that are likely to be performed similarly across different business units or operational areas. Greater variation may be expected for core IT processes and support functions in organizations with different data centers, facilities, service providers, or types of systems, or in organizations with decentralized management structures. The capability to implement and leverage entity-level controls offers potential benefits to organizations from financial and administrative efficiency and also in terms of enabling more effective execution of enterprise IT governance, risk management, and compliance activities.

Auditing different IT assets

Many types of IT audits require the examination of IT assets and associated technical controls, either as a primary focus in IT-centric auditing or in the context of auditing management functions, business processes, and operational programs and projects supported by IT assets. Auditors tasked with examining specific technologies and technical controls need to select the appropriate audit procedures and, in many cases, tailor their audit approach to reflect particular characteristics of different types of IT assets. The questions IT auditors seek to answer also vary according to the type of audit to be conducted, so auditors must have applicable technical knowledge about the IT components and technical controls they audit. They also need sufficient understanding of the context in which IT assets are used or the business processes and control objectives they support to be sure; relevant evidence is gathered and appropriate examination procedures are used. Auditors examining multiple IT components within the scope of a single audit balance technology-specific criteria and audit procedures with the need for a consistent approach to collecting and analyzing information and reporting audit findings. Across most types of IT assets, there are common areas of focus or audit procedures that can help provide this consistency, as summarized in Table 6.2. Collectively, these procedures highlight the combined use of documentation, inquiry, observation, and direct test methods to provide the evidence necessary to support audit findings.

Table 6.2 IT Audit Procedures Used Across Subjects or Components

IT Audit Focus	Audit Procedures
Technical architecture	Review existing architecture documentation and diagrams to understand the operating environment, infrastructure, and hardware and software associated with the audit subject
Product versions	Establish current versions for all products and components (whether commercially acquired or internally developed) and compare actual versions to applicable policies, standards, and license agreements
Patch management	Review procedures for maintaining awareness of patches or upgrades and processes for implementing them, including prerequisite unit and regression testing
Necessary services	Scan or query to identify all services enabled, compare actual services to policy specifications, and confirm no additional unnecessary services are running
Configuration	Scan or otherwise analyze asset configuration and compare actual configuration to policy, approved baselines, and standards
Logging and monitoring	Confirm logging is enabled at an appropriate level of detail and that log output is monitored and regularly reviewed or analyzed
Account provisioning	Review processes and procedures for creating, updating, and removing accounts and, where applicable, confirm provisioned accounts reflect valid current users
Access control	Review policies, procedures, and mechanisms for controlling access to the audit subject, including granting and revoking access privileges and authenticating and authorizing access
Capacity utilization	Compare resource needs and corresponding resource allocation to actual usage of the audit subject and review policies and procedures for expanding or reducing capacity as required
Performance measurement	Review practices for measuring and reporting performance to support findings related to meeting efficiency and effectiveness targets or other objectives

IT component decomposition

Organizations can facilitate planning and efficient performance of IT audits by clearly identifying IT assets and technical controls to be addressed within each type of audit. Decomposing IT audit subject areas into individual technologies helps to more accurately determine the scope of each audit, the skill sets and competencies needed by the auditors, and the level of resources necessary to complete the audit process. IT audit plans reflect the type of audit and its intended purpose, the IT components it will examine, and the procedures, protocols, standards, or criteria auditors will use. Decomposing the IT assets and corresponding controls included in an audit is analogous to the business-centric process of clearly defining the organizational level (e.g., enterprise, business unit, operational function, and project) to which the audit applies. Many approaches to information technology decomposition use architectural frameworks or reference models to categorize different technologies and determine the appropriate audit procedures to use for each component under examination. Such frameworks typically distinguish among IT systems, the environments in which those systems operate, and models or views describing the details of underlying technology components and their interaction [10].

There is no single standard or "best" method to evaluating systems or technical environments. One approach involves decomposing a system into its constituent parts and auditing each component individually, applying similar audit protocols across all major elements but also using technology-specific procedures or checklists where appropriate. Organizations may use their own system architecture standards or models as a guide for decomposing their systems in a consistent manner or follow available external standards applicable to the types of systems they maintain. Commonly used models for system decomposition include the seven-layer Open Systems Interconnection model described in ISO/IEC 7498-1 [11], the software architecture design specified in ISO/IEC 12207 [12], or other systems and software architecture description languages conforming to ISO/IEC/IEEE 42010 [10]. To audit a typical n-tier architected system, for example, an auditor using such an approach might separately examine the web server, application server, database, middleware or other integration technology as well as the administrators, support personnel, and end users who access the system. An alternative approach to auditing systems at the individual component level considers all components, points of integration, and data flows together as the basis for an end-to-end examination, sometimes called *path analysis* (or critical path analysis, or transaction path analysis). As illustrated in Figure 6.3, this approach—informed by methods used in varied contexts such as network traffic analysis and behavioral analytics—defines the system scope by tracing the flow of information from initiation by a user or other system through all points of interaction. Path analysis may offer a more appropriate audit approach for transactional systems or those supporting processes with clearly correlated inputs and outputs.

Common categories or IT components representing audit subject areas include the eight IT elements shown in the center of Figure 6.1. Some special audit

FIGURE 6.3

One approach to auditing IT systems focuses on the end-to-end flow of information associated with a transaction or other type of user or system interaction.

considerations also apply in certain types of operating environments such as cloud computing or other uses of server virtualization technology, and system or application access using web browsers, mobile devices, or other types of client applications and interfaces. The following sections briefly describe the context and audit considerations applicable to different IT components.

Systems and applications

The terms *system* and *application* are used interchangeably in many organizations to refer to the software and computing capabilities that perform specific functions in support of business processes. The diverse nature of systems or applications and underlying technologies implemented in many organizations poses a challenge to defining and auditing systems in a uniform manner. Systems and applications vary in characteristics such as technical architecture, operating systems, programming languages, points of integration, and intended function. The choice of appropriate audit procedures for systems and applications depends on their architecture and the different types of technical components deployed for each system or application subject to examination. For example, auditors apply different criteria, tests, and audit procedures to client–server systems than to web-based applications relying on web servers, web browser–based access, and corresponding protocols and communication channels. Organizations often focus on auditing systems and applications that are fully operational, but they may also be audited during other phases of the system development life cycle. Auditors apply different criteria for systems or applications undergoing planning, design, or development than for those in production operation. System or application audits focus on functional and nonfunctional capabilities and controls. Functional concerns include ensuring that what the organization puts into operation meets specified requirements. Nonfunctional aspects include performance, usability, reliability, and security, where auditors often test for or review evidence demonstrating the implementation of controls appropriate for the intended use of the system or application and the ways in which users will interact with it. For example, audits of web-based applications often examine the use of controls to guard against known vulnerabilities, misconfiguration, and unauthorized disclosure of sensitive information.

Databases

The term *database* generically means any collection or repository of information maintained by an organization, but in practice most often connotes a specific type of technology that stores and provides access to data in support of one or more applications and business processes. Databases house many types of information, often including information considered highly sensitive such as personal information about individuals, intellectual property, transactional records and other financial data, and confidential or proprietary internal information about an organization. Databases represent a specialized type of application software, subject to many of the same audit procedures and examination criteria as applications and systems. The nature and sensitivity of the data stored in organizational databases influences the criteria used to audit them, particularly with respect to examining security or privacy controls such as data encryption, access control, and data backup and recovery. Auditors may examine databases in isolation or in the broader context of the applications, systems, or business processes that rely on the information the databases contain. Database audits typically focus on controls that help ensure current, accurate information is available to the organization and that the confidentiality, integrity, and availability of information in databases is protected by appropriate security and privacy safeguards.

Operating systems

Modern organizations often use multiple operating systems to support different systems and computing needs, most commonly including Microsoft Windows, various versions of Unix or Linux, and vendor- and platform-specific alternatives such as z/OS for IBM mainframe computers. Operating systems are highly customizable and can be implemented differently across organizations or within the same organization. To improve maintainability, administration, security, and support, organizations often standardize operating system configurations for servers, desktop and laptop computers, and mobile devices. Many operating system vendors offer configuration recommendations intended to optimize security or suitability for different uses. In the United States, both the military and civilian branches of government maintain secure configuration standards for specific operating system versions and publish configuration specifications that any organization can use [13,14]. Operating system audits confirm the use and appropriate configuration of operating systems on different computing platforms deployed within organizations.

Hardware

Hardware comprises the physical devices used to build networks, telecommunications infrastructure, computer systems, end-user computing clients, and many components of physical security. In many technical architecture decompositions, hardware connotes the servers, desktop and laptop computers, and mobile devices organizations deploy as well as the routers, switches, firewalls, and other components used in networks. Audits of hardware IT assets typically focus on consistent and correct configuration and adherence to internal policies and standards.

Compared to software, a greater proportion of an organization's IT hardware is likely to be acquired commercially, so hardware audits also consider the vendors and internal processes used to acquire hardware.

Networks

Networks provide connectivity and enable communications and information exchange for most if not of an organization's IT assets. Networks comprise hardware assets such as routers, hubs, switches, and firewalls that enable the flow of information between IT components and communications and security controls that protect the quality of service in network communications and the confidentiality, integrity, and availability of data traversing network infrastructure. Network audits examine the implementation and configuration of hardware devices, services and protocols running on the network, and security controls such as firewalls and network intrusion detection systems. These audits also consider the nature of the communication within the network so that auditors can select appropriate audit procedures to address the use of wireless, satellite, cellular, frame relay, and other network technologies. The specific audit procedures used to examine networks depend on the types of hardware, services, security controls, and telecommunications infrastructure implemented by an organization and on the scale of the network in terms of its geographic reach and the number and variety of systems and facilities connected to it. While much of the underlying technology is substantially similar regardless of the scale of a network, there are practical differences in auditing conventional or virtual local area networks deployed in a single physical location versus wide area networks spanning multiple sites.

Storage

Although organizations store substantial amounts of data in relational databases, content and document management systems, and similar IT components, the increasingly pervasive use of dedicated storage technologies makes storage platforms, networks, and infrastructure a distinct subset of IT subject to audit. Storage solutions use specialized hardware, software, communication protocols, and data storage and access methods, although the areas of emphasis for storage audits overlap substantially with those for databases. Audit procedures and criteria for storage depend both on the specific types of storage technology used by an organization and the nature and sensitivity of the data housed in storage environments. Storage may be audited in isolation or in a broader operational context—such technology is typically provisioned as a supporting component of data centers or other technical operating environments, where a single storage infrastructure can receive data from multiple systems. Depending on the systems operation and maintenance procedures organizations follow and the security control standards or regulations that apply to them, the scope of storage technology subject to audit may include alternate data storage locations or third-party providers of off-site data backup services. These external storage facilities, services, and technical mechanisms need to be included within the scope of IT audits addressing storage.

Data centers

As the facilities in which many IT systems, hardware, network infrastructure, and associated technologies reside, data centers provide an essential foundation for IT operations. In addition to serving as the physical location for many IT components, data centers are also the point of execution for many IT processes, procedures, and support functions. Organizational IT assets typically rely on a wide variety of common controls implemented at the data center level and shared or inherited by the systems and technologies that operate in data center environments. Examples include physical and environmental controls—such as backup power generation, fire suppression, building access control, security guards, and telecommunications—and disaster recovery and business continuity, including services and capabilities provided through the use of redundant or alternate processing facilities. Audits of data center facilities focus on these specialized types of controls and the operational support processes, resources, and personnel that ensure that IT components residing in the data center operate normally to support the business processes and functions that depend on IT. Whether owned and managed by an organization or by third parties, data centers are often considered service providers and are therefore subject to explicit standards prescribed for auditing service organizations [15].

Virtualized environments

Virtualization technology provides an alternative technical approach to delivering infrastructure, platforms and operating systems, servers, software, and systems and applications. Most virtualized computing environments have much in common with conventional data centers, but employ high-performing hardware and specialized software that enables a single physical server to function as multiple concurrently running instances. This approach increases capacity utilization and, in IT service-based models such as cloud computing, allows organizations to make more efficient use of their IT resources by scaling up or down as business needs warrant. Auditing virtualized computing environments uses many of the same procedures and criteria used for data center audits, with additional emphasis on the provisioning, deprovisioning, management, and maintenance of multiple virtual servers that share computing, network, and infrastructure resources.

The use of cloud computing and associated third-party service providers is becoming sufficiently common that IT audits may address such services distinct from other audited components. In many respects—including significant use of virtualization technology—cloud computing services are quite similar to conventional outsourced application hosting and managed infrastructure services long used by some organizations. Distinctions emphasized by cloud service vendors include on-demand service provisioning, ubiquitous network access, resource pooling, elastic capabilities and services, and metered usage and associated billing and payment models. The anticipated growth in cloud computing is one factor motivating the development of cloud-specific control frameworks, intended in particular to address concerns about information security in cloud computing. Available frameworks include the Cloud Controls Matrix)[16] developed by the nonprofit Cloud

Security Alliance and the Federal Risk and Authorization Management Program (FedRAMP) [17] administered by the General Services Administration for use by cloud service providers serving US government agencies. These control frameworks offer IT auditors additional points of reference on the types of controls that should be present in cloud computing environments.

Interfaces

Interfaces are points of integration or connectivity mechanisms among two or more IT components, enabling the transmission of information between systems or exposing services or functional capabilities from one system or application to others. Organizations often use many different types of interfaces, each of which may have different communication methods, technical protocols, or standards associated with it. As a subject for IT audit, key considerations for interfaces include confirming that system interconnections are authorized, conform to technical specifications, and satisfy functional and technical requirements. Auditors often emphasize the security measures implemented to protect information in transit across interfaces and to control access to interfaces exposed by each system. Interface audits rely on both documentation such as formal interface specifications and tests that demonstrate the correct function of each interface, taking into consideration the intended purpose, information flows, technical access mechanisms, and user- or system-level authentication and authorization processes.

Auditing procedural controls or processes

The scope of information technology auditing is every bit as broad and varied in as the domain of organization IT itself, encompassing a wide range of technologies, technical capabilities, and controls as well as the policies, processes, and procedures associated with operational and governance functions. Depending on the type and scope of IT audits planned by an organization, auditors may examine process-based or procedural controls in conjunction with the IT assets and components that support them, or separately in process-specific audits. The relative emphasis an organization places on auditing IT processes is influenced to some extent by the governance, risk, compliance, and IT management frameworks it chooses to implement. Popular governance frameworks such as COBIT and the Information Technology Infrastructure Library (ITIL) are largely process-oriented, while enterprise architecture and information security management frameworks align more closely to organizational descriptions or decompositions that are more technical in nature. Many types of external audits—including those intended to achieve certification or demonstrate regulatory compliance—require auditors to consider administrative, technical, and physical controls within the scope of the same audit. Organizations typically have more discretion to plan, define the scope of, and conduct internal audits in ways that separate audits of processes and procedural controls from audits of IT assets, systems, and technologies. There are many reasons to pursue such an approach, including the ability to more closely match skills and competencies of auditors to the subject matter of the audits they conduct.

IT operations

As noted in Chapter 5, operational IT audits focus on processes and procedures executed by an organization and the alignment of those activities with the systems, infrastructure, and other information technology resources. Internal audits undertaken to support IT governance also emphasize the operational processes or services implemented by an organization and the extent to which those operational aspects comply with policies, standards, and other requirements [8]. To successfully perform these types of audits, organizations need to develop an inventory of the processes and procedural controls it uses (or identify this information within existing documentation of its audit universe) and prepare an audit strategy and corresponding audit plans similar to those used in other types of IT audits. Relevant processes for examination include those in both IT-specific and more general business areas, including:

- Strategic and tactical planning
- Risk management
- Quality management
- Financial management
- Human resources management
- Acquisition or procurement
- Supply chain management
- Program and project management
- Change management
- Service management
- Customer and technical support
- Security management
- Facilities management
- Vendor management

Operational processes and procedural controls are also subject to prioritization so that audit resources can be allocated effectively. Prioritization in this context considers criteria such as the level of resources involved, complexity, dependent relationships with other processes, and the criticality of each process to the organization overall or to the mission or business functions it supports.

As an alternative to developing an organizational process inventory from scratch, organizations may choose to use available process reference models as a basis for their own. The wide variety of existing process reference models apply to broadly defined enterprise perspectives as well as more narrowly focused IT domains. Examples include models in COBIT 5 [8] for IT governance, ITIL [18] or CMMI [19] for service management, and the US Federal Enterprise Architecture [20] for government sector organizations.

Process audits can present a challenge for organizations in that, unlike other aspects of IT operations, there is no established set of audit standards to guide the conduct of process audits. Many standards and documented best practices define process expectations or describe characteristics or metrics associated with effective and efficient process execution, where processes under examination represent security provisions or other types of internal controls, numerous sources exist to guide their implementation and assessment. Organizations also have the benefit of abundant guidance on effective management of many types of processes—including those leveraged in IT governance and internal control frameworks—and on process improvement, process maturity, and other aspects of quality management. Organizations seeking to use these sources to guide process auditing efforts must first transform model processes or recommendations into explicit criteria auditors can use as a baseline to compare actual organizational processes as implemented. More prescriptive sources of guidance apply to types of IT processes addressed in formally specified standards such as ISO/IEC 20000 for IT service management or any of the many standards on systems and software engineering.

Program and project management

The sphere of IT operations in most organizations includes many ongoing purpose-specific activities, known generally as *programs* or *projects*. Although these terms are often used interchangeably, standards and guidance on managing these activities typically distinguish between them in terms of scope, duration, and results, where programs comprise one or more projects, have less discretely defined time frames, and are intended to achieve one or more long-term outcomes, projects are more narrowly focused, temporary endeavors with clearly defined starting and ending points intended to produce a specific product or service [21–23]. Organizations often manage IT programs and projects using formal plans that specify the allocation of organizational resources and the roles and responsibilities of personnel that execute applicable processes and activities. Programs and projects may be subject to operational audits; audits associated with certification, compliance, or quality assurance; or IT-specific audits focused on technologies, systems, infrastructure, or processes that support effective program or project execution. IT audits of programs or projects conducted from an IT governance perspective focus on effective resource allocation, satisfaction of requirements, and the achievement of expected outcomes. Because many IT projects follow standard systems or software development life cycle methodologies, project-focused IT audits may also examine aspects of the project corresponding to the life cycle phase or stage of completion the project has attained at the time of audit. Auditors conducting audits of this type typically base audit criteria at least in part on the expectations established in life cycle methodologies or standards that the organizations define or adopt, such as those listed in Table 6.3.

Although many IT programs and projects focus on the deployment and operation of systems, software, or other technologies, program or project audits are concerned with effective management, not on the operational or technical aspects of the information technology. These characteristics fall within the scope of system-specific or IT component audits described previously in this chapter. Program and project audits, in contrast, center on the processes, controls, and artifacts produced in the course of executing program or project activities and the compliance of those

Table 6.3 Life Cycle Processes in Commonly Used Project Methodologies			
ISO 12207 [12]	**ISO 15288 [24]**	**SP 800-64 [25]**	**PMBOK [21]**
Software development	System development	System development	Project management
Acquisition	Concept	Initiation	Initiating
Supply	Development	Development/acquisition	Planning
Development	Production	Implementation/assessment	Executing
Operation	Utilization	Operations and maintenance	Monitoring and controlling
Maintenance	Support		
Disposal	Retirement	Disposal	Closing

activities with organizational policies, standards, and requirements. Auditors focusing on IT audits of this type tend to rely on examination of documentary evidence, direct observation, and interviews with program or project staff, as testing methods are less applicable to management activities. Some examination of program and project management capabilities is often included in operational or compliance audits, or in certification audits addressing standards for quality, service management, or process maturity.

System development life cycle

IT projects in many organizations conform to phased sets of processes and activities known as a system (or software) development life cycle (SDLC). As the project moves through different phases of the SDLC, the project team undertakes different activities, produces different outputs, and satisfies requirements or criteria necessary to complete one phase and move on to the next. There is surprisingly little uniformity in the SDLC methodologies employed by different organizations, with wide variation in the number of life cycle phases and the names and expected durations of those phases, even among SDLC standards. From a holistic perspective, however, most SDLC models comprise similar activities and objectives. Whether organizations use as few as four phases or as many as 10 (or more), essentially all SDLCs include activities corresponding to project initiation, preimplementation design and development, operations and maintenance, and project termination. Organizations adopting a single, standard SDLC may nonetheless adapt the life cycle phases to address distinct needs, such as projects intended to select and implement commercially available software or technical solutions versus those involving design, development, and implementation of custom solutions. Audits of IT projects may be conducted at any point in the life cycle—or potentially span multiple life cycle phases for large or complex projects or those using iterative methodologies—meaning IT auditors must adapt their examination criteria to reflect the different activities, outputs, and intended accomplishments of each phase. The following sections follow the system life cycle phase names specified in

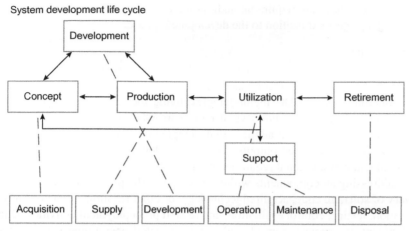

FIGURE 6.4

Project audits vary in scope and focus depending on the project phase when the audit is conducted and the type of IT project under examination.

ISO/IEC 15288 [24] and illustrated in Figure 6.4, but the IT audit points of emphasis apply to similar phases in other methodologies, notably including the software development-focused life cycle in ISO/IEC 12207 [12].

Concept

Every IT project begins with an idea, suggestion, requirement, or other recognized organizational need. The project concept or initiation phase starts when an organization identifies a need for a new or enhanced capability and begins to determine how it might meet that need. During the concept phase, an organization may identify and evaluate multiple alternatives, considering technical and nontechnical characteristics such as cost, complexity, time frame, acquisition strategies, and feasibility. Projects require commitment of budgetary and other resources, so the concept phase may also include the development of a business case, cost/benefit analysis, or other means of justifying the investment required by the organization to move forward with a proposed project. Audits of IT projects in the concept phase typically examine project management processes, standards, and methodologies to ensure they conform to organizational policies and standards and verify the completeness and approval (where required) of necessary project documentation such as a project charter project management plan, business case, alternatives analysis, and project schedule. The concept phase may also result in functional and technical requirements specifications, high-level solution designs, initial control selection, and drafts of project artifacts to be completed in later phases such as a security plan, risk management plan, contingency plan, or quality assurance plan. Organizations may require an audit at the concept phase as a prerequisite for approving a project's transition to the development phase.

Development

The development phase encompasses a wide range of activities intended to satisfy the full set of requirements specified for a system, software application, or other solution. Many SLDC methodologies divide the single development phase defined in ISO/IEC 15288 into several more narrowly defined phases for requirements analysis and design in addition to development. Whether spanning one phase or several, the key intended outputs from the development phase include complete functional and nonfunctional requirements specifications, detailed design documentation addressing all components within the scope of the project, test plans, and the delivery of software code, acquired technology, or other solution elements ready for integration, testing, control evaluation, and related predeployment activities. During development, the project team also identifies expected operational needs in terms of infrastructure, hardware and network capacity, computing platforms, and operations, maintenance, and support needs. Audits of IT projects in the development phase focus on the accuracy and completeness of documentation and key artifacts, ensuring that the approved design meets all requirements, includes sufficient internal controls, and complies with applicable internal and external standards and criteria. Audits of IT projects using commercially acquired technology seek to confirm that the intended use of the technology conforms to licensing terms, contractual obligations, or service-level agreements. For projects involving custom software development, the scope of an IT project audit may include code reviews or other software quality control processes. Regardless of the source or type of technology used in the project, at the conclusion of the development phase, all design documentation, integration interfaces, and technical specifications must be complete and system components or software applications need to be ready for evaluation and approval prior to full deployment.

Production

The term *production* as used in ISO/IEC 15288 corresponds to a set of activities intended to test a technical solution or confirm the organization's capability to deliver the product or service resulting from the project. For projects deploying systems or software applications, the scope of the production phase comprises performing unit, integration, and acceptance testing to confirm that the technology satisfies functional requirements; verifying the implementation and proper configuration of internal controls; and assessing security and privacy protective measures necessary to receive approval for the system or software to go into full operation. IT project audits during the production phase examine testing plans and procedures to ensure that testing activities are sufficient to determine the satisfaction of requirements. Because production is the last phase before a system or software application is deployed for use, auditors also check that the project has received all necessary approvals, potentially including functional test results, user acceptance, system integration, environmental readiness, risk acceptance, and authorization to operate. To the extent that administrators or support resources require training to support the system or software application once it is operational, project auditors may also verify the allocation of adequate resources with sufficient skills and capabilities to support the project.

Utilization

In the utilization phase, the system or services the project is intended to deliver are available for use, where the focus of the project shifts from preparing for deployment to actively operating and maintaining the system in a manner that continuously satisfies user needs. A system in the utilization phase is typically subject to routine operational audits to evaluate the ongoing efficiency and effectiveness of the system and the business processes it supports. Organizations may also perform a variety of IT-specific audits addressing the system overall or any of its components. In contrast, audits of IT projects in the utilization phase focus on verifying that the system when deployed will provide the intended functionality and comply with applicable technical requirements and standards, relying on documented evidence such as test results, control assessments, and approvals from authorized personnel within the organization. Project audits at this phase also seek to ensure that the resources specified and provisioned for the operational system are correct and sufficient and that necessary support functions are in place so that administrative and support responsibilities can successfully be transitioned.

Support

For an operational system, support comprises monitoring, technical administration, troubleshooting and problem resolution, and routine maintenance activities such as backup, configuration control, patch management, and upgrade and release management for software or other technical components. Depending on organizational policies, procedures, and standards, support may also include information security management activities such as vulnerability analysis, automated or manual verification of configuration settings, and security information and event management. The support phase of an IT project typically runs in parallel with utilization; phases analogous to support in many SDLC methodologies are termed *maintenance*, with the combination of utilization and support known collectively as *operations and maintenance*. Audits of IT project support activities examine technical documentation such as administrative manuals and system configuration information; adherence of the project's support processes to organizational policies, procedures, standards, and guidelines; and the ability of support resources allocated to the project to satisfy service-level agreements or other performance objectives specified for operational systems and services. An organization's technical support capabilities have a direct impact on the operational effectiveness of its systems, so although support-phase activities can be audited in isolation, the scope of audits focusing on the utilization phase often includes support functions.

Under the umbrella function of continuous monitoring used in many organizational IT environments, capabilities such as intrusion detection and incident response are often performed for the organization as a whole rather than for specific projects or programs. Similarly, organizations that have standardized on particular hardware, software, operating systems, or other technologies may have a centralized function for managing updates, correcting vulnerabilities, or making other changes. Project-specific responsibilities in these support areas may be limited to ensuring that appropriate changes have been made and that technical documentation has been updated accordingly to accurately reflect the operational status of each system.

Retirement

Projects by definition have a well-defined end point, typically coinciding with an organization's decision to decommission or replace a system or service. The retirement phase of the project life cycle involves activities necessary to remove an operational capability and to ensure the proper disposition of equipment, hardware and software, data, and other resources previously allocated to operating and supporting the system. Key priorities for the retirement phase align directly to the areas of emphasis for audits of IT projects that reach this final phase: disposing of or repurposing technology assets; releasing resources committed to the system so that they can be applied elsewhere within the organization; and sanitizing fixed and removable storage media to ensure that no residual data remains on decommissioned components. IT auditors examining projects in the retirement phase look for thorough documentation detailing the disposition of project resources and IT assets and for authorized approvals of such documentation that typically constitute a prerequisite for formally closing out a project.

The acronym SDLC can refer to either *system* or *software* development life cycle, raising the potential for confusion when auditing IT projects when the focus of the life cycle methodology is not clearly specified. Prevailing life cycle standards do little to resolve this ambiguity in terminology, as the names assigned to SDLC phases in standards such as ISO/IEC 15288, ISO/IEC 12207, and the PMI Project Management Body of Knowledge (PMBOK) are quite similar. IT auditors determine at the outset of a project audit the scope and focus of the project, precisely what methodology is being followed, the phase of the project within the SDLC, and the expectations or implications corresponding to that phase.

Relevant source material

Guidance and useful references for identifying, categorizing, and auditing different IT components include IT governance and management frameworks such as COSO's *Internal Control—Integrated Framework*[2] and ISACA's COBIT model [8]. Relevant standards and guidance on decomposing IT architecture, systems, processes, or capabilities include:

- ISO/IEC/IEEE 42010, *Systems and Software Engineering—Architecture Description* [10].
- ISO/IEC 7498-1, *Open Systems Interconnection* [11].
- ISO/IEC 12207, *Systems and Software Engineering—Software Life Cycle Processes* [12] and ISO/IEC 15288, *Systems and Software Engineering—System Life Cycle Processes* [24].

Information technology auditing in many organizations encompasses a very broad scope of subject areas, controls, components, and other elements subject to examination. This chapter reiterated the critical importance of inventorying IT assets and defining an audit universe to use as the basis for prioritizing audit activities and associated resource commitments. It presents an overview of key organizational, architectural, and technological components to highlight similarities and differences in the ways different IT elements are used and audited within organizations. Influenced by standards and frameworks from IT governance and risk management as well as from internal auditing, this chapter identified relevant standards, processes, and tools used to audit various IT-related processes, systems, and components, whether organizations approach such audits from process-centric, technical, or hybrid perspectives.

References

[1] Committee of Sponsoring Organizations of the Treadway Commission Enterprise risk management—Integrated framework. New York, NY: Committee of Sponsoring Organizations of the Treadway Commission; 2004.

[2] Committee of Sponsoring Organizations of the Treadway Commission Internal control—Integrated framework. New York, NY: Committee of Sponsoring Organizations of the Treadway Commission; 2013.

[3] IT Governance Institute COBIT 4.1. Rolling Meadows, IL: IT Governance Institute; 2007.

[4] ISACA COBIT 5 for assurance. Rolling Meadows, IL: ISACA; 2013.

[5] Sarbanes–Oxley Act of 2002, Pub. L. No. 107-204, 116 Stat. 745.

[6] ISO/IEC 27002:2005. Information technology—Security techniques—Code of practice for information security management.

[7] Security and privacy controls for federal information systems and organizations. Gaithersburg, MD: National Institute of Standards and Technology, Computer Security Division; 2013 April. Special Publication 800-53 revision 4.

[8] ISACA COBIT 5: a business framework for the governance and management of enterprise IT. Rolling Meadows, IL: ISACA; 2012.

[9] Managing information security risk: organization, mission, and information system view. Gaithersburg, MD: National Institute of Standards and Technology, Computer Security Division; 2011 March. Special Publication 800-39.

[10] ISO/IEC/IEEE 42010:2011. Systems and software engineering—Architecture description.

[11] ISO/IEC 7498-1:1994. Information technology—Open systems interconnection—Basic reference model: the basic model.

[12] ISO/IEC 12207:2008. Systems and software engineering—Software life cycle processes.

[13] Security Technical Implementation Guides [Internet]. Defense Information Systems Agency, Information Assurance Support Environment [updated 2011 February 14; cited 2012 February 18]. Available from: <http://iase.disa.mil/stigs/index.html>.

[14] U.S. Government Configuration Baseline (USGCG) [Internet]. Gaithersburg, MD: National Institute of Standards and Technology, Information Technology Laboratory [created 2010 February 19; updated 2013 June 3; cited 2013 June 7]. Available from <http://usgcb.nist.gov>.

[15] See for example and Statement on Standards for Attestation Engagements No. 16, International Standard on Auditing 402, or International Standards for Assurance Engagements 3402.

[16] Cloud Controls Matrix version 1.4. Seattle, WA: Cloud Security Alliance; 2013.

[17] FedRAMP Security Controls Baseline version 1.1. Washington, DC: General Services Administration; 2012.

[18] Orr AT Introduction to the ITIL service life cycle. London, UK: Cabinet Office; 2011.

[19] CMMI for services, version 1.3. Pittsburgh, PA: Software Engineering Institute; 2010 November.

[20] FEA consolidated reference model version 2.3. Washington, DC: Office of Management and Budget; 2007 October.

[21] Project Management Institute A guide to the project management body of knowledge, 4th ed. Newtown Square, PA: Project Management Institute; 2008.

[22] Guidance on Exhibit 300—Planning, budgeting, acquisition, and management of IT capital assets. Washington, DC: Office of Management and Budget; 2011 August.

[23] ISO/IEC TR 24748-1:2010. Systems and software engineering—Life cycle management.

[24] ISO/IEC 15288:2008. Systems and software engineering—System life cycle processes.

[25] Kissel R, Stine K, Scholl M, Rossman H, Fahlsing J, Gulick J. Security considerations in the system development life cycle. Gaithersburg, MD: National Institute of Standards and Technology, Computer Security Division; 2008 October. Special Publication 800-64 revision 2.

IT Audit Drivers

INFORMATION IN THIS CHAPTER:

- Laws and regulations
- Certification standards
- Operational effectiveness and governance
- Quality and process improvement

The rationale for IT auditing reflects externally driven requirements as well as internal organizational objectives. Some audit drivers—particularly external sources such as regulatory requirements and certification standards—explicitly obligate organizations to conduct formal auditing activities. The success of organizational programs described in Chapter 2 such as IT governance, risk management, compliance, and quality assurance depends to some extent on periodically performing IT audits, even where such examinations are not absolutely required. Organizations are often subject to multiple internal and external drivers, making more complex the prospect of satisfying audit needs and potentially presenting a challenge to maintaining awareness of all applicable external drivers and corresponding audit requirements. Many parts of this book highlight reasons organizations choose to conduct or are required to undergo audits. This chapter summarizes IT audit drivers applicable to most types of organizations, including legal and regulatory requirements, certification standards and criteria, operational effectiveness and governance objectives, and quality management and process improvement. As illustrated conceptually in Figure 7.1, these different categories of drivers influence organizations' IT audit strategies for both external and internal auditing. Few, if any, of these drivers affect every organization, as the applicability of many drivers varies by size and type of organization, ownership, industry, operating environment, and geographic location. Most of the drivers presented in this chapter impose many types of requirements or sources of behavioral motivation on organizations; the emphasis here is on describing their impact on IT auditing.

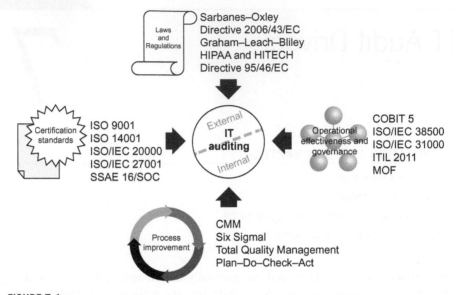

FIGURE 7.1

Multiple factors drive the need for IT audits and influence the ways organizations conduct internal and external IT auditing.

Laws and regulations

The set of laws and regulations influencing IT audit activities are numerous, varying significantly across sectors, industries, and countries but generally including requirements related to financial management and accounting, organizational and IT management, and privacy and information security. Multiple management functions or organizational units often need to maintain awareness of and compliance with applicable laws and regulations, separately or through efforts coordinated under a centralized compliance or internal auditing program. The descriptions of legal and regulatory audit drivers listed below include brief summaries of their purpose or intent, types of organizations subject to them, and provisions or requirements addressed through internal or external audits. Table 7.1 summarizes major laws and their applicability in terms of sector or industry specificity (if any) and subject matter. There are no international laws or regulations that are universally applicable to organizations in all countries, but strong similarities exist among audit-related provisions in many laws and regulations in the United States, the European Community (EC), and industrialized nations including China, Japan, India, Canada, Australia, and Russia. Substantial areas of commonality exist for international regulatory treatment of specific types of organizations, especially with respect to issuers of securities to be traded in public markets.

Table 7.1 Legal Audit Drivers and Organizational Applicability

Law	Applicability
Sarbanes–Oxley Act of 2002 (SOX)	Regulates public companies and their auditors; applies to all issuers of securities exchanged in US markets
European Council Directive 2006/43/EC	Sets standards for auditors and audits in the public interest; applies to organizations subject to statutory audit requirements
Graham–Leach–Bliley Act of 1999 (GLBA)	Enabled consolidation of different types of financial services firms within a single holding company; applies to financial institutions
Health Insurance Portability and Accountability Act of 1996 (HIPAA)	Protects the privacy and security of health-related personal information; applies to health-care providers, plans, and clearinghouses
Health Information Technology for Economic and Clinical Health Act of 2009 (HITECH)	HIPAA-covered entities, business associates, and contractors and subcontractors
European Council Directive 95/46/EC	Protects personal data privacy; applies to all organizations in European Union countries
Computer Fraud and Abuse Act of 1986	Criminalizes unauthorized access or damage to protected computers; applies to all computing devices used in interstate or international commerce or communications
Electronic Communications Privacy Act of 1986 (ECPA)	Protects the content of personal communications; applies to electronic communications service providers, government organizations
Federal Information Security Management Act of 2002 (FISMA)	US federal executive agencies; applies to systems and information operated by the government or on the government's behalf
The Privacy Act of 1974	US federal executive agencies; protects personally identifiable information for US citizens and legal resident aliens
State Privacy and Security Breach Notification Laws	Requires protection of personal information about state residents; in many states laws apply to organizations operating within or outside state borders whose customers include state residents

Securities industry laws and regulations

Laws and regulations applicable to issuers of securities (commonly known as publicly traded organizations) are one of the most prominent sources of audit requirements. Securities-related regulations influence internal and external IT audits as well as many other types of auditing because they impose requirements on organizations and their auditors in terms of auditor independence, mandatory use of standards, and qualifications and competencies needed for auditors, audit firms, and the organizational stakeholders that select auditors and receive and respond to audit results. Laws such as the Sarbanes–Oxley Act in the United States, the European Council Directive on statutory audits, and comparable legislation in other countries also explicitly include internal controls over accounting and financial reporting within the scope of audit reports to which organizations must attest. The set of internal controls encompasses IT infrastructure, systems, operational processes, and security mechanisms implemented to protect the confidentiality and integrity of corporate financial data and other information assets.

Securities and Exchange Commission laws and regulations

Participation of organizations in the US securities markets is regulated by the Securities and Exchange Commission (SEC) under authority granted by the Securities and Exchange Act of 1934 [1]. The regulations stemming from this law, the Securities Act of 1933 that preceded it, and subsequent legislation including the Sarbanes–Oxley Act of 2002, impose requirements on the behavior of publicly traded companies and many types of financial institutions. The SEC prescribes the implementation of many provisions in securities industry law, providing more explicit guidance and compliance criteria than the text of the legislation enacted by Congress. With respect to auditing, the key organizational aspects addressed in legislation, regulations, and SEC rules include requirements on the maintenance, disclosure, and mandatory reporting of financial information; the conduct of audits of public companies, and the use of generally accepted auditing standards. Securities regulations apply to organizations that participate in US securities markets, including foreign-based and multinational firms as well as domestic companies. Many countries outside the United States have similar securities laws governing participation in national securities exchanges.

Sarbanes–Oxley Act of 2002

Enacted to reform accounting and financial reporting practices in publicly traded organizations and to restore public confidence in the wake of several high-profile instances of corporate and accounting fraud, the Sarbanes–Oxley Act of 2002 initiated sweeping changes in corporate governance and financial accounting practices in US companies [2]. The law established the Public Company Accounting Oversight Board and required all firms performing audits of US companies to register with the Board. It included provisions to help ensure auditor independence, assigned greater responsibility to executives and directors of public companies, and revised the reporting requirements for financial transactions. All of these provisions significantly affect auditing practice for public companies and other securities-issuing organizations. Many of the key requirements in Sarbanes–Oxley do not apply to privately held organizations, although nonpublic organizations that may consider issuing securities in the future or engaging in a major financial transaction such as a sale or acquisition may voluntarily adopt some or all of the law's requirements. From an IT auditing perspective, the most significant part of the law is the requirement that organizations maintain internal controls over financial reporting and audit the effectiveness of those controls.

European Council Directive 2006/43/EC

Organizations that issue securities for sale to the public in EC nations are subject to both country-specific legislation and laws and regulations established by the European Parliament that harmonizes statutory audit requirements in EC member countries. Directive 2006/43/EC established new minimum qualifications for auditors and audit firms and requires all such firms to register with the appropriate oversight authority in the country or countries where they perform audits. The directive emphasizes auditor independence, objectivity, ethical behavior, education and testing standards, and theoretical and practical knowledge that collectively seek to ensure that auditors have knowledge and competence to effectively conduct audits [3]. In addition to delegating member countries the responsibility for auditor quality assurance, Directive 2006/43/EC mandates that statutory audits follow international auditing standards. Similar to the provision in the Sarbanes–Oxley Act, the European Council Directive requires that the scope of statutory audits include formal audit of the effectiveness of internal controls, internal audit function, and risk management. EC member countries use the requirements in Directive 2006/43/EC and other EC policies and guidance to structure national laws applicable to publicly traded companies and to implement requirements such as registries of audit firms and national oversight bodies.

Graham–Leach–Bliley Act

The Financial Services Modernization Act of 1999 [4], known more commonly as the Graham–Leach–Bliley Act (GLBA) after its major sponsors, removed long-standing regulatory barriers to consolidation of different types of financial services firms and specified new requirements for bank holding companies and other combined services entities. The law and the rules and regulations established to implement its provisions apply only to certain types of financial institutions. GLBA requires annual independent audits of the 12 Federal Reserve banks and explicitly emphasizes the use of external audit reports, attesting to compliance with internal risk management and control objectives, to satisfy bank holding company supervision requirements. Audits of GLBA compliance are one of several supervisory and oversight functions that use Federal Financial Institutions Examination Council (FFIEC) principles, standards, and reporting guidance such as the FFIEC IT Examination Handbook.

Health industry-specific laws

Organizations operating in the health-care industry need to comply with a variety of laws and regulations in areas such as patient safety, meaningful use of health information technology, information security, patient privacy, and compliance with laboratory and medical device standards. Affected organizations include hospitals and other provider organizations, insurance carriers, health-care plans, billing and claims processors, and many types of health service providers. Many of the laws obligating health industry organizations to conduct internal audits or undergo external audits leverage formal auditing practices as a means of demonstrating or verifying compliance with legal or regulatory requirements. Because the health-care delivery and administration generally entails the use of health-related personal information about patients or insurance plan beneficiaries and personal health data is usually considered especially sensitive, health industry organizations in many countries are subject to regulations intended to protect the privacy and security of personal health information.

Health Insurance Portability and Accountability Act

The Health Insurance Portability and Accountability Act of 1996 (HIPAA) was enacted in part to protect health insurance coverage for employees of US companies when they are no longer employed by an organization that provides their health insurance. The law also mandates the use of a variety of technical standards used in electronic health-care transactions and established a set of requirements for protecting the privacy and security of health data. Only specific types of organizations are subject to HIPAA privacy and security regulations: health-care providers, health-care plans, and health-care clearinghouses, collectively known as "covered entities," as well as business associates that provide services to those covered entities. The legislative requirements for privacy and security contained in Title II of HIPAA were implemented as federal regulations known as the HIPAA Privacy Rule and the HIPAA Security Rule, which took effect in 2003 and 2005, respectively. HIPAA's privacy and security requirements apply to *protected health information*, which is any information transmitted or maintained electronically or in any other medium about the health of an individual, health care provided to an individual, or payment for health care provided to an individual [5]. The US Department of Health and Human Services (HHS) Office for Civil Rights (OCR) is responsible for enforcing compliance with HIPAA privacy and security requirements, which since 2012 includes operating a formal auditing program that proactively examines the compliance of a small number of HIPAA-covered entities.

Health Information Technology for Economic and Clinical Health Act

Enacted as Title XIII of the American Recovery and Reinvestment Act of 2009, the Health Information Technology for Economic and Clinical Health (HITECH) Act strengthened many HIPAA regulations, including making changes to enforcement guidelines and increasing the civil and criminal penalties that may be imposed on entities found to be in violation of HIPAA security and privacy rules [6]. The law expanded the set of organizations subject to HIPAA regulations, making business associates and contractors of covered entities directly responsible for compliance. HITECH also mandated new practices among covered entities, business associates, and contractors requiring notification and public disclosure of breaches of protected health information. The federal health data breach standards complement the laws in place in the vast majority of US states addressing breaches of personal information (including but not limited to personal health data) and preempt contradictory state laws. The HIPAA audit program established by the HHS OCR implements a HITECH requirement that OCR perform periodic audits of organizations' compliance with the HIPAA privacy, security, and breach notification regulations.

The HIPAA compliance audit program mandated by HITECH and initiated in 2012 by the HHS OCR examines covered entities and business associates for compliance with HIPAA requirements, including requirements added or amended by the HITECH Act. Although many HIPAA regulations have been in force for more than 10 years, prior to 2012 audits of HIPAA compliance were only performed when the government initiated an investigation into an organization's practices following a formal complaint or other notification to OCR alleging a HIPAA violation. To help covered entities and business associates prepare for potential audits under the new program, OCR publishes the complete audit protocol used in HIPAA compliance audits [7]. This provides organizations potentially subject to audits detailed information about each audit criterion, including how auditors will assess criteria and the specific audit procedures to be used.

International health data privacy protection laws

Following provisions in the European Council Directive on personal data protection [8], many European countries have laws constraining the collection, use, and disclosure of many types of personal data, including health data. The processing or use of health data is often subject to explicit requirements and protective measures such as the special considerations for processing health data included in the EC data protection directive and the General Data Protection Regulation proposed to replace the existing 1995 regulations. Not all countries enact legislation explicitly to address protection of health data, but most countries with any type of data protection laws include health data within their statutory definitions of sensitive personal data that warrants special attention under the law. Many countries in all regions of the world have data privacy laws, the majority of which impose restrictions on when and under what circumstances organizations may collect sensitive information such as personal health data, the purposes for which it can be used, and whether or not individuals first need to give consent before their personal data can be stored, processed, or disclosed. While relatively few national laws require formal audits to determine compliance with privacy protection requirements, audits are often used in support of investigations into regulatory violations and, in some countries, government oversight bodies or other authorities have the right to conduct audits of organizations within their jurisdictions [9]. The scope of such audits typically includes information technology resources, making IT auditing directly relevant to compliance and enforcement of data privacy laws in many countries.

Security and privacy laws

Outside the public sector, most organizations are not subject to legal or regulatory requirements about information technology management or other aspects of business operations. Organizations are generally free to perform their IT processes and functions in whatever manner they find most effective, whether they choose to adopt externally developed models, frameworks, or practices or to design and implement their own. Similarly, most organizations have wide latitude to select and implement the internal controls they determine to be adequate to achieve governance, risk management, and compliance objectives. Security and privacy laws represent important exceptions to organizational discretion, as many organizations are legally obligated to implement specific types of controls to protect confidentiality, integrity, and availability of their information technology systems, infrastructure, and data. Security and privacy legislation rarely specifies technologies or standards within the text of enacted laws, and most rules and regulations promulgated to implement or explain provisions in the laws similarly emphasize types of controls that should be used or security objectives that the laws are intended to achieve. Organizations choose specific controls, including security-related products, processes, standards, and technologies and rely on internal or third-party IT audits to determine if controls are correctly implemented and effective in meeting objectives.

In addition to types of security and privacy controls specified in legislation and regulations or explicit security and privacy objectives that should be achieved, organizations need to consider standards of due care when determining what controls to implement. With a series legal precedents (in the United States) dating back more than 80 years, the standard of due care in American tort law says that organizations can be held liable if they fail to implement readily available technologies or practices that could mitigate or prevent loss or damage. A 1932 federal appeals court ruling held that owners of two tugboats conveying barges that sank in a storm were liable for the loss of the cargo the barges were carrying because the tugboats were not equipped with radios that could have been used to alert the tugboat pilots to the impending storm [10]. The same federal judge, delivering the court's opinion on a subsequent case in 1947, also involving cargo lost when a barge sank, introduced a formula for determining liability: if the probability of loss times the magnitude of loss is greater than the burden of providing adequate protection against the loss, the standard of care has not been met [11]. This formula (known in legal contexts as the "Hand rule" after its author, Justice Learned Hand) is pervasive in risk-based management models, which generally state that the cost of mitigating a risk should not be greater than the negative impact to the organization associated with the risk.

European Council Directive 95/46/EC

Privacy of personal information in member countries of the European Union is addressed primarily through European Council Directive 95/46/EC, which addresses "protection of individuals with regard to the processing of personal data and on the free movement of such data [8]." The rules in the directive regulate all processing of personal data in member countries, where *processing* is defined broadly to encompass essentially all actions taken on covered information, including collection, organization, storage, alteration, retrieval, disclosure, dissemination, and destruction. Like other European Council Directives, the provisions in the Data Protection Directive do not directly apply to individuals and organizations in member countries until each country enacts its own legislation reflecting the requirements in the directive. The Data Protection Directive works from the perspective that no processing of personal data should be allowed unless appropriate conditions are met, making it much more restrictive by default than privacy regulations in the United States and many other countries. It also prescribes rules for sending data to countries outside the EC jurisdiction, in general prohibiting transfers of personal data to non-EC countries unless the country where the recipient is located provides comparable privacy protections. To enable personal data transmissions between EC countries and the United States, the directive allowed for the establishment of a safe harbor process under which organizations in the United States can attest to and certify their adherence to adequate privacy protection principles to satisfy EC requirements on an organization-by-organization basis. The EC has proposed a new General Data Protection Directive to replace Directive 95/46/EC as early as 2014, which is intended to unify personal data protection across all member countries under a single, central authority and set of rules [12]. It will also apply to organizations outside the European Union if they process personal data about residents of member countries. In this respect, the new proposed directive is similar to the personal data security laws in many US states that apply based on the residency of individuals whose personal information an organization collects or uses rather than the state in which the organization operates.

Computer Fraud and Abuse Act

The Computer Fraud and Abuse Act of 1986 makes it a crime for anyone to access without authorization a computer or computer system used by a financial institution, US government agency, or any organization or individual involved in interstate or foreign commerce or communication. In addition to criminalizing many forms of computer hacking, intrusion, or actions that exceed authorized use, the law also addresses computer espionage, computer trespassing, committing fraud using a computer, or causing or threatening to cause damage to a computer [13]. Although the law focuses on behavior by outsiders against an organization or its computing infrastructure, it highlights the need for organizations to establish effective security controls and to monitor their own environments to protect against outside attacks and to ensure that none of its own computing resources are used in ways that would violate the law. The Computer Fraud and Abuse Act has been amended several times by subsequent legislation, increasing the number and types of actions considered crimes under the law and resulting in a broader definition of computers subject to its provisions. Because the statutory definition of "protected computer" includes any computing device used in interstate or international communication, the law can be interpreted to include mobile equipment such as cellular phones or other devices capable of Internet connectivity.

Electronic Communications Privacy Act

Public and private sector organizations in many countries are subject to restrictions on intercepting or recording telephone communications with other parties. In the United States, the Electronic Communications Privacy Act (ECPA) of 1986 extended such restrictions to cover electronic data transmissions, and the law imposes strict constraints on the storage and disclosure of electronic communications and the ability of government agencies to access the contents of those communications [14]. Under the provisions of the Stored Communications Act (Title II of ECPA), organizations that provide electronic communications services to consumers must safeguard the privacy of the contents of any communications, both while in transit and while stored by the service provider, and must not disclose the contents of such communications without the consent of the sender (subject to several exceptions such as when the disclosure is previously authorized, directed to the recipient, incidental to the provision of the service, or for law enforcement purposes). Complying with ECPA regulations requires organizations subject to the law to implement strong operational and technical controls to prevent the unintended or unauthorized disclosure of information they hold. Covered organizations use internal IT audits to assess their own compliance and ensure the continual effectiveness of the internal controls protecting communications data.

State security and privacy laws

In the United States, the vast majority of states have enacted laws imposing security and privacy protection requirements on organizations operating with particular states or maintaining business relationships with state residents. Many state laws and regulations focus on protecting personal information, with provisions including mandatory security practices and safeguards to prevent inadvertent or unauthorized disclosure of personal information and requirements for notifying affected individuals (and state or national authorities) when such breaches occur. The personal data protection provisions in state laws are substantially similar, with many adopting language following the example of the California Security Breach Information Act often cited as the first state law to address security breach notification [15]. To focus this and other similar state laws require that organizations disclose breaches of personal information unless the information is rendered unusable through mechanisms such as encryption. Subsequent state data breach laws, such as 201 CMR 17 enacted in Massachusetts in 2010, mandate the use of various types of security controls to protect personal information from unauthorized access or disclosure [16]. There is no federal law requiring nongovernment organizations generally to protect the security or privacy of personal information (although data breach notification regulations exist in specific industry sectors such as health care), so organizations operating in the United States or conducting business with or maintaining personal information on customers in the United States need to look at individual state regulations when determining requirements and ensuring compliance.

Organizations operating in or conducting business with customers in the United States need to consider state security laws and regulations when assessing compliance. According to information aggregated by the National Conference of State Legislatures, in the United States, security breach notification laws have been enacted in 46 states, the District of Columbia, and the territories of Guam, Puerto Rico, and the US Virgin Islands [17]. Most of these laws center on the residency of the individuals affected by a breach rather than the location in which an organization suffering a breach operates. This means that an organization offering products or services to customers in multiple states is likely subject to multiple similar but not identical sets of requirements specifying how they must respond to a breach of personal information.

Government sector laws

Government organizations in the United States, Canada, European Union member nations, and many other countries are subject to separate security, privacy, and information technology management laws that strongly influence their internal and external IT auditing activities. Legislation focused on IT management or operations, such as the Information Technology Management Reform Act of 1996 in the United States, emphasizes the effective allocation of government resources in acquiring, implementing, operating, maintaining, and disposing of information technology [18]. The same IT governance and service management frameworks used in commercial organizations are available for use in the public sector (indeed, Information Technology Infrastructure Library (ITIL) was originally developed by an agency of the government of the United Kingdom), but in many countries formal implementation of such frameworks in government agencies is uncommon. Instead, many government organizations develop and implement information resources management strategies seeking to increase the efficiency of IT operations, particularly by reducing duplication of IT investment across multiple agencies where government-wide laws or regulations do exist, agencies' IT management practices are subject to both internal examination and external audit by designated national oversight authorities or "supreme audit institutions" such as the US Government Accountability Office, Canada's Office of the Auditor General, China's National Audit Office, India's Comptroller and Auditor General, and Russia's Accounts Chamber [19]. Government organizations in many countries are also subject to explicit public sector security and privacy legislation that gives special emphasis to protecting government infrastructure and information systems and safeguarding information collected, used, or held by government about their citizens.

The range of sector-specific laws imposing operational requirements or audit needs on organizations means that large or complex organizations with operations that cross industries are subject to multiple, potentially overlapping, sets of laws and regulations. For example, publicly traded diversified services companies like AXA Group, Cigna, and UnitedHealth Group operate as financial services and health insurance firms, subject to laws including Sarbanes–Oxley, GLBA, and HIPAA. Similarly, a government agency involved in health-care delivery or administration is subject to HIPAA in addition to the Federal Information Security Management Act (FISMA), the Privacy Act, and other laws applicable only to government agencies.

Federal Information Security Management Act

FISMA, enacted in the United States as part of the E-Government Act of 2002, requires federal executive branch agencies to implement, maintain, and continuously monitor controls sufficient to provide security protection commensurate with the risk to agencies from the loss of confidentiality, integrity, or availability of information. The law mandates compliance with federal information processing standards and associated guidance issued by the National Institute of Standards and Technology (NIST), including selecting security controls from an extensive framework defined in NIST Special Publication 800-53, *Recommended Security Controls for Federal Information Systems and Organizations*[20]. Government agencies must provide detailed documentation of the security measures taken to protect their information systems and provide regular reports on security practices to the Office of Management and Budget and Department of Homeland Security. Among other provisions, FISMA requires agencies to undergo annual independent evaluations of their information security programs, where such evaluations are conducted by agency Inspectors General or, for agencies without that position, by an external auditor [21]. Agency information systems are also subject to audit, alone or as part of a broader performance or financial audit, by the Government Accountability Office, which uses a standard audit methodology documented in the *Federal Information System Controls Audit Manual* [22]. Although compliance with FISMA is mandatory for federal agencies and contractors that operate IT systems or infrastructure on their behalf, there are no civil or criminal penalties for violating the law's provisions. The consequences for failing to comply with FISMA or for weaknesses or deficiency findings in audit reports may include greater scrutiny of an agency's IT or information security management practices or conditioning approval of budget requests on adequate remediation of noncompliant controls or practices.

The Privacy Act

The Privacy Act of 1974 codified a set of fair information practices originally issued by the US Department of Health, Education, and Welfare in 1973. These practices provide the basis for a variety of privacy guidelines and regulatory schemes found in other laws, including the ability for individuals to prevent the use of their personal information for purposes other than which it was originally collected. The core provisions in the Privacy Act reflect the fair information principles incorporated in widely followed international privacy frameworks such as the Organization for Economic Cooperation and Development Guidelines on the Protection of Privacy and Transborder Flows of Personal Data [23]. The Privacy Act applies to all federal agencies and covers personally identifiable information about US citizens and resident aliens. The Privacy Act is also voluntarily followed by some states and other nonfederal government authorities. The law requires agencies to provide public notice before collecting personal information from individuals and before implementing any system containing personally identifiable information about individuals (technically called a "system of records") from which information is retrieved using the name or other identifying attribute of individuals [24]. The Privacy Act is not sector-specific; it covers all types of personal information collected, stored, used, or disclosed by government agencies. The implementation of a US privacy law with jurisdiction only over government agencies differs from the approach taken in other countries, such as Canada's Personal Information Protection and Electronic Documents Act [25] or European Council Directive 2006/43/EC [3], both of which cover private sector as well as public sector personal data protection practices.

Certification standards

Certification is a formal process conducted by a qualified, independent external auditor intended to confirm compliance with a standard or prescribed set of criteria. The International Organization for Standardization (ISO) highlights the value of certification to organizations by giving assurance that its management practices or other aspects of its operations conform to applicable standards. Certification "provides independent demonstration that the management system of the organization conforms to specified requirements, is capable of consistently achieving its stated policy and objectives, and is effectively implemented [26]." Certification standards often do not constitute audit drivers by themselves, but the need for certification to meet internal organizational objectives or to satisfy external requirements has the effect of making the corresponding standards important audit drivers for certification-seeking organizations. As noted in previous chapters, organizations often pursue certification for a variety of business reasons that include enhancing market positioning or establishing competitive advantage, or to support the achievement of internal objectives for governance, operational effectiveness, quality management, or process maturity. In some cases, organizations may need to achieve certification in order to gain access to business opportunities. For instance, some solicitations for IT outsourcing or contracts for IT-related services may require responding organizations to have achieved a specified capability maturity model level. Similarly, manufacturing processes or technical capabilities organizations offered to external consumers or business partners may need to be ISO 9001 or ISO/IEC 20000 certified. Table 7.2 summarizes common certification standards and the subject areas to which they apply.

Table 7.2 Organizational Certifications and Associated Subject Areas

Certification	Subject Area
CMMI for Services	Maturity of service provider capabilities and processes
ISO 9001	Quality management systems
ISO 14001	Environmental management systems
ISO/IEC 15408	IT security evaluation of computer systems and software
ISO/IEC 20000	IT service management
ISO/IEC 27001	Information security management systems
Service Organization Control (SOC) Reports	Security, privacy, and system controls implemented by service providers

Quality certification

Organizations implement quality management programs to satisfy a range of internal objectives, including process improvement and performance enhancement to increase operational efficiency and effectiveness. For organizations offering products or services to customers, quality management is an important component of customer satisfaction, where customer requirements are incorporated into product or service specifications and organizations' ability to meet those requirements is reflected in customer acceptance, sales, and market share. Modern business environments and markets change frequently, leading organizations to implement quality management to help them adapt to drivers such as changes in customer requirements, market competition, and advancing technological capabilities [27]. Organizations have many alternatives when consider ways to implement quality management and choosing externally developed methodologies and standards. Quality is both an explicit goal and process area emphasis in IT governance frameworks such as COBIT and ITIL, and is the focus of dedicated business methodologies such as Six Sigma and Total Quality Management. None of these sources of guidance on quality are subject to organizational-level certification.

The most prominent certification standard in the area of quality management is ISO 9001, which specifies requirements for quality management systems focused on delivering products that meet customer requirements while also satisfying applicable legal and regulatory requirements. The emphasis in ISO 9001 is on establishing and maintaining a quality management system that supports continuous improvement that includes [28]:

- determining the processes needed for quality management and the scope of their application;
- determining the sequence and points of interaction among quality management processes;
- determining operational and control effectiveness criteria and evaluation methods;

- providing resources and information necessary to support operation and monitoring of quality management processes;
- monitoring, measuring, and analyzing quality management processes;
- taking necessary actions to achieve desired results and enable continuous process improvement.

ISO 9001 is explicitly intended for use in certification, where accredited certifying bodies use the requirements in the standard as a basis for assessing an organization's ability to meet external legal and customer requirements as well as the organization's internal requirements.

Information security

Organizations implement a wide range of security controls to achieve governance, risk management, and compliance objectives associated with IT systems, infrastructure, and operational processes, including complying with security and privacy laws and regulations such as the ones described previously in this chapter. With the exception of demonstrating compliance, examinations of security-specific IT controls tend to focus on assessing the effectiveness of implemented security measures and their ability to reduce or mitigate risk to a level that an organization finds acceptable. Although there are many voluntary and mandatory security standards affecting organizations' selection of security controls, compliance to most security standards is determined through internal audit or assessment. Formal certification by third-party auditors is available for relatively few security standards. With the exception of ISO/IEC 27001, organizational certification of compliance with security standards typically focus on a narrowly defined scope of operations such as the Service Organization Control Reports used to attest to the security controls implemented in data centers or other types of IT service providers. Organizations still look to standards and externally developed frameworks and methodologies to help establish and maintain effective information security management programs and supporting processes.

Publicly available standards such as NIST Federal Information Processing Standards and ISO/IEC 15408 (familiarly known as Common Criteria) are required only for certain types of organizations—such as government agencies—but potentially offer useful guidance to any organization. One of the most widely applicable voluntary security standards is the ISO/IEC 27000 series, which focuses on formal establishment of an information security management system (ISMS) and many related aspects of organizational security. For the ISO/IEC 27000 series of standards, organizations can only achieve certification against the ISO/IEC 27001 standard for ISMS requirements, but this standard is rarely adopted in isolation. In particular, the code of practice and corresponding security controls defined in ISO/IEC 27002 is often implemented in conjunction with the ISMS. What are now published separately as ISO/IEC 27001 and 27002 were previously designated as two parts of the same standard, ISO/IEC 17799. Although nothing in the current

ISMS requirements mandates the use of ISO/IEC 27002 or any other specific security control framework [29], many organizations choose to implement ISO/IEC 27001 and 27002 together. In addition to these standards, the 27000 series includes separate standards for implementing ISMS (ISO/IEC 27003), measuring information security management (ISO/IEC 27004), information security risk management (ISO/IEC 27005), and information security governance (ISO/IEC 27014). Standards with specific applicability to auditing including ISO/IEC 27007 and 27008 on auditing ISMS and information security controls, respectively, and ISO/IEC 27006 that specifies requirements for ISMS auditors and certification bodies.

Service management

Organizations structuring their operations using service-based models such as ITIL or Capability Maturity Model Integration (CMMI) for Services describe and manage their business processes and operational capabilities in terms of the services they provide for internal and external customers. Many organizations believe that the customer-centricity of service-oriented management models is aligned more closely to quality management and process improvement objectives and facilitates effective governance by ensuring organizational resources are allocated appropriately to meet service delivery needs. Organizations can certify their IT service management capabilities using the ISO/IEC 20000 standard, which addresses the initial establishment of service management capabilities as well as service operations, maintenance, and improvement [30]. ISO/IEC 20000 certification can provide an independent evaluation of an organization's implementation of an external service management framework such as ITIL or of the compliance (and presumed effectiveness) of internally developed capabilities. Certification based on the Software Engineering Institute's CMMI for Services model appraises the relative maturity of a service provider's processes and capabilities for delivering services to internal or external customers [31].

Operational effectiveness

In contrast to legal and regulatory requirements and certification of compliance with standards, operational effectiveness objectives represent primarily internal drivers for organizations. Operational effectiveness is a core objective of enterprise and IT governance where organizations seek to maximize the efficient use of resources in their business operations and to improve quality, productivity, or competitive positioning in markets in which they participate. Many well-accepted organizational management theories consider an organization's ability to effectively use resources to be a source of competitive advantage, particularly where operational effectiveness includes capabilities enabling an organization to rapidly adapt to changing customer requirements or environmental factors [32,33]. These and other motivations lead organizations to establish formal governance, quality management, and process improvement functions, each of which relies to some extent on effective internal IT auditing. Organizations often pursue operational effectiveness by following governance frameworks such as COBIT or quality management approaches such as Six Sigma, Total Quality Management, or activities described in standards such as ISO 9004 [34] and ISO 15504 [35].

Quality assurance and continuous improvement

Quality management initiatives such as quality assurance, quality control, and continuous improvement represent significant internal drivers for many organizations. In an IT management context, organizations can apply general quality management guidance and standards to help them establish and operationalize effective approaches to quality. Leading quality management methodologies emphasize the importance of implementing formally documented, repeatable IT processes based on accepted standards and practices and of consistently following those processes throughout the organization. Detailed standards and guidance are available for many core IT functions and processes, including ISO/IEC standards for systems and software engineering life cycle processes and assurance [36,37]. In addition to broad-based quality management standards such as ISO 9001 that help guide quality management practices, organizations can also leverage standards and guidance specific to conducting internal or external quality audits, such as ISO 19011 [38] and ISO/IEC 17021 [39]. The American Society for Quality provides detailed guidance on implementing and operating quality audit programs in its *ASQ Auditing Handbook* [40]. Collectively, IT-focused quality standards and guidance provide organizations a foundation for developing and maintaining IT processes and capabilities that conform to accepted practices and influence the internal execution of IT quality audits.

Relevant source material

As the information in this chapter demonstrates, IT auditing in many organizations is influenced by a wide variety of external and internal drivers. Relevant sources of information about external drivers such as laws and regulations listed in Table 7.1 include the text of laws themselves and analyses or interpretations of those laws. The most comprehensive information on standards providing the basis for certification, such as those in Table 7.2, comes from the specifications published by the respective standards development organizations and the information they provide on certification [41]. Many accredited certifying bodies also offer guidance on standards and the process of achieving certification, in part to establish their credibility to perform certification audits to organizations that need to engage the services of external auditors. Applicable guidance on service management includes major frameworks and process models such as ITIL and CMMI for Services and certification requirements for IT service management in ISO/IEC 20000. In addition to requirements and performance considerations described in the ISO 9000 series of quality standards, prominent professional associations and standards organizations publish detailed guidance on quality management and quality-focused auditing, including handbooks from the ASQ [40] and the International Audit and Assurance Standards Board [42].

Summary

This chapter identified and explained major external drivers of IT auditing, particularly legal and regulatory requirements, as well as internal drivers related to organizational strategic goals and management objectives including operational effectiveness, quality assurance, and process improvement. Collectively, these drivers influence the ways in which organizations structure and operate their internal auditing programs, prepare for and actively participate in external audits, and use both internal and external forms of IT auditing to support organizational objectives focused on governance, certification, regulatory and standards compliance, and process improvement or other forms of quality management. The categories of drivers addressed in this chapter apply to international and multinational organizations across public and private sector contexts. Where relevant, the information presented highlights both similarities and differences in the applicability of different drivers and corresponding requirements to various types of organizations operating in different countries and industries.

References

[1] Securities Exchange Act of 1934, Pub. L. No. 73-291, 48 Stat. 881.

[2] Sarbanes–Oxley Act of 2002, Pub. L. No. 107-204, 116 Stat. 745.

[3] Directive of the European Parliament and of the Council on statutory audits of annual accounts and consolidated accounts, Directive 2006/43/EC; 2006 May.

[4] Financial Services Modernization Act of 1999, Pub. L. No. 106-102, 113 Stat. 1338.

[5] Health Insurance Portability and Accountability Act of 1996, Pub. L. No. 104-191, 110 Stat. 1936.

[6] Health Information Technology for Economic and Clinical Health Act of 2009, Pub. L. No. 111-5, 123 Stat. 226.

[7] Audit Program Protocol [Internet]. Washington, DC: Department of Health and Human Services, Office for Civil Rights [cited 2013 July 18]. Available from <http://www.hhs.gov/ocr/privacy/hipaa/enforcement/audit/protocol.html>.

[8] Directive of the European Parliament and of the Council on the protection of individuals with regard to the processing of personal data and on the free movement of such data, Directive 95/46/EC; 1995 October.

[9] Examples include Canada's Personal Information Protection and Electronic Documents Act (PIPEDA) and India's Information Technology Rules for reasonable security practices and procedures and sensitive personal data or information.

[10] *The T.J. Hooper* (1932) 60 F.2d 737.

[11] United States v. Carroll Towing (1947) 159 F.2d 169.

[12] Proposal for a regulation of the European parliament and of the council on the protection of individuals with regard to the processing of personal data and on the free movement of such data (General Data Protection Regulation). COD 2012/0011; 2012 December.

[13] Computer Fraud and Abuse Act of 1986, Pub. L. No. 99-474, 100 Stat. 1213.

[14] Electronic Communications Privacy Act of 1986, Pub. L. No. 99-508, 100 Stat. 1848.

[15] California Security Breach Information Act, S.B. 1386; 2002.

[16] Standards for the protection of personal information of residents of the commonwealth, 201 CMR 17.00; 2010.

[17] State security breach notification laws [Internet]. Washington, DC: National Conference of State Legislatures [updated 2012 August 20; cited 2013 July 18]. Available from: <http://www.ncsl.org/issues-research/telecom/security-breach-notification-laws.aspx>.

[18] Information Technology Management Reform Act of 1996, Pub. L. No. 104-106, 110 Stat. 679.

[19] INTOSAI.org: Membership List [Internet]. Vienna: International Organization of Supreme Audit Institutions [cited 2013 May 4]. Available from: <http://www.intosai.org/organisation/membership-list.html>.

[20] Recommended security controls for federal information systems and organizations. Gaithersburg, MD: National Institute of Standards and Technology, Computer Security Division; 2009 August. Special Publication 800-53 revision 3.

[21] Federal Information Security Management Act of 2002, Pub. L. No. 107-347, 116 Stat. 2946. §3545.

[22] Federal information system controls audit manual (FISCAM). Washington, DC: Government Accountability Office; 2009 February.

[23] OECD Guidelines on the protection of privacy and transborder flows of personal data. Paris, France: Organization for Economic Cooperation and Development; 1980 September 23.

[24] Privacy Act of 1974, Pub. L. No. 93-579, 88 Stat. 1896.

[25] Personal Information Protection and Electronic Documents Act, S.C. 2000, c.5; 2000.

[26] ISO/IEC 17021:2011. Conformity assessment—Requirements for bodies providing audit and certification of management systems.

[27] ISO 9000:2005. Quality management—Fundamentals and vocabulary.

[28] ISO 9001:2008. Quality management systems—requirements.

[29] ISO/IEC 27001:2005. Information—Security techniques—Information security management systems—Requirements.

[30] ISO/IEC 20000-1:2011. Information technology—Service management—Part 1: Service management system requirements.

[31] CMMI for services, version 1.3. Pittsburgh, PA: Software Engineering Institute; 2010 November.

[32] Barney JB, Clark DN. Resource-based theory. Oxford, UK: Oxford University Press; 2007.

[33] Teece D. Dynamic capabilities and strategic management. New York, NY: Oxford University Press; 2009.

[34] ISO 9004:2009. Managing for the sustained success of an organization—A quality management approach.

[35] ISO/IEC 15504:2004. Information technology—Process assessment.

[36] ISO/IEC 12207:2008. Systems and software engineering—Software life cycle processes.

[37] ISO/IEC 15026:2011. Systems and software engineering—Systems and software assurance.

[38] ISO 19011:2011. Guidelines for auditing management systems.

[39] ISO/IEC 17021:2011. Conformity assessment—Requirements for bodies providing audit and certification of management systems.

[40] Russell JP, editor. (4th ed.). Milwaukee, WI: ASQ Quality Press; 2013.

[41] Certification—ISO [Internet]. Geneva: International Organization for Standardization [cited 2013 June 7]. Available from: <http://www.iso.org/iso/home/standards/certification.htm>.

[42] Handbook of international quality control, auditing review, other assurance, and related services pronouncements. New York, NY: International Auditing and Assurance Standards Board; 2012 June.

IT Audit Processes

8

INFORMATION IN THIS CHAPTER:

- Audit planning
- Preparation and evidence collection
- Audit performance
- Reporting findings
- Responding to audit results
- Process life cycles and methodologies

Organizations invest substantial time and resources to identify their IT auditing needs, establish their audit programs, choose auditors, and prioritize audit activities. All of this effort leads to the process of conducting IT audits, which is the subject of this chapter. Organizations use a variety of audit methodologies, frameworks, and standards, often following different processes for different types of audits or to guide the conduct of internal versus external audits. Despite the many available sources of guidance, the core process steps and activities performed in IT auditing are generally quite similar, comprising stages focused on audit planning, audit performance or execution, reporting findings, and remediating findings with corrective action. Regardless of the names used to designate these steps in different methodologies, the nature of activities performed and their intended outcomes can be traced back to the Deming cycle and its four-stage (plan-do-check-act or PDCA) process for continuous improvement. This model, described in Chapter 2 and illustrated in Figure 2.6, is pervasive in quality management methodologies and also provides the basis for numerous management standards, including the auditing guidelines prescribed in ISO 19011 [1]. Variations on the PDCA process life cycle sometimes simplify the process to just three steps or expand it to half a dozen or more, but for audit practitioners and organizations and personnel undergoing IT audits, the exact number or names of major process stages is less important than understanding the activities and expectations for the process as a whole. Figure 8.1 provides a conceptual representation of the audit process as described in this chapter, using audit-relevant labels for the major steps: "plan," "perform," "report," and "respond."

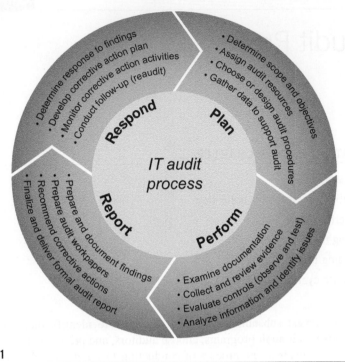

FIGURE 8.1

Most IT audit approaches include one or more activities conducted within the process areas of audit planning, audit performance, audit reporting, and responding to audit findings and recommendations.

Successfully implementing IT audit processes depends to a large extent on organizational commitments and the existence of a structural foundation supporting audit activities. For external audits, such commitments consist of executive decisions to engage outside auditors, allocate necessary financial resources, and receive and appropriately respond to audit findings. With respect to internal auditing, an organization's internal audit program provides the primary structure and direction for conducting internal audits. The internal audit program formulates the organization's audit strategy and develops audit plans for each type of IT audit to be performed by internal auditors. Audit plans developed at the program level define the scope, priority, frequency, and anticipated resource requirements for each type of audit, and often recommend or specify audit protocols and sources of audit criteria internal auditors will use. This information is incorporated as a starting point and refined, expanded, or adapted to meet the contextual requirements and constraints specific to each IT audit the organization performs. Tailoring relevant audit plans produced by the organizational audit program to reflect the needs of a particular audit is the focus of audit planning, the first step in the IT audit process.

Audit planning

Audit planning encompasses all the activities necessary to ensure that a specific audit—whether performed by internal or external auditors—can be executed completely and efficiently to satisfy the organization's audit objectives. Planning an audit is conceptually similar to planning IT projects or other discretely defined initiatives, in that an audit typically has intended start and finish dates, requires organizations to assign appropriate personnel and sufficient resources, and produces tangible outputs in the form of documentation, findings, and recommendations. Planning an individual audit is informed by, but separate from, the broader activity of developing audit plans within the internal audit program. In a single-audit context, the need for an audit has already been determined, as has its relative priority, so planning emphasizes the preparatory activities that, when done properly, facilitate the successful achievement of the organization's objectives and ensure that the audit team has everything it needs to begin executing the audit. Single-audit planning also takes general guidelines and inputs about scope, resource requirements, timelines, protocols, and supporting information into consideration and determines explicit needs, deadlines, audit criteria, and evidentiary and procedural requirements. During audit planning, organizations also set expectations about audit reports or other work products that will be delivered by the end of the audit.

Audit preparation

Organizations with established audit programs assess mission and business processes, operational capabilities, and IT assets to develop the audit universe, comprising all aspects of the organization potentially subject to audit, and align the contents of the audit universe to the most applicable audit types or approaches. Each type of IT audit has different sources of motivation, expected outcomes, and organizational objectives. Many audits also have explicit criteria, standards, or protocols associated with them. These factors collectively drive the definition of the audit scope. As part of audit planning, audit program personnel refer to the organizational audit strategy and identify audit-specific needs to explain in detail what will be examined during the audit and what the organization hopes to achieve by performing the audit. With a clearly defined scope and set of objectives, the audit team and the people within the organization who will support the audit process can prepare for audit execution by identifying and assigning necessary auditors and other resources, reviewing the relevant existing controls and information that will be used during the audit, and determining the appropriate procedures, standards, and protocols to be followed.

Resource allocation

Depending on the scope and complexity of the audit being conducted, IT audits can be very resource-intensive. Organizations assign auditors and allocate resources sufficient to support each audit based on the scope and type of audit, the nature of the examination required for different assets, processes, or controls, and the timeline for completion. Audit plans should establish the intended start and finish dates for an audit as well as any interim milestones or checkpoints required during the project. If audit results must be delivered by a specific date to the audit committee, executive management, or external audiences such as regulatory authorities, then the assignment of resources should prioritize finishing the audit within the time available to satisfy internally or externally specified deadlines. When operating under less strict time constraints, organizations may be able to schedule audits or allocate resources based on the availability of auditors with the requisite skills and experience. Many organizations develop formal project plans to manage IT audits, itemizing all tasks, activities, and milestones with scheduled start and finish dates and personnel and other resources assigned to each item. Establishing a project baseline allows audit managers or team leaders to track the completion of tasks, determine the level of effort needed to complete the remaining work, and adjust staff or resourcing as necessary.

Preliminary data gathering

Evidence collection is a primary focus of performing IT audits, but organizations can help ensure timely and effective audit execution by gathering information during the planning stage that auditors will need to examine during the audit. Depending on the type and scope of the audit, relevant sources of information typically include:

- policies, procedures, standards, and guidelines;
- system or application documentation, including operational manuals;
- configuration settings for servers, devices, or technology components;
- descriptions of implemented controls, including security controls; and
- audit reports and corrective action plans from previously completed audits.

To the extent that the organization knows the audit procedures and specific audit criteria to be applied by the auditors, the outputs of audit planning can include preliminary summaries of evidence needs or audit checklists. Personnel with supporting roles for the audit can use this information to prepare readily available information and to ensure that necessary logistical arrangements have been made, such as provisioning facility or system access rights, for auditors and designating and providing contact information for personnel that will serve as resources for auditors during the performance of the audit.

Audit procedures and protocols

Audits by definition differ from assessments and other more general types of reviews, in that they compare organizational characteristics with formal audit criteria. Whether specified in published standards, rules, or regulations or developed internally, audit criteria must be explicitly defined and documented so that auditors can use them as the basis for examining processes, controls, capabilities, or organizational behavior falling within the scope of an audit. The selection of audit

Table 8.1 Sources of Audit Procedures and Protocols for Major Audit Types

Audit Type	Audit Procedures and Protocols
Financial audits	• Statements on Auditing Standards (SAS) [2] • Statement on Standards for Attestation Engagements (SSAE) [3] • International Standards on Auditing (ISA) [4] • International Professional Practices Framework (IIPF) [5]
Operational audits	• Standard Audit Program Guides [6]
Certification audits	• ISO/IEC 17021 [7] • ISO 19011 [1]
Quality audits	• ASQ Quality Auditor Body of Knowledge [8]
Information systems audits	• ISACA IT Audit Framework [9] • ISO/IEC 27006 [10], 27007, [11] and 27008 [12] • Federal Information System Controls Audit Manual (FISCAM) [13]

criteria used for a given audit depends on the type of audit, its intended purpose or outcomes, and the set of subjects to be examined. Similarly, the choice of audit procedures and protocols that auditors will use reflects the type and purpose of the audit and what is being audited. Table 8.1 identifies some prominent sources of audit procedures for different major types of audits. The definition of audit scope and objectives during audit planning typically correlates to the audit criteria that auditors will apply to the applicable procedures and protocols. In an internal audit, the organization's audit program personnel generally have the discretion to determine procedures and protocols best suited to their audit objectives. When engaging the services of external auditors, organizations are less likely to dictate audit procedures, although recommended or proposed procedures may be among the criteria organizations consider when selecting external auditors.

When performing certain types of IT audits, such as those intended to achieve or maintain certification or demonstrate compliance with regulatory requirements, an organization's choice of audit procedures and protocols may be constrained by the need to conform to externally specified standards. External audits performed by accredited certifying bodies—or internal audits used by organizations to self-assess their qualifications for certification—are in many cases subject to additional standards about how audits are performed [1,7]. Organizations need to ensure that their audits are conducted in compliance with such standards to have confidence in the reliability and validity of the audit results.

Planning internal and external audits

In organizations with established audit programs, planning for internal audits benefits from the consideration given in organizational audit strategy to audit scope, objectives, priority, resource requirements, and scheduling. The reliance on internal auditors and resources means that audit managers responsible for assigning and overseeing personnel and audit performance can leverage knowledge about different auditors' qualifications and backgrounds to make sure each audit team includes the skills and abilities necessary to successfully conduct the audit. For types of audits an organization performs repeatedly audit managers can also use prior experience and audit results to identify relevant sources of information and to gauge the procedure and protocols that will be most effective in future iterations. In many cases organizations have the ability to choose their auditors—designating employees from the internal audit program for internal audits, and selecting audit firms for external audits. Where possible, organizations can improve overall prospects for successful audit engagements by choosing auditors with whom the organization has a collaborative, rather than adversarial, working relationship. Planning for external audits differs in many respects from planning internal audits. Organizations often have the flexibility to select their external auditors (from among a pool of qualified firms), but may have little or no role in assigning individual auditors or audit team leaders other than specifying necessary qualifications. External audit firms typically bring audit procedures, protocols, and tools to audit engagements, reflecting their own preferences or prior experience. With respect to preliminary data gathering, the primary focus for organizations working with external auditors is to ensure that the organization can furnish all necessary information at (or before) the point in the audit when the information is needed. From this perspective, one measure of success for external audit planning is what proportion of documentation or other evidentiary information required by auditors the organization can provide at the beginning of audit execution.

Engaging the services of an external auditor generally involves a formal contractual agreement between the audit firm and the audited organization that sets expectations and obligations for the resources and kinds of support each party contributes to the audit process. Organizations typically have a vested interest in ensuring that external audits proceed as planned, fully address all aspects within their scope, and conclude within the time frame specified. Many types of internal audits produce findings or other results that external auditors use as evidence of the relative effectiveness of internal controls. Organizations can more effectively support external audit activities if they plan their internal audits to deliver audit reports prior to the start of external audit engagements.

Audit performance

Audit performance is the stage in the audit process in which the audit team executes the plan developed for the audit and conducts a detailed examination of processes, IT assets, and controls, comparing evidence collected about the organization and its capabilities and practices to the requirements specified in audit criteria, relevant protocols, or applicable standards. The activities associated with performing an IT audit include the examination by auditors of all documentation and contextual information available about the subject of the audit, the collection of evidence through observation, interviews, and tests, and the analysis of that evidence to identify weaknesses, control deficiencies, or other issues. The nature of many audit performance tasks often requires auditors to be physically present at one or more locations maintained by the organization undergoing the audit. Working on-site facilitates interaction with organizational personnel supporting the audit or responsible for furnishing information to auditors and enables direct access to and observation of IT assets and associated controls examined within the scope of the audit. During the audit performance part of the process the audit team and organizational personnel involved in the audit meet to kick off the audit, set expectations about what will be examined and when, and explain the audit methods to be used with the relevant information and sources of evidence. Audit performance comprises both the collection and analysis of evidence, as auditors may need to iterate these tasks multiple times, to ensure that sufficient evidence is reviewed to substantiate audit findings.

Evidence collection

Auditors rely on evidence collected from the organization to determine the extent to which the elements examined in the audit satisfy specified criteria. Audit standards distinguish between *information* provided by an organization or gathered by auditors and *evidence*, the latter consisting of information that auditors are able to verify using methods appropriate for the scope, objectives, and criteria of the audit and for the type of information under examination [1]. In IT audits, key evidence collection activities typically include those shown in Figure 8.2: reviewing documentation provided by the organization or gathered from interviews with personnel, observing operational procedures or activities, testing controls, and checking technical configuration settings for IT components. Sources of information therefore become sources of evidence when and if auditors are able to fully evaluate the information, confirm its accuracy and completeness, and correlate it to audit criteria. Evidence collected by auditors provides the basis for audit findings, including indications of insufficient or ineffective controls or determinations of conformity. Auditors record the types of information they examine and the methods they use to collect evidence in work papers that—separate from audit findings that result from evidence collection and analysis—document the procedural steps each auditor follows. Describing the audit process in detail, in this manner, helps ensure the reliability and validity of the audit results by enabling review of each auditor's work by the audit manager or other auditors on the team.

Relevant sources of IT audit evidence vary among different types of audits and their purposes and objectives. To fully examine a process, system, or environment that implements administrative, technical, and physical controls, auditors typically need to consider a wide range of criteria corresponding to many sources of information and evaluation methods. The audit guidelines provided in ISO 19011

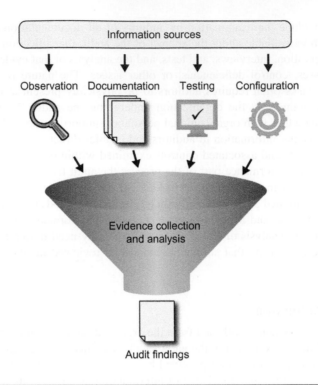

FIGURE 8.2

IT auditors collect evidence from multiple sources using a variety of methods, examining procedural and technical documentation, observing process execution and personnel behavior, testing controls, and checking system and environment configuration settings.

identify many information sources auditors may select depending on audit scope, complexity, and the criteria that must be satisfied, including [1]:

- documents such as policies, plans, procedures, standards, guidelines, technical specifications, contracts, licenses, and service level agreements;
- interviews with organizational personnel responsible for operating or managing the subject under examination;
- direct observation of activities occurring in the organizational environment;
- applications, databases, user interfaces, and other technical components;
- performance data such as customer and supplier satisfaction ratings or quality reports produced by third parties; and
- simulated or actual control testing, modeling, or exercises.

When conducting audits of large or complex organizations or subject matter, the volume of information auditors must consider in the evidence collection process may exceed the capacity of the audit team. In such cases auditors may engage in information sampling, applying audit methods to a subset of the available information, and using the results to perform analysis and develop audit findings. The use of sampling

Table 8.2 Applicability of Audit Methods for Different Types of Evidence

Methods	Applicability
Examination	• System documentation, specifications, diagrams • Plans, policies, procedures, instructions, guidelines • Standards, frameworks, methodologies
Interviewing	• Employees with operational responsibility for audit subjects • Managers responsible for governance, risk, and compliance • Customers, support personnel, system end users
Observation	• Software or hardware functionality • Operational activities, processes, practices, exercises • Personnel behavior
Testing	• Technology components • Hardware devices • Application software and systems • Procedural controls and technical capabilities

can improve the feasibility and cost effectiveness of an audit, but imposes additional procedural requirements on auditors to make sure that sampling methods used in an audit are sound, appropriate for the type of audit, and statistically valid and that the sample taken is representative of the entire set of information.

Analysis of evidence

The primary purpose of collecting evidence is to enable auditors to correlate the evidence to applicable audit criteria and analyze the evidence to determine the extent to which those criteria are satisfied. Practices for analyzing audit evidence encompass a broad range of methods; auditors select the most appropriate methods based on the type of control under examination and the type of audit and its purpose and objectives. Available guidance on analyzing evidence recommends different methods, used alone or in combination, for evaluating administrative, technical, and physical controls. Table 8.2 lists representative methods and the sources of evidence to which they apply. Terminology varies across standards and sources of guidance, but commonly described methods include examination or review of documentation-based evidence; interviews with operations or supervisory personnel; observation of organizational practices and personnel behavior; and testing implemented controls [14,15]. The choice of audit methods also takes into account the amount and quality of interaction between the auditor and personnel in the organization being audited, the level of access the auditor has to IT components or other audit subjects, and the location of the auditor (e.g., on-site or off-site) during the examination [1]. Analytical methods can also be performed at different levels of rigor; audit objectives and requirements regarding the use of audit results drive the comprehensiveness of examination or testing activities. Auditors are responsible for describing the specific analytical procedures they use in work papers or other documentation which are made available to audit managers and organizational executives to help substantiate audit quality.

Criteria used in IT auditing typically include requirements that can be determined objectively as well as those that involve the judgment of the auditors who collect and analyze the evidence. Auditors consider both the type of evidence and its source to judge its reliability and sufficiency to support audit findings. External auditors often give more credence to evidence collected through direct observation or analysis or produced by qualified third parties than for internal information and evidence provided by the organization undergoing the audit. The focus of IT audits often includes technical characteristics, such as system and device configuration and control implementation, that can be confirmed through automated testing methods. Examining these elements requires auditors to have sufficient knowledge of applicable testing procedures and tools, but the interpretation of results generally entails an objective comparison between test results and audit criteria. In contrast, auditors reviewing documentation or analyzing information gathered through interviewing or observation need to exercise judgment to evaluate evidence, consistent with professional practice standards for objectivity, competence, and due care [14].

Reporting findings

Audit findings result from comparing evidence to audit criteria. Depending on the type of audit and its objectives, reported findings may address all criteria or only those elements the auditors determine to be deficient or insufficiently supported by evidence. Almost all audit methodologies emphasize the importance of reporting findings of weaknesses or nonconformity to audit criteria, as these areas represent the sources of risk to which the audited organization needs to respond. Depending on the audit objectives and the intended audience for the audit report, the contents of the report may include satisfactory findings and areas of conformance as well as weaknesses or deficiencies. For example, audit protocols for compliance and certification audits often entail the use of checklists or requirements templates with which auditors record the organization's satisfaction or failure-to-satisfy of all compliance requirements or certification criteria. The specific format and content required in an audit report—which influence the level of detail the report includes—are driven by the purposes for which the report will be used and the internal and external stakeholders with whom it will be shared. As the primary output from an audit engagement, the audit report needs to provide enough information to stand on its own as an artifact. Full details of the audit process are captured in audit work papers, which provide an accounting of the evidence each auditor considered, the criteria to which it applied, and the audit methods used. The level of detail reflected in work papers is rarely included in audit reports, but this supporting documentation may be referenced from the audit report if necessary. In addition to an overall summary of the audit and its results, an audit report typically contains information including [1]:

- purpose and objectives for performing the audit;
- audit scope, including organizational, functional, or technical elements to which the audit applies;

- identification of the audit client;
- identification of audit participants, including auditors and those subject to the audit;
- time frame during which the audit took place;
- locations where auditing occurred, including organization facilities and auditor work sites outside the organization, if any;
- criteria specified for the audit;
- audit findings and supporting evidence;
- audit conclusions, including auditor recommendations; and
- audit results, potentially including overall success or failure determination or the extent to which the organization satisfies the audit criteria.

Most audit methodologies and guidance distinguish between audit *findings* and audit *conclusions*—findings correspond directly to audit criteria and indicate whether or not the subject of the audit satisfies each criterion, while conclusions are evidence- and experience-based opinions from auditors regarding the implications of the findings to the organization. Conclusions may include inferences about why different findings occurred, recommendations for mitigating risk or remediating deficiencies indicated in findings, whether audit objectives have been achieved, or the effectiveness of the organizational capabilities under examination. Organizational objectives for IT audits do not always include corrective actions or identifying opportunities for operational improvement, particularly if a determination of "success" for the organization does not require a response to audit findings. Prevalent auditing standards and guidance for internal auditors emphasize the importance not only of making recommendations for corrective action to resolve audit findings, but also to verify that corrective actions are taken [2,7,9]. Many types of external audits include recommendations for corrective action and responses from the audited organization's management, such as concurrence or disagreement with recommendations and commitments to implement plans of action to remediate weaknesses.

Audit findings describe in detail control weaknesses, operational deficiencies, and other sources of risk to an organization. Audit reports often include sensitive or confidential information that the subject organization does not want to be made public or disclosed to competitors, customers, business partners, or to regulators or oversight authorities unless such disclosure is explicitly required. Organizations need to ensure that audit reports and work papers detailing auditor findings are strictly access controlled to limit disclosure to only those authorized and with a legitimate need to have the information, such as members of the audit committee and others, with fiduciary responsibilities to the organization. Audited organizations typically execute confidentiality agreements with their external auditors to protect internal information, but once audit reports are delivered the organization has the primary responsibility to ensure that only authorized parties have access.

Using information in audit reports

At the conclusion of the audit process, the auditors finalize the audit report and deliver it to the audited organization. Primary recipients of the audit reports produced in both internal and external audits include the audit committee and executive management of the audited organization. The results of external audits must be typically communicated to authorized third parties such as regulators, but the information distributed outside the organization may not include the entire audit report. One key objective for external audits is achieving a successful result, where success may mean an audit that addresses all elements defined within its scope, that produces few or no significant findings warranting corrective action, or that improves on prior audit outcomes in terms of the number or significance of findings and recommendations. Organizations completing audits that endorse their operational effectiveness, business processes, or internal controls may publicize the overall results or, in the case of publicly traded companies, summarize the results in regulatory filings. Some specialized types of IT audits produce reports intended for public, rather than internal, consumption, such as the Trust Services Report for Service Organizations issued to organizations by external auditors following the Statements on Standards for Attestation Engagements (SSAE) No. 16 [16]. Audit reports from internal audits may also be provided to regulators or external auditors as evidence to support external audits. In addition to delivering audit results to external stakeholders to support compliance and oversight requirements, organizations use the information in internal audit reports to make improvements in the effectiveness of their operational capabilities and correct weaknesses or areas of nonconformance.

Organizational control weaknesses, deficiencies, or areas of nonconformity identified in audit findings present some level of risk. Organizations need to understand the severity of the impact that could occur or the magnitude or risk associated with each finding to determine the most appropriate response. In some types of IT audits, auditors provide a risk estimate or assign relative levels (e.g., high, moderate, low) to risk or determining factors such as likelihood and impact. Accurately characterizing risk for a given organization, however, typically requires detailed knowledge of the organization's assets and control objectives as well as its risk tolerance—the level of risk the organization is willing to accept. Internal auditors may therefore be better positioned than external auditors to assess risk for audit findings. Both internal and external auditors often need to work collaboratively with risk managers and the organizational personnel responsible for audited systems, IT assets, and business processes to accurately assess the risk posed by audit findings.

Responding to audit results

Audits reports with findings and conclusions warranting corrective action, monitoring, or follow-up by the audited organization become a significant input to the process of planning and executing appropriate organizational responses. The best-case scenario for an organization undergoing IT audits in conjunction with financial, compliance, or certification audits is that the auditors will determine the organization is compliant with requirements or certify (or recertify) its adherence to applicable criteria. Operational or quality audits have similar desired outcomes, in that organizations typically would not welcome results showing extensive areas of nonconformity to standards or inefficient processes. One fundamental principle in continuous improvement, however, is that there are always ways to perform better, so organizations engaging in these types of audits are motivated at least in part by the need to identify opportunities to improve. Beyond increasing the level of conformance with audit criteria or the standards and practices they represent, organizational improvements can come from a variety of sources, potentially including business process reengineering or optimization, or the introduction of new technologies or procedural controls to existing operational processes. Organizations can also plan improvements in capabilities or processes by aligning their internal practices to maturity models such as Capability Maturity Model Integration (CMMI) where the adoption and effective management of standard processes and procedures corresponds to higher levels of maturity.

Audit findings of control weakness or organizational nonconformance represent some level of risk to the organization if they do not resolve identified issues. Organizations need to assess the risk associated with audit findings and determine the best response to that risk. Just as risk assessment—within the broader context of risk management—helps organizations prioritize their audit activities, risk assessment of threats or vulnerabilities associated with audit findings supports the prioritization of risk responses. The set of possible responses to risk include mitigation, avoidance, transference, or acceptance. Risk transference and acceptance require no direct changes to the organization's operations or controls, but mitigation and avoidance both require changes in controls or operational capabilities implemented by organizations. Mitigation reduces or eliminates risk through the addition or enhancement of controls, while avoidance limits or removes functions the organization performs so that excessively risky activities are no longer within its sphere of operations. Corrective actions organizations intend to take to respond to audit findings and mitigate risk are documented in a remediation plan—known in information security management as a plan of actions and milestones (POA&M)—that enumerates what and when the organization will do and assigns responsibility within the organization seeing each action is through to completion. Organizations need to track their responses to audit findings through monitoring and follow-up activities, to ensure that they fulfill commitments documented in final audit reports or remediation plans and to provide information to subsequent audit teams about changes implemented since the prior audit.

Process life cycles and methodologies

Although individual audit engagements typically have a defined scope, set of objectives, and initiation and completion dates, few audits are truly isolated events. Whether or not an organization achieves its intended objectives from an IT audit, from the findings and conclusions in the audit report it learns aspects of its controls or capabilities that are not operating as intended, fail to conform to applicable standards or criteria, or are insufficient or ineffective to support the organizational purposes for which they are intended. Such findings represent opportunities for improvement as well as potential focus areas for subsequent audits covering the same controls or capabilities. With the possible exception of audits conducted as part of an investigation, virtually all types of IT audits are conducted more than once in an organization, at regular intervals specified in laws, regulations, or certification requirements or at a frequency determined by organizations in their internal audit strategies. The cyclical and iterative nature of most audit processes reflects an expectation that audits will be repeated. This repetition is a defining characteristic of continuous improvement initiatives and corresponding methodologies, notably including the PDCA cycle on which many auditing processes are based.

The PDCA model attained prominence as a central element of a theory of management in manufacturing companies and firms in service industries that emphasized continuous improvement and highlighted the benefits to organizations from effecting change that leads to higher quality products or services [17]. Although the process in practice can be applied to almost any type of organizational change, it is particularly well suited to auditing and other types of assessments that identify areas of relative weakness or inefficiency that, if corrected, can result in gains in productivity, operational efficiency and effectiveness, market position, or competitive advantage. An organization's ability to realize these outcomes on an ongoing basis rests on its execution of the "check" and "act" phases of the process, in which it analyzes results such as IT audit findings and commits to corrective action not only to mitigate risk, but also to improve operational quality and enhance the value IT delivers to the organization in supporting the achievement of mission and business objectives. Beyond its pervasive use in quality management standards and methodologies, the PDCA process cycle features prominently in governance, risk, and compliance frameworks and in control evaluation and assessment methodologies, particularly for information security management.

Available methodologies and guidance on auditing offer many process life cycles to organizations that differ in terms of the number of steps they include and their areas of emphasis, but these alternatives feature more similarities than differences, in part, due to their reliance on similar standards and foundational concepts. For instance, ISO 19011, *Guidelines for Auditing Management Systems*, applies the PDCA life cycle model to the process of managing an audit program and prescribes a six-step process for performing individual audits [1]. Both of these elements are incorporated by reference into other standards, including those addressing requirements for auditors providing certification audits and [7] and audits of information security management systems [11]. Not all audit methodologies explicitly include steps for closing out the audit and following up on audit findings and corrective actions, but both audit-specific and more general control assessment processes specify activities for planning, performing, and reporting the results of formal evaluations such as IT audits. Relevant examples include:

- The Institute of Internal Auditors' (IIA) *International Professional Practices Framework* (IPPF) specifies performance standards for planning and performing audit engagements and communicating results of such engagements [5];
- The American Society for Quality's *ASQ Auditing Handbook* describes a four-step audit process including preparation, performance, reporting, and follow-up [6];
- ISACA's *IT Audit Framework* defines information system audit and assurance guidelines in three major categories: general (preparatory), performance, and reporting [9];
- The Federal Information System Controls Audit Manual (FISCAM) used in audits of U.S. government agencies defines an audit methodology organized into the three core steps of plan, perform, and report [13];
- National Institute of Standards and Technology (NIST) special publication 800-30, *Guide for Conducting Risk Assessments*, prescribes a three-step process of preparing, conducting, and maintaining assessments [18]; and
- ISACA's *COBIT 5 for Assurance* approach includes three primary phases: determining the scope of, performing, and communicating about an assurance initiative [19].

Chapter 9 provides more detailed descriptions of major frameworks and methodologies used in auditing, IT governance, risk management, and security control assessment.

Relevant source material

Key sources of guidance on audit processes include major governance and risk management methodologies as well as audit-specific standards and protocols. Many of these sources implicitly or explicitly reference the PDCA model, providing some consistency for organizations considering or incorporating multiple sources. In addition to the sources of audit and assessment process life cycles described in the previous section, relevant procedural guidance comes from auditing standards and the process and system management guidelines and methodologies that incorporate those auditing standards. These include:

- ISO 19011:2011, *Guidelines for Auditing Management Systems* [1].
- ISO/IEC 17021:2011, *Conformity Assessment—Requirements for Bodies Providing Audit and Certification of Management Systems* [7].
- ISO/IEC TR 27008:2011, *Information Technology—Security Techniques—Guidelines for Auditors on Information Security Controls* [11].
- ISO 9001:2008, *Quality Management Systems—Requirements* [20].

More prescriptive guidance is also available to organizations on performing individual process steps and activities related to audit execution, analysis of findings, and development of audit reports. Relevant sources include audit procedures and protocols defined in the IPPF [4] and standards and guidance for developing reports in the Statements on Auditing Standards (SAS) [2] and International Standards on Auditing (ISA) [3].

Summary

This chapter described the overall audit process and the primary phases or steps found in most major audit methodologies and life cycles. The audit process covers all activities from the point at which an organization makes a decision to conduct a particular audit through to the delivery of findings and formulation and initiation of plans for corrective action, compliance, operational effectiveness, or business process improvement. It addresses key activities and roles and responsibilities for IT auditors as well as those subject to or tasked with supporting audits, distinguishing where applicable between internal and external audit perspectives. The chapter also highlights the similarities among processes specified in different governance, risk management, quality management, and audit-specific frameworks, methodologies, and standards. Many of these sources of process guidance on IT auditing share a common foundation, making the choice of methodology among different organizations somewhat less important than the understanding of the end-to-end process life cycle and the expectations or obligations associated with key activities performed as part of essentially all types of audits.

References

[1] ISO 19011:2011. Guidelines for auditing management systems.
[2] Statements on Auditing Standards [Internet]. Durham (NC): American Institute of Certified Public Accountants [cited 2013 May 4]. Available from: <http://www.aicpa.org/Research/Standards/AuditAttest/Pages/SAS.aspx>.
[3] Statements on Standards for Attestation Engagements [Internet]. Durham (NC): American Institute of Certified Public Accountants [cited 2013 May 4]. Available from: <http://www.aicpa.org/Research/Standards/AuditAttest/Pages/SSAE.aspx>.
[4] International Auditing and Assurance Standards Board Handbook of international quality control, auditing review, other assurance, and related services pronouncements. New York (NY): International Auditing and Assurance Standards Board; 2012 June.
[5] Institute of Internal Auditors International Professional Practices Framework (IPPF) 2013 Edition. Altamonte Springs (FL): Institute of Internal Auditors; 2013.
[6] Chambers A, Rand G. The operational auditing handbook: auditing business and IT processes. West Sussex (UK): John Wiley & Sons; 2010.
[7] ISO/IEC 17021:2011. Conformity assessment—Requirements for bodies providing audit and certification of management systems.
[8] Russell JP, editor. The ASQ auditing handbook (4th ed.). Milwaukee (WI): ASQ Quality Press; 2013.

[9] ISACA ITAF: a professional practices framework for IS audit/assurance, 2nd ed. Rolling Meadows (IL): ISACA; 2013.

[10] ISO/IEC 27006:2011. Information technology—Security techniques—Requirements for bodies providing audit and certification of information security management systems.

[11] ISO/IEC 27007:2011. Information—Security techniques—Guidelines for information security management systems auditing.

[12] ISO/IEC TR 27008:2011. Information technology—Security techniques—Guidelines for auditors on information security controls.

[13] Government Accountability Office Federal information system controls audit manual (FISCAM). Washington (DC): Government Accountability Office; 2009 February.

[14] Institute of Internal Auditors International standards for the professional practice of internal auditing. Altamonte Springs (FL): Institute of Internal Auditors; 2012 October.

[15] National Institute of Standards and Technology Guide for assessing the security controls in federal information systems and organizations. Gaithersburg (MD): National Institute of Standards and Technology, Computer Security Division; 2010 June. [special publication 800-53A revision 1].

[16] American Institute of Certified Public Accountants Reporting on controls at a service organization. Durham (NC): American Institute of Certified Public Accountants; 2011. [Statement on Standards for Attestation Engagements No. 16].

[17] Deming WE. Out of the crisis. Cambridge (MA): MIT Center for Advanced Educational Services; 1986.

[18] National Institute of Standards and Technology Guide for conducting risk assessments. Gaithersburg (MD): National Institute of Standards and Technology, Computer Security Division; 2012 September. [special publication 800-30 revision 1].

[19] ISACA COBIT 5 for assurance. Rolling Meadows (IL): ISACA; 2013.

[20] ISO 9001:2008. Quality management systems—Requirements.

Methodologies and Frameworks

INFORMATION IN THIS CHAPTER

- Audit-specific methodologies and frameworks
- IT governance and management frameworks
- Government-focused audit methodologies
- Security control assessment frameworks

Consistency and reliability are the hallmarks of a well-functioning internal audit program. With few exceptions, organizations are typically not obligated to use an externally developed or standards-based framework or set of procedures to conduct audits. Even when organizations develop their own approaches and methodologies, however, they should be well defined so that different auditors can follow the same processes and procedures, document their findings and results the same way, and make their results usable for other auditors and examiners working in the organization and for the audit committees, executive management, regulators, or other audiences for audit reports. Fortunately for organizations lacking the interest, capability, or expertise to develop their own audit methodologies—or those in closely regulated industries or subject to a high level of oversight or scrutiny regarding their IT operations—there are many frameworks and methodologies available from leading audit, governance, and IT management standards bodies, professional associations, and other organizations. This chapter introduces and describes the key features and benefits of some of the most widely used and influential frameworks and methodologies. Table 9.1 lists the frameworks and methodologies covered in this chapter and the source, type, and focus of each.

Not all of the frameworks and methodologies applicable to IT auditing are explicitly designed for audit purposes; some specify controls applicable to process or service management, IT governance methods, or IT asset and component management that organizations may use to try to more efficiently manage their IT operations or to establish effective IT governance or process orchestration. Auditing against these IT control frameworks offers some consistency and conceptual alignment between the audit approach and the way the organizations view and structure their IT operations. Other frameworks presented here are designed specifically for auditing and describe methods auditors can use to critically examine different aspects of IT operations and internal IT assets.

Table 9.1 Methodologies and Frameworks Covered in This Chapter

Methodology/Framework	Source	Type	Focus
Generally Accepted Auditing Standards (GAAS)	AICPA	Auditing	External audits
International Standards on Auditing (ISA)	IFAC/IAASB	Auditing	External audit
Internal Control—Integrated Framework	COSO	Internal controls	Internal audit
International Professional Practices Framework (IPPF)	IIA	Auditing	Internal audit
ISO 19011	ISO	Auditing	Management systems
ISO/IEC 27007	ISO and IEC	Auditing	ISMS
Control Objectives for Business and Related Information Technology (COBIT)	ISACA	IT governance	Processes controls
Information Technology Infrastructure Library (ITIL)	Cabinet Office (UK)	IT service management	Service controls
ISO/IEC 38500	ISO and IEC	IT governance	Corporate governance
ISO/IEC 20000	ISO and IEC	Service management	Service processes
Federal Information System Controls Audit Manual (FISCAM)	GAO (US)	System auditing	Government organizations
Information System Security Review Methodology (ISSAI 5310)	ISSAI	System auditing	Government organizations
ISO/IEC 27001 and 27002	ISO and IEC	Security controls	ISMS
Special Publication 800-53A	NIST (US)	Security control assessment	Government organizations

Audit-specific methodologies and frameworks

Given the breadth of IT auditing, the large number of organizational elements potentially subject to audits, and the many types of audit procedures, designing, implementing, and operating an effective audit capability presents a challenge for many organizations. Although many types of audits can be performed satisfactorily using internally developed or externally sourced auditing processes, not all organizations have the capacity or the understanding to design their own audit programs and structures. A common alternative to developing unique internal processes or relying on ad hoc approaches is to identify and adopt suitable audit methodologies or frameworks offered by prominent professional associations or standards bodies, such as those described below.

Generally Accepted Auditing Standards

Generally Accepted Auditing Standards (GAAS) are a set of principles and requirements that provide the basis for how an auditor prepares for, performs, and reports the results of audits. Originally developed and issued by the American Institute of Certified Public Accountants (AICPA) in 1972, the current GAAS comprises 10 standards with which AICPA member auditors are required to comply. In its Statement on Auditing Standards No. 95, the AICPA's Accounting Standards Board distinguishes between auditing standards and audit procedures by stating that "Auditing procedures are acts that the auditor performs during the course of an audit to comply with auditing standards" [1]. From this perspective, auditing standards in general and the GAAS in particular apply to any type of audit or audit methodology executed by auditors who choose or are obligated to follow the GAAS. Although the AICPA is an American organization, its membership comprises auditors in many different countries; as these members agree to follow GAAS as part of adhering to the AICPA's code of professional conduct, the GAAS is in practice a global framework for auditing. Auditors typically use the GAAS as a minimum baseline for auditing activities, recognizing that depending on the country, industry, type of audit, and auditor affiliations, there may be multiple other principles or requirements an auditor needs to satisfy.

The 10 standards in the GAAS are grouped into three categories: general standards, standards of field work, and standards of reporting. These standards appear in Table 9.2.

In addition to the GAAS, the AICPA's Statements on Auditing Standards (SAS) provide more detailed guidance to member auditors on many more specific elements of auditing and audit procedures, including several directly applicable to IT auditing, summarized in Table 10.1. Some SAS documentation imposes additional auditing requirements in addition to providing explicit instructions regarding audit planning, performance, and reporting. AICPA offers additional prescriptive guidance in the form of statements on standards for attestation engagements (SSAE) for use with different types of organizations and audit environments, such as the Service Organization Control (SOC) assessments described in Chapter 5. Where such standards apply to a particular audit, adherence to GAAS and the AICPA Code of Professional Conduct generally means following all applicable SAS guidance.

International Standards on Auditing

International Standards on Auditing (ISA), developed by the independent International Auditing and Assurance Standards Board (IAASB) under the authority of the International Federation of Accountants (IFAC), specify auditor objectives and responsibilities related to conducting financial audits. Much like the GAAS, the directives in the ISA apply to the individual auditors that conduct audits, rather than to the organizations the auditors represent or that are the subject of an audit. Numerous ISA documents provide additional objectives and requirements related

Table 9.2 Generally Accepted Auditing Standards [1]

Category	Standards
General	1. The audit is to be performed by a person or persons having adequate technical training and proficiency as an auditor.
	2. In all matters relating to the assignment, an independence in mental attitude is to be maintained by the auditor or auditors.
	3. Due professional care is to be exercised in the performance of the audit and the preparation of the report.
Standards of Field Work	1. The work is to be adequately planned and assistants, if any, are to be properly supervised.
	2. A sufficient understanding of internal control is to be obtained to plan the audit and to determine the nature, timing, and extent of tests to be performed.
	3. Sufficient competent evidential matter is to be obtained through inspection, observation, inquiries, and confirmations to afford a reasonable basis for an opinion regarding the financial statements under audit.
Standards of Reporting	1. The report shall state whether the financial statements are presented in accordance with generally accepted accounting principles (GAAP).
	2. The report shall identify those circumstances in which such principles have not been consistently observed in the current period in relation to the preceding period.
	3. Informative disclosures in the financial statements are to be regarded as reasonably adequate unless otherwise stated in the report.
	4. The report shall contain either an expression of opinion regarding the financial statements, taken as a whole, or an assertion to the effect that an opinion cannot be expressed. When an overall opinion cannot be expressed, the reasons therefore should be stated. In all cases where an auditor's name is associated with financial statements, the report should contain a clear-cut indication of the character of the auditor's work, if any, and the degree of responsibility the auditor is taking.

to various aspects of performing audits which should apply to an auditor seeking to comply with the ISA when conducting any type of audit. IAASB specifies the core objectives and requirements for auditors complying with International Standards on Auditing in ISA 200, *Overall Objectives of the Independent Auditor and the Conduct of an Audit in Accordance with International Standards on Auditing*. Under ISA, an auditor's overarching objectives are first "to obtain reasonable assurance about whether the financial statements as a whole are free from material misstatement," and second, "to report on the financial statements, and communicate as

Table 9.3 Auditor Requirements Under International Standards on Auditing [2]	
Category	**Standards**
Ethical Requirements	• The auditor shall comply with relevant ethical requirements, including those pertaining to independence, relating to financial statement audit engagements.
Professional Skepticism	• The auditor shall plan and perform an audit with professional skepticism recognizing that circumstances may exist that cause the financial statements to be materially misstated.
Professional Judgment	• The auditor shall exercise professional judgment in planning and performing an audit of financial statements.
Audit Evidence and Risk	• To obtain reasonable assurance, the auditor shall obtain sufficient appropriate audit evidence to reduce audit risk to an acceptably low level and thereby enable the auditor to draw reasonable conclusions on which to base the auditor's opinion.
Conducting Audits	• The auditor shall comply with all ISAs relevant to the audit. An ISA is relevant to the audit when the ISA is in effect and the circumstances addressed by the ISA exist. • The auditor shall have an understanding of the entire text of an ISA, including its application and other explanatory material, to understand its objectives and to apply its requirements properly. • The auditor shall not represent compliance with ISAs in the auditor's report unless the auditor has complied with the requirements of this ISA and all other ISAs relevant to the audit. • To achieve the overall objectives of the auditor, the auditor shall use the objectives stated in relevant ISAs in planning and performing the audit. • The auditor shall comply with each requirement of an ISA unless, in the circumstances of the audit, the entire ISA is not relevant; or the requirement is not relevant because it is conditional and the condition does not exist. • In exceptional circumstances, the auditor may judge it necessary to depart from a relevant requirement in an ISA. In such circumstances, the auditor shall perform alternative audit procedures to achieve the aim of that requirement. • If an objective in a relevant ISA cannot be achieved, the auditor shall evaluate whether this prevents the auditor from achieving the overall objectives of the auditor and thereby requires the auditor, in accordance with the ISAs, to modify the auditor's opinion or withdraw from the engagement.

required by the ISAs, in accordance with the auditor's findings" [2]. ISA guidance requires auditors who cannot satisfy these objectives to refuse to render an opinion or to withdraw from the audit engagement. Auditors following ISA are subject to 10 requirements related to auditor behavior and to conducting audits in accordance with the International Standards, as listed in Table 9.3.

In contrast to the SAS, none of the current ISA documentation explicitly addresses IT auditing, although ISA 402, *Audit Considerations Relating to an Entity*

Using a Service Organization, addresses the use of external services provided as part of an entity's financial management and reporting systems [3]. ISA 402 is comparable in focus and intent to the AICPA's Statement on Auditing Standards No. 70, *Service Organizations*, although the ISA guidance only considers matters related to auditing financial statements, not to IT, management, or information security controls more generally. For this reason, auditors may find SAS guidance more applicable to many types of IT audits than ISA guidance. Audit professionals who represent members of IFAC are required under the Federation's Statement of Membership Obligations to "adopt and implement" IAASB standards including the ISA [4].

Committee of Sponsoring Organizations integrated framework

The Committee of Sponsoring Organizations of the Treadway Commission (COSO) is a collaborative body focused on understanding, analyzing, and developing and disseminating guidance on effective organizational governance. Originally established in 1985 to sponsor the National Commission on Fraudulent Financial Reporting, COSO gets its current familiar full name in part by association with its first commissioner, James Treadway. The sponsoring organizations COSO comprises include the American Accounting Association, the American Institute of Certified Public Accountants, Financial Executives International, the Institute of Internal Auditors, and the Institute of Management Accountants. With the active participation of many private sector firms in accounting, investment banking, securities trading, and financial services, COSO develops management frameworks and industry guidance on internal controls, fraud deterrence, and enterprise risk management. The Commission has published formal guidance on all three subjects, including the *Enterprise Risk Management—Integrated Framework* referenced in Chapter 2, two research studies on fraud in financial reporting, and multiple guidance documents on internal controls. COSO's most significant internal control guidance is its *Internal Control—Integrated Framework*, first published in 1992 and significantly updated in 2013, which defines a structured framework and set of processes for implementing, managing, and overseeing an enterprise-wide system of internal controls [5]. The internal control framework provides both a foundation for effective operational management and a basis for auditing internal controls implemented in an organization, including those related to information technology.

The COSO internal control framework begins with a focus on organizational objectives for operations, reporting, and compliance and identifies five components of internal control—a control environment, risk assessment, control activities, information and communication, and monitoring activities—that support the achievement of those objectives. Consideration of these objectives and components occurs not only at the enterprise level, but also at the level of subsidiaries, divisions, operating units, and business or functional areas of operation. COSO's framework integrates the three dimensions of objectives, components, and organizational structure, represented graphically in the multilevel cube shown in Figure 9.1 and considers the relationships among these elements.

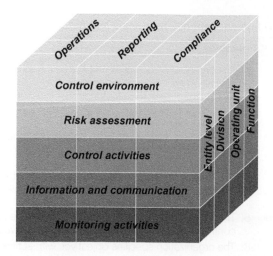

FIGURE 9.1

The COSO Internal Control Integrated Framework [5] reflects the close interrelationship among control objectives and components and organizational structure.

Source: Internal Control — Integrated Framework, Committee of Sponsoring Organizations
of the Treadway Commission, ©2013. All rights reserved. Used by permission.

Beneath this conceptual view of the framework, COSO defines 17 principles of internal control associated with each component and 81 attributes of the control principles. Audits of internal controls in an organization that has adopted the COSO framework focus on evaluating the extent to which the organization effectively implements and operationalizes the control principles. To do so, auditors look for evidence of each attribute associated with a given control principle to arrive at a subjective but evidence-based opinion as to the effectiveness of each internal control, the five control components, and the overall system of organizational internal controls. The principles associated with each internal control component are listed in Table 9.4.

International Professional Practices Framework

The Institute of Internal Auditors (IIA) consolidates a large volume of standards and guidance for auditing in its International Professional Practices Framework (IPPF). This conceptual framework offers a point of reference for internal auditors about expectations and obligations for professionals engaged in auditing, including requirements for auditors certified by IIA or other individual members of the organization. (Nonmembers are not bound by the same obligation to follow the standards and code of ethics in the IPPF, but may choose to do so.) It also provides detailed guidance on conducting different kinds of audits and on the relationship

Table 9.4 COSO Internal Control Components and Associated Principles [5]

Component	Principles
Control Environment	1. The organization demonstrates commitment to integrity and ethical values. 2. The Board of Directors demonstrates independence of management exercises oversight for the development and performance of internal control. 3. Management establishes, with board oversight, structure, reporting lines, and appropriate authorities and responsibilities in the pursuit of objectives. 4. The organization demonstrates a commitment to attract, develop, and retain competent individuals in alignment with objectives. 5. The organization holds individuals accountable for their internal control responsibilities in the pursuit of objectives.
Risk Assessment	6. The organization specifies objectives with sufficient clarity to enable the identification and assessment of risks relating to objectives. 7. The organization identifies risks to the achievement of its objectives across the entity and analyzes risks as a basis for determining how the risks should be managed. 8. The organization considers the potential for fraud in assessing risks to the achievement of its objectives. 9. The organization identifies and assesses changes that could significantly impact the system of internal control.
Control Activities	10. The organization selects and develops control activities that contribute to the mitigation of risks to the achievement of objectives to acceptable levels. 11. The organization selects and develops general control activities over technology to support the achievement of objectives. 12. The organization deploys control activities as manifested in policies that establish what is expected and in relevant procedures to effect the policies.
Information and Communication	13. The organization obtains or generates and uses relevant, quality information to support the functioning of other components of internal control. 14. The organization internally communicates information, including objectives and responsibilities for internal control, necessary to support the functioning of other components of internal control. 15. The organization communicates with external parties regarding matters affecting the functioning of other components of internal control.
Monitoring Activities	16. The organization selects, develops, and performs ongoing and/or separate evaluations to ascertain whether the components of internal control are present and functioning. 17. The organization evaluates and communicates internal control deficiencies in a timely manner to those parties responsible for taking corrective action, including senior management and the board of directors, as appropriate.

between internal auditing practices and different governance and operations processes such as risk management and quality assurance. The IPPF includes some guidance designated as mandatory—the IIA definition of internal auditing, the code of ethics, and the international standards in the framework—and additional "strongly recommended" guidance including position papers, practice advisories, and practice guides. The guidance the IPPF comprises is summarized graphically in Figure 9.2.

The IPPF mandates a set of International Standards for the Professional Practice of Internal Auditing, comprising attribute, performance, and implementation standards for both assurance and consulting services. Attribute standards specify characteristics or aspects of individual auditors and organizations that conduct internal audits, while performance standards describe audit activities and performance criteria used to measure quality (of the audit services performed, not the organization being audited). Many attribute and performance standards are further decomposed into implementation standards that specify requirements used in assurance or consulting audit services. According to the IIA, the purpose of the international standards in the IPPF is to "delineate basic principles that represent the practice of internal auditing; provide a framework for performing and promoting a broad range of value-added internal auditing; establish the basis for the evaluation of internal audit performance; and foster improved organizational processes

FIGURE 9.2

The International Professional Practices Framework comprises both mandatory standards and practice expectations and strongly recommended guidance in the form of several types of documentation [6].

Source: IPPF, Institute of Internal Auditors ©2013. All rights reserved. Used by permission.

and operations" [7]. With 18 attribute standards, 33 performance standards, and 53 implementation standards (32 assurance and 21 consulting), listing all of them here is impractical due to space constraints; Table 9.5 lists the major categories of attribute and performance standards in the IPPF, with the subordinate standards and implementation standards designations associated with each.

Individual auditors and organizations seeking to conduct audits following the IPPF may be primarily interested in the international standards prescribed in

Table 9.5 IPPF International Standards [7]

Primary Standards	Subordinate	Implementation
1000—Purpose, Authority, and Responsibility	1010	1000.A1, 1000.C1
1100—Independence and Objectivity	1110, 1111, 1120	1110.A1
1130—Impairment to Independence or Objectivity	None	1130.A1, 1130.A2, 1130.C1, 1130.C2
1200—Proficiency and Due Professional Care	1210, 1220, 1230	1210.A1, 1210.A2, 1210.A3, 1210.C1, 1220.A1, 1220.A2, 1220.A3, 1220.C1
1300—Quality Assurance and Improvement Program	1310, 1311, 1312, 1320, 1321, 1322	None
2000—Managing the Internal Audit Activity	2010, 2020, 2030, 2040, 2050, 2060, 2070	2010.A1, 2010.A2, 2010.C1
2100—Nature of Work	2110, 2120, 2130	2110.A1, 2110.A2, 2120.A1, 2120.A2, 2120.C1, 2120.C2, 2120.C3, 2130.A1, 2130.C1
2200—Engagement Planning	2201, 2210, 2220, 2230, 2240	2201.A1, 2201.C1, 2210.A1, 2210.A2, 2210.A3, 2210.C1, 2210.C2, 2220.A1, 2220.A2, 2220.C1, 2220.C2, 2240.A1, 2240.C1
2300—Performing the Engagement	2310, 2320, 2330, 2340	2330.A1, 2330.A2, 2330.C1,
2400—Communicating Results	2410, 2420, 2421, 2430, 2431, 2440, 2450	2410.A1, 2410.A2, 2410.A3, 2410.C1, 2440.A1, 2440.A2, 2440.C1, 2440.C2
2500—Monitoring Progress	None	2500.A1, 2500.C1
2600—Communicating the Acceptance of Risks	None	None

the framework and the available practice guides. The position papers in the IPPF describe the role and importance of internal auditing in the broader context of risk management and governance. Practice advisories directly correlate to many of the international standards mandated under the IPPF, providing clarification and offering instruction on the proper use of those standards. Practice advisories are identified using the same numbering scheme as the International Standards for the Professional Practice of Internal Auditing. Practice guides offer detailed guidance to help auditors correctly perform audit activities, with explicit procedures, recommended tools and techniques, and sample outputs. In addition to 16 Global Technology Audit Guides (GTAG) intended to address IT management, controls, and information security, the IPPF includes some two dozen additional practice guides covering a wide range of auditing and risk management topics.

International Organization for Standardization

The broad scope of activities and domains covered by the International Organization for Standardization (ISO) and its global sphere of influence make it a bit challenging to categorize the entire organization and its contributions to methodologies and frameworks applicable to IT auditing. Various ISO standards address quality management, environmental management, information security management, risk management, and IT governance. ISO also publishes standards related to auditing, including ISO 19011 on auditing management systems and ISO/IEC 27007 on auditing information security management systems (ISMS). ISO auditing standards can be used generally to support audits of many types of organizational systems, but they apply most directly to organizations implementing or operating systems complying with requirements for explicit types of systems specified in other ISO standards. For instance, the ISO 19011 standard is included in packaged ISO guidance for quality management systems and environmental management systems, requirements for which appear in ISO 9001 and ISO 14001, respectively. Similarly, ISO/IEC 27007 aligns directly to the ISO requirements for ISMS prescribed in ISO/IEC 27001. (Further details about the ISMS and the security control framework addressed in ISO/IEC 27001 and 27002 appears later in this chapter.)

Both ISO 19011 and ISO/IEC 27007 provide a general foundation for conducting audits, grounded in a set of audit principles and working from an expectation that organizations have established or will establish a formal, repeatable audit program. ISO audit standards also emphasize the importance of establishing criteria to assess auditor competence and using evidence that demonstrates such competence, including prior experience, completion of relevant training, and achievement of appropriate certifications attesting to the auditor's knowledge and expertise [8,9]. Activities performed as part of an ISO-defined audit include overall audit program management as well as discrete phases for initiating, planning, conducting, reporting, completing, and following up on audits, as reflected in Figure 9.3.

FIGURE 9.3

The ISO auditing process defines six sequential steps in addition to overall audit program management [8,9].

IT governance and management frameworks

IT auditing plays an essential supporting role in IT governance by helping organizations, their executive management teams, and their boards of directors ensure that IT assets, processes and services, and management functions operate as intended and in accordance with the IT goals and objectives established by the organization [10]. The interdependent relationship between IT auditing and governance, described in some detail in Chapter 2, extends to the internal controls implemented in an organization to enable effective IT governance. Although all organizations arguably perform at least some degree of IT governance, not all organizations choose to standardize governance through the use of formal frameworks. IT auditors working for or evaluating organizations that adopt formal IT governance or IT management frameworks can use the structure defined by those frameworks to facilitate establishing the scope and relative priority of IT audit activities and identifying the relevant set of business processes and internal controls to be audited.

Control Objectives for Business and Related Information Technology

The Control Objectives for Business and Related Information Technology (COBIT®), originally developed by ISACA in 1996 and updated several times, most recently in 2012, is among the most widely used models for IT governance and management, including the management of internal controls used to satisfy legal and regulatory requirements such as those mandated under Sarbanes–Oxley and Directive 2006/43/EC. Its primary focus is on good governance practices, rather than audit or compliance, but its detailed hierarchy of principles, enablers, and processes provides a basis for conducting IT audits of organizations that implement COBIT. Two versions of COBIT are widely used in organizational governance programs: the current COBIT 5 framework and the 4.1 version that preceded it. COBIT 5 reflects an integrated approach combining key principles and objectives from version 4.1 with several other ISACA domain-specific frameworks—including Val IT (focused on business investments), Risk IT (focused on IT risk management), the Business Model for Information Security (BMIS), and the IT Assurance Framework (ITAF)—and elements of Information Technology Infrastructure Library (ITIL®) and several ISO standards [11].

COBIT 4.1 remains applicable to IT auditing because many organizations that implemented the governance framework since its release in 2005 did so to help achieve compliance with requirements in the Sarbanes–Oxley Act and associated rules, and continue to describe their operations in terms of the processes and control objectives COBIT 4.1 defined. Those control objectives, while not included in COBIT 5, help define the scope for audits of processes in the COBIT framework. COBIT 5 also identifies seven categories of enablers—principles, policies, and frameworks; processes; organizational structures; culture, ethics, and behavior; information; services, infrastructure, and applications; and people, skills, and competencies—each of which could represent subject areas for IT audits. COBIT 4.1 also emphasizes the cyclical pattern of executing governance processes in each domain, shown in Figure 9.4, reflecting the familiar plan–do–check–act (PDCA) pattern used in audits of governance, risk, and compliance functions, information security management, and quality management.

As a governance framework, COBIT first considers the business goals of an organization and the IT goals, objectives, and processes that support those business goals. The COBIT 5 framework is organized around five main principles [11]:

1. Meeting stakeholder needs
2. Covering the enterprise end-to-end
3. Applying a single integrated framework
4. Enabling a holistic approach
5. Separating governance from management.

COBIT 5 emphasizes core governance activities of setting enterprise goals and objectives, prioritizing IT investments, making strategic decisions to further progress toward those goals and objectives, and assessing performance in their achievement. From the IT auditor's perspective, COBIT 5 offers less explicit direction than version 4.1, in large part because auditing is not a primary focus of the newer guidance. ISACA publishes several more specialized documents providing guidance to organizations on applying COBIT 5 in different governance contexts, including assurance, information security, and assessment [13]. The enterprise-level perspective COBIT 5 uses also come into play when evaluating entity-level controls, as those controls typically include governance processes. COBIT is a process-based

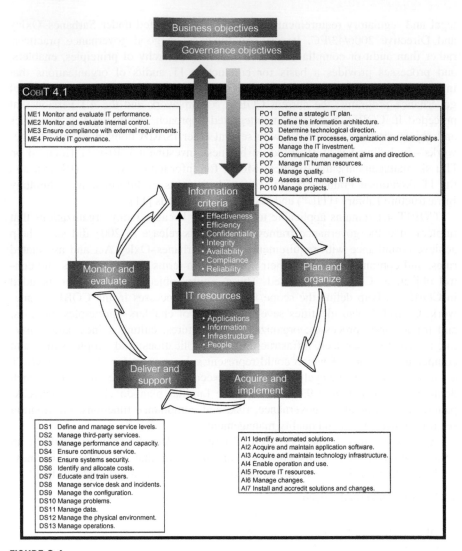

FIGURE 9.4

The COBIT 4.1 framework defines an interrelated set of processes and control objectives for use in IT governance [12].

governance framework organized into five distinct yet related domains: evaluate, direct, and monitor; align, plan, and organize; build, acquire, and implement; deliver, service, and support; and monitor, evaluate, and assess. Each domain contains multiple processes. For each process, COBIT offers a description and guidance on assessment, the latter derived in large part from ISO/IEC 15504. The COBIT 5 structure comprises the five domains and 37 processes listed in Table 9.6.

Table 9.6 COBIT 5 Domains and Processes [11]

IT Domain	Processes
Evaluate, Direct, and Monitor	EDM01 Ensure Governance Framework Setting and Maintenance
	EDM02 Ensure Benefits Delivery
	EDM03 Ensure Risk Optimization
	EDM04 Ensure Resource Optimization
	EDM05 Ensure Stakeholder Transparency
Align, Plan, and Organize	APO01 Manage the IT Management Framework
	APO02 Manage Strategy
	APO03 Manage Enterprise Architecture
	APO04 Manage Innovation
	APO05 Manage Portfolio
	APO06 Manage Budget and Costs
	APO07 Manage Human Resources
	APO08 Manage Relationships
	APO09 Manage Service Agreements
	APO10 Manage Suppliers
	APO11 Manage Quality
	APO12 Manage Risk
	APO13 Manage Security
Build, Acquire, and Implement	BAI01 Manage Programs and Projects
	BAI02 Manage Requirements Definition
	BAI03 Manage Solutions Identification and Build
	BAI04 Manage Availability and Capacity
	BAI05 Manage Organizational Change Enablement
	BAI06 Manage Changes
	BAI07 Manage Change Acceptance and Transitioning
	BAI08 Manage Knowledge
	BAI09 Manage Assets
	BAI10 Manage Configuration
Deliver, Service, and Support	DSS01 Manage Operations
	DSS02 Manage Service Requests and Incidents
	DSS03 Manage Problems
	DSS04 Manage Continuity
	DSS05 Manage Security Services
	DSS06 Manage Business Process Controls
Monitor, Evaluate, and Assess	MEA01 Monitor, Evaluate, and Assess Performance and Conformance
	MEA02 Monitor, Evaluate, and Assess the System of Internal Control
	MEA03 Monitor, Evaluate, and Assess Compliance with External Requirements

Although ISACA is responsible both for the COBIT framework and the Certified Information Systems Auditor (CISA) certification; CISA-certified auditors are not obligated to follow COBIT. CISAs use ISACA's audit standards and guidelines, in much the same way that membership in some other professional organizations comes with a requirement to use the organization's audit standards, but COBIT is aimed at a different level. Implementing COBIT is an organizational decision about governance, and the governance domains described in the framework apply to organizations and their IT processes, not to individuals. Auditors with the CISA credential may assess the information system controls of an organization following any governance approach, formal or otherwise, so while the CISA auditing and governance processes align well to COBIT, their applicability is not limited to organizations using COBIT.

Information Technology Infrastructure Library

The ITIL® is a governance model for IT service management developed by the government of the United Kingdom that defines an end-to-end life cycle and integrated set of practices and guidance in the areas of service strategy, service design, service transition, service operation, and continual service improvement. In the ITIL context, a *service* is defined as "A means of delivering value to customers by facilitating outcomes customers want to achieve without the ownership of specific costs and risks" [14] where outcomes are the result of executing processes or supporting activities to achieve a specific objective or produce specific outputs. Although ITIL covers many of the same business domains and operational processes as other governance and control frameworks, its service orientation differentiates ITIL from COBIT, ISO standards, and most IT management frameworks. Presenting a detailed comparison of process versus service orientations in IT governance is beyond the scope of this book, but auditors and others working with organizations adhering to ITIL should recognize that its service-based perspective impacts the nature and suitable approaches for IT audits in those organizations.

Since its initial development more than 20 years ago, ITIL has undergone several major revisions, first using numbered versions and now designated by the year in which updates are published. The most current version is ITIL 2011, although it is common to see references to ITIL v3 and ITIL 2007 (both designations refer to the same version), as the core structure of the framework has remained the same since ITIL v3. The ITIL framework defines a service life cycle comprising the five main practices illustrated in Figure 9.5. For each phase of the service life cycle, ITIL defines key processes and activities, their inputs and outputs, and roles and responsibilities integral to successfully executing those processes. Table 9.7 lists the processes defined for each service phase in ITIL.

ITIL also includes four functions within service operations: application management, technical management, IT operations management, and service desk. Some references to ITIL also include service measurement and service reporting within the continuous service improvement phase; these processes were part of ITIL 2007 but are not so designated in ITIL 2011. In organizations adopting ITIL, the service

FIGURE 9.5

ITIL approaches effective IT management through a formal services life cycle emphasizing continuous improvement [16].

catalogue—which lists all services defined and offered by the organization—provides an important point of reference for developing the IT audit universe and for establishing the scope of specific types of IT audits.

> The term "ITIL certification" applies only to individuals, not to organizations. Several levels of ITIL certification are available to individuals, denoting increasing knowledge of and expertise in ITIL-based service management best practices. These include foundation, intermediate, expert, and master qualifications. Organizations cannot be "ITIL certified" although they can pursue and achieve IT service management certification against the ISO/IEC 20000 standard.

International Organization for Standardization

As noted previously in this chapter, ISO publishes standards applicable to many different aspects of IT implementation, operations, and management, including those directly related to IT governance, risk management, service management, and information security management and associated controls. With respect to IT governance and management, the most relevant standards include ISO/IEC 38500 addressing corporate governance of IT and the ISO/IEC 20000 family of standards on IT service management. The ISO/IEC 38500 standard offers guidance to

Table 9.7 ITIL 2011 Service Lifecycle Phases and Processes [15]

Phase	Processes
Service Strategy	• Strategy Management • Service Portfolio Management • Financial Management • Demand Management • Business Relationship Management
Service Design	• Design Coordination • Service Catalogue Management • Service Level Management • Availability Management • Capacity Management • IT Service Continuity Management (ITSCM) • Information Security Management • Supplier Management
Service Transition	• Transition Planning and Support • Change Management • Service Asset and Configuration Management (SACM) • Release and Deployment Management • Service Validation and Testing • Change Evaluation • Knowledge Management
Service Operation	• Event Management • Incident Management • Request Fulfillment • Problem Management • Access Management

Continuous Service Improvement	• Service Improvement:
	  1. Define what to measure
	  2. Define what can be measured
	  3. Gather the data
	  4. Process the data
	  5. Analyze the data
	  6. Present and use the information
	  7. Implement corrective action

organizational leaders on using information technology effectively and efficiently and in a manner that support regulatory compliance and other governance objectives. The corporate governance framework in ISO/IEC 38500 provides definitions of key terms and offers six core principles for good governance: responsibility, strategy, acquisition, performance, conformance, and human behavior [17]. In contrast to detailed governance models like COBIT and ITIL, ISO/IEC 38500 emphasizes guidance for how those responsible for governance should act when evaluating, directing, and monitoring the use of IT in their organizations. This

Table 9.8 ISO/IEC 20000 Processes by Category [19]	
Process Category	**Processes**
Service Delivery	• Capacity Management • Services Continuity and Availability Management • Service Level Management • Service Reporting • Information Security Management • Budgeting and Accounting for Services
Relationship	• Business Relationship Management • Supplier Management
Resolution	• Incident and Services Request Management • Problem Management
Control	• Configuration Management • Change Management • Release and Deployment Management

high-level perspective makes the standard complementary to more finely grained, prescriptive frameworks.

ISO/IEC 20000, published in five parts, specifies requirements for service management systems, including those service providers need to satisfy "to plan, establish, implement, operate, monitor, review, maintain and improve" their service management systems [18]. It also defines a process reference model for service management, describing processes necessary to deliver the requirements in Part 1 of the standard and the purpose and intended outcomes for each process. ISO/IEC 20000 groups processes into four primary categories: service delivery, relationship, resolution, and control. The reference model is also intended to provide a basis for process assessment to support performance measurement and continuous service improvement. The processes defined in ISO/IEC 20000 overlap substantially with those in ITIL 2011, as should be evident from comparing the ISO processes in Table 9.8 with the ITIL processes in Table 9.7.

Government-focused audit methodologies

Although the basic processes and procedures used in IT auditing are much the same across industries, sectors, and even countries, there are considerations unique to government organizations that some organizations address through government-specific methodologies. In contrast to the broad scope of IT governance and internal control frameworks described previously in this chapter, formal government audit methodologies tend to focus more narrowly on controls for information systems, particularly including security controls. This topical concentration—and the explicit focus on government organizations and auditors—does not mean that federal-specific guidance has no value for other types of organizations, although some of the assumed objectives and priorities underlying the frameworks may not resonate in commercial enterprises. Government auditing standards and guidance also include position descriptions and personnel qualification requirements for IT auditors [20], including those performing specialized audits such as those for computer network defense [21]. Another point to consider is that, at least in the United States, government-produced guidance and standards tend to be available to anyone free of charge.

Federal Information System Controls Audit Manual

The US Government Accountability publishes the Federal Information System Controls Audit Manual (FISCAM) [22], which prescribes a simple, three-step process for auditing information system controls and provides detailed guidance for evaluating and testing two major types of controls—general controls and business process application controls. General controls include five categories: security management, access control, configuration management, segregation of duties, and contingency planning. Business process application controls span four categories: application level general controls, business process controls, interface controls, and data management system controls. For each control category, FISCAM identifies critical elements considered essential to implementing adequate controls and achieving control objectives, as well as recommended control techniques and procedures for auditing each element. As a US government audit manual, the guidance in FISCAM conforms to the Government Auditing Standards (commonly known as the Yellow Book) [20] and to the audit standards specified by the AICPA. The control hierarchy in FISCAM closely aligns to the federal security and privacy control framework defined by the US National Institute of Standards and Technology (NIST) in its Special Publication 800-53 Revision 3, *Recommended Security Controls for Federal Information Systems and Organizations*. This framework is also the basis for security control assessments required for federal information systems subject to FISMA and associated regulations, but in contrast to assessment procedures, FISCAM is explicitly intended to facilitate information system control audits.

The audit process defined in FISCAM, shown in Figure 9.6, comprises just three steps: plan the information system controls audit, perform information system control audit tests, and report audit results. The manual includes detailed guidance on a set of activities prescribed within each process step and listed in Table 9.9.

As might be expected for a government audit manual, the primary intended use of FISCAM is to support audits of information systems performed in accordance with the Government Auditing Standards. Auditors or organizations not subject to these standards and not committed to some other control framework may find FISCAM guidance useful to help understand the general IT audit process and determine potential methods to use to test various information system controls.

FIGURE 9.6

The FISCAM process involves three iterative phases—plan, perform, and report—and a set of audit activities within each phase [22].

Table 9.9 FISCAM Audit Processes and Activities [22]	
Process Step	**Activities**
Plan the Information System Controls Audit	• Understand the overall audit objectives and related scope of the information system controls audit • Understand the entity's operations and key business processes • Obtain a general understanding of the structure of the entity's networks • Identify key areas of audit interest • Assess information system risk on a preliminary basis • Identify critical control points • Obtain a preliminary understanding of information system controls • Perform other audit planning procedures
Perform Information System Control Audit Tests	• Understand information systems relevant to the audit objectives • Determine which IS control techniques are relevant to the audit objectives • For each relevant IS control technique determine whether it is suitably designed to achieve the critical activity and has been implemented
Report Audit Results	• Evaluate the effects of identified IS control weaknesses • Consider other audit reporting requirements and related reporting responsibilities

International Standards of Supreme Audit Institutions

Among the International Standards of Supreme Audit Institutions (ISSAI) issued by the International Organization of Supreme Audit Institutions, the standard most directly applicable to auditing IT controls is ISSAI 5310, *Information System Security Review Methodology*. Like other INTOSAI publications, ISSAI 5310 addresses government institutions and their information systems. This guidance document provides two distinct methodologies: a "top-down" approach and a more finely grained detailed assessment approach [23]. The former uses qualitative risk management practices to prioritize auditor activities on information systems based on their value to the organization, threats to the system, and the potential adverse impact if threats materialize. The detailed information system security approach relies on asset valuation and quantitative risk analysis to attempt to place a monetary value on impacts to systems and the organizations they support. To many observers, the security assessment process in ISSAI 5310 will seem more like conventional information security risk management than an audit methodology, as its prescribed steps mirror well-known risk management approaches. The process entails the development of a sensitivity statement, a business impact assessment, a threat and risk assessment, an exposure assessment (a function of impact and probability), and a decision regarding what security provisions to implement or other actions to take to mitigate exposure risk [23]. The ISSAI 5310 guidance includes an appendix describing numerous threats and countermeasures relevant to many types of government information systems, similar to information provided in NIST Special Publication 800-30 Revision 1, *Guide for Conducting Risk Assessments*[24]. These risk-centered methodologies may help IT auditors determine the extent to which organizations have accurately identified and addressed threats to their systems and other IT assets.

Security control assessment frameworks

IT audits assess the proper and effective implementation and operation of internal controls and the extent to which controls implemented by an organization achieve their intended objectives. Information security—the protection of information and assets from harm due to a loss of confidentiality, integrity, or availability—is an important control objective in virtually all organizations, making the assessment of security controls a key component of many IT audits. Organizations in many industries and both public and private sector contexts are also subject to a variety of legal, regulatory, and policy requirements related to security. Such organizations often implement security control standards or frameworks intended to help achieve compliance with applicable requirements and to demonstrate the use of industry best practices, provision of adequate security, or fulfillment of the principle of due care. Auditors working in organizations that manage their information security using formal control frameworks can leverage the underlying control structures (and, typically, associated documentation) to guide IT audit activities. In many cases, the control frameworks also include or make reference to explicit assessment procedures, testing methods, and other guidance that help auditors accurately evaluate implemented security controls.

ISO/IEC 27000 series

The ISO and International Electrotechnical Commission (IEC) jointly publish a set of standards describing organizational ISMS and the security controls such systems contain. In the ISMS context, the word *system* denotes a set of explicit, standard, repeatable processes and activities for security management, not a type of technology solution. Originally created in 1995 as British Standard 17799, this framework was revised in 1998 and adopted by the International Standards Organization in 1999 as ISO 17799. After being significantly revised again in 2005, the 17799 standard was formally converted to two related ISO/IEC standards, 27001 and 27002, and became the cornerstone of a broader set of information security management standards collectively known as the 27000 series. ISO/IEC 27001 specifies requirements for an information security management system, while ISO/IEC 27002 provides the security control framework. ISO/IEC 27001 incorporates the PDCA process flow introduced in Chapter 2, adapted to become an ISMS life cycle [25]:

- Plan → Establish the ISMS
- Do → Implement and operating the ISMS
- Check → Monitor and review the ISMS
- Act → Maintain and improve the ISMS

ISO/IEC 27002 specifies a security control hierarchy comprising 11 main security "clauses," 39 security categories, and 133 distinct security controls. Table 9.10 lists the security categories in the framework, grouped by clause.

From an auditing perspective, the ISO/IEC security management standards have a role in both internal and external audits. In internal audits, organizations that implement ISMS conforming to the ISO/IEC standards can use the standards as a baseline for evaluating security controls as implemented in the organization. Some organizations choose to seek ISO/IEC 27001 certification of their ISMS—essentially an objective determination that their ISMS satisfies the requirements in ISO/IEC 27001. To achieve such certification, an organization needs to have its ISMS evaluated (i.e., audited for compliance) by an external organization with the authority to award certification. These certifying bodies must be accredited by ISO, a prerequisite that invokes compliance with other standards, including ISO/IEC 27006 and ISO/IEC 17021, both of which specify requirements for organizational entities performing audit and certification of management systems [27,28]. ISO/IEC 17021 is more general, covering all types of management systems (quality, environmental, etc.), while ISO/IEC 27006 explicitly covers ISMS.

Table 9.10 ISO/IEC 27002 Security Clauses and Categories [26]

Security Clause	Security Categories
Security Policy	• Management Direction
Organizing Information Security	• Internal Organization • External Parties
Asset Management	• Responsibility for Assets • Information Classification
Human Resources Security	• Prior to Employment • During Employment • Termination of Employment
Physical and Environmental Security	• Secure Areas • Equipment Security
Communications and Operations Management	• Operational Procedures and Responsibilities • Third Party Service Delivery Management • System Planning and Acceptance • Protection Against Malicious and Mobile Code • Back-up • Network Security Management • Media Handling • Exchange of Information • Electronic Commerce Services • Monitoring
Access Control	• Business Requirement for Access Control • User Access Management • User Responsibilities • Network Access Control • Operating System Access Control • Application and Information Access Control • Mobile Computing and Teleworking
Information Systems Acquisition, Development and Maintenance	• Security Requirements of Information Systems • Correct Processing in Applications • Cryptographic Controls • Security of System Files • Security in Development and Support Processes • Technical Vulnerability Management
Information Security Incident Management	• Reporting Information Security Events and Weaknesses • Management of Information Security Events and Improvements
Business Continuity Management	• Information Security Aspects of Business Continuity Management
Compliance	• Compliance with Legal Requirements • Compliance with Security Policies and Standards, and Technical Compliance • Information Systems Audit Considerations

When discussing ISO/IEC 27001 certification, it is important to distinguish the subject of the certification to avoid potential confusion. Organizations can seek ISO/IEC 27001 certification for their ISMS through an evaluation process conducted by a certifying body accredited by ISO. Separate from any organizational designation, individuals can obtain professional certifications related to the standard, such as ISO/IEC 27001 Lead Auditor or ISO/IEC 27001 Lead Implementer, which attest, respectively, to knowledge and qualifications related to auditing organizations for compliance against the standard or implementing ISMS in conformance with the standard.

NIST security control assessment guidance

Under authority delegated by a provision of the Federal Information Security Management Act (FISMA), the NIST develops and publishes numerous standards and guidance documents on information security and privacy management for use by federal government agencies. The security control framework mandated for use in agencies subject to FISMA is documented in Special Publication 800-53 (SP 800-53) [29], which specifies different sets of controls to be used to safeguard federal information systems. NIST also publishes guidance for conducting security control assessments of information systems and the organizations that own or operate them in SP 800-53A [30]. As the similar document numbers imply, the assessment guidance in SP 800-53A matches the structure of the control framework defined in SP 800-53, making it an obvious choice for evaluating security controls in government agencies or other organizations that choose to adopt the NIST control framework. The security control assessment procedures in SP 800-53A are organized to match the 18 control families and 198 controls in the framework defined in SP 800-53. The SP 800-53 control families appear in Table 9.11 along with counts of the controls and control enhancements defined within each family.

NIST released the latest update to the framework in SP 800-53 in April 2013 with Revision 4, reflecting significant changes in some structural aspects as well as adding many controls and control enhancements and removing or consolidating some others. The most current version of the SP 800-53A assessment guidance was published in June 2010 and so aligns to Revision 3 of the security control framework. The 18 control families remain the same, but the set of controls within some families has changed in the latest revision to SP 800-53. From a practical perspective, federal agencies and other organizations using the framework as a control reference are unlikely to transition fully to the new version until an matching update to 800-53A occurs.

Not all controls and control enhancements addressed in SP 800-53A are required; the specific requirements for a given system under evaluation depend on its assigned security categorization, organizational policy, and the perceived risk to the system. For a system categorized at a "high" impact level, a full assessment using SP 800-53A would cover 167 controls and 161 control enhancements

Table 9.11 NIST Controls and Control Enhancements by Control Family [29]

Control Family	Number of Controls	Number of Enhancements
Access Control	19	65
Awareness and Training	5	3
Audit and Accountability	14	29
Security Assessment and Authorization	6	7
Configuration Management	9	32
Contingency Planning	9	34
Identification and Authentication	8	25
Incident Response	8	14
Maintenance	6	17
Media Protection	6	13
Physical and Environmental Protection	19	29
Planning	5	3
Personnel Security	8	4
Risk Assessment	4	9
System and Services Acquisition	14	27
System and Communications Protection	34	61
System and Information Integrity	13	41
Program Management	11	0
Total	198	413

or 328 discrete items to be assessed [30]. For each item to be assessed, NIST guidance specifies assessment methods (examine, interview, and test) and the subjects of those assessment methods (specifications, mechanisms, activities, individuals, and groups). This guidance includes optional controls and control enhancements as well, with a total of over 600 assessment procedures documented in SP 800-53A [30]. The clear benefit to an IT auditor evaluating controls implemented according to NIST guidance is a detailed, prescriptive set of instructions intended to help assess the extent to which each security control effectively satisfies its control objectives.

Security control frameworks like ISO/IEC 27002 and SP 800-53 are incomplete if the goal is to assess all IT controls; security controls are vitally important to IT, but do not represent the full set of controls applicable to IT operations and governance. Security control frameworks remain both relevant and beneficial given the emphasis in many IT audits on evaluating the compliance or effectiveness of security controls, but they are insufficient foundation for comprehensive IT auditing.

Relevant source material

Each of the methodologies and frameworks described in this chapter is available as documentation in electronic and, in most cases, published hard-copy formats. Information on downloading or otherwise obtaining such documentation is available on the web sites of the organizations responsible for each document or set of documents. Readers should be aware that while a great deal of information is typically publicly available about methodologies, frameworks, and associated standards and guidance, obtaining complete versions often requires purchasing the documentation. Some organizations make information available free or at a reduced cost to members or to individuals willing to register with them. Of the information covered in this chapter, documentation published by government agencies or government-focused organizations is generally available publicly at no cost, with the exception of ITIL. Relevant source material on major audit-relevant methodologies and frameworks includes:

- Statement on Auditing Standards 95, *Generally Accepted Auditing Standards* [1]
- IAASB's International Standards on Auditing, available individually as downloads from http://www.ifac.org or consolidated in the annually updated *Handbook of International Quality Control, Auditing Review, Other Assurance, and Related Services Pronouncements* [31]
- COSO's *Internal Control—Integrated Framework* [5]
- IIA's *International Professional Practices Framework (IPPF)* [6]
- ISACA's COBIT 4.1 [12] and COBIT 5 frameworks [11]
- Information Technology Infrastructure Library (ITIL) Service Lifecycle, available for purchase at http://www.best-management-practice.com
  - *ITIL Service Strategy*
  - *ITIL Service Design*
  - *ITIL Service Transition*
  - *ITIL Service Operation*
  - *ITIL Continuous Service Improvement*
- ISO and ISO/IEC Standards, available for purchase at http://www.iso.org/ or through national standards bodies
  - ISO 19011:2011, Guidelines for Auditing Management Systems [8]
  - ISO/IEC 20000:2011, Information Technology Service Management [18]
  - ISO/IEC 27001:2005, ISMS Requirements [25]
  - ISO/IEC 27002:2005, Code of Practice for Information Security Management [26]
  - ISO/IEC 27007:2011, Guidelines for ISMS Auditing [9]
  - ISO/IEC 38500:2008, Corporate Governance of Information Technology [17]
- GAO's *Federal Information System Controls Audit Manual (FISCAM)* [22]
- ISSAI 5310, *Information System Security Review Methodology* [23]
- NIST Special Publication 800-53A, *Guide for Assessing the Security Controls in Federal Information Systems and Organizations* [30]

Summary

This chapter identified and briefly described the major methodologies and frameworks available to assist auditors and organizations effectively conduct different types of audits, including audits of internal controls, information technology, security controls, and processes and services used in IT management and governance. With many alternative frameworks, approaches, and sources of information available, organizations that look externally for guidance can choose the methodology (or methodologies) that best suit the organization, the types of audits it needs to perform, and its audit objectives.

References

[1] Generally Accepted Auditing Standards. New York, NY: American Institute of Certified Public Accountants, Auditing Standards Board; 2001 December. Statement on Auditing Standards No. 95.

[2] Overall objectives of the independent auditor and the conduct of an audit in accordance with International Standards on Auditing. New York (NY): International Federation of Accountants; 2012. International Standard on Auditing 200.

[3] Audit considerations relating to an entity using a service organization. International Standard on Auditing 402. New York (NY): International Federation of Accountants; 2012.

[4] Board of the International Federation of Accountants. Statement of membership obligations. New York (NY): International Federation of Accountants; 2012 November.

[5] Committee of Sponsoring Organizations of the Treadway Commission. Internal control—Integrated framework. Durham (NC): American Institute of Certified Public Accountants; 2013.

[6] International Professional Practices Framework (IPPF) 2013 Edition. Altamonte Springs (FL): Institute of Internal Auditors; 2013.

[7] International standards for the professional practice of internal auditing. Altamonte Springs (FL): Institute of Internal Auditors; 2012 October.

[8] ISO 19011:2011. Guidelines for auditing management systems.

[9] ISO/IEC 27007:2011. Information—Security techniques—Guidelines for information security management systems auditing.

[10] IT Governance Institute. Board briefing on IT governance. 2nd ed. Rolling Meadows (IL): IT Governance Institute; 2003.

[11] ISACA. COBIT 5: A business framework for the governance and management of enterprise IT; Rolling Meadows (IL): ISACA; 2012. IT Governance Institute. COBIT 4.1. Rolling Meadows (IL): IT Governance Institute; 2007.

[12] IT Governance Institute. COBIT 4.1. Rolling Meadows (IL): IT Governance Institute; 2007.

[13] COBIT 5 Product Family [Internet]. Rolling Meadows (IL): ISACA [cited 2013 May 4]. Available from: <http://www.isaca.org/COBIT/Pages/Product-Family.aspx>.

[14] ITIL glossary and abbreviations. London (UK): Cabinet Office; 2011.

[15] Orr AT. Introduction to the ITIL service lifecycle. London (UK): Cabinet Office; 2011.

[16] Cartlidge A, Hanna A, Rudd C, Macfarlane I, Windebank J, Rance S. An introductory overview of ITIL® V3. Wokingham (UK): IT Service Management Forum, UK Chapter; 2007.

[17] ISO/IEC 38500:2008. Corporate governance of information technology.

[18] ISO/IEC 20000-1:2011. Information technology—Service management—Part 1: Service management system requirements.

[19] ISO/IEC 20000-4:2011. Information technology—Service management—Part 4: Process reference model.

[20] Government auditing standards. Washington (DC): Government Accountability Office; 2011 December.

[21] Information assurance workforce improvement program. Washington (DC): Department of Defense; 2005 December 19. DoD Manual 8570.01-M.

[22] Federal Information System Controls Audit Manual (FISCAM). Washington (DC): Government Accountability Office; 2009 February.

[23] International Organisation of Supreme Audit Institutions. Information system security review methodology. Copenhagen (DK): INTOSAI Professional Standards Committee; 1995. ISSAI 5310.

[24] Guide for conducting risk assessments. Gaithersburg (MD): National Institute of Standards and Technology, Computer Security Division; 2012 September. Special Publication 800-30 revision 1.

[25] ISO/IEC 27001:2005. Information—Security techniques—Information security management systems—Requirements.

[26] ISO/IEC 27002:2005. Information technology—Security techniques—Code of practice for information security management.

[27] ISO/IEC 17021:2011. Conformity assessment—Requirements for bodies providing audit and certification of management systems.

[28] ISO/IEC 27006:2011. Information technology—Security techniques—Requirements for bodies providing audit and certification of information security management systems.

[29] Recommended security controls for federal information systems and organizations. Gaithersburg, (MD): National Institute of Standards and Technology, Computer Security Division; 2009 August. Special Publication 800-53 revision 3.

[30] Guide for assessing the security controls in federal information systems and organizations. Gaithersburg (MD): National Institute of Standards and Technology, Computer Security Division; 2010 June. Special Publication 800-53A revision 1.

[31] Handbook of international quality control, auditing review, other assurance, and related services pronouncements. New York (NY): International Auditing and Assurance Standards Board; 2012 June.

Audit-Related Organizations, Standards, and Certifications

INFORMATION IN THIS CHAPTER

- National and international perspectives
- Audit-focused standards and certification organizations
- Organizations offering IT-related assessment or audit guidance

As should be clear from the information in the preceding chapters, there are many dimensions to IT auditing organizations should consider and there is no single "right" or "best" auditing approach or strategy that will work effectively for all organizations. No single authoritative standard or source of IT audit knowledge exists, even within one country, sector, or operational domain; instead there are many, stemming from organizations focused on IT assurance as well as more general accounting and financial management, quality management, IT management, software engineering, and information security. The large number and variety of sources of audit information, guidance, and professional expertise can be both a help and a hindrance to organizations trying to determine the most appropriate approach for their IT auditing. The optimal approach for a given organization is a function of many factors, including the nature of the organization, its business functions, and its information systems and infrastructure; the industry in which it participates; its regulatory environment and the extent to which it is subject to external audits; the sphere of its geographical locations and operations; the importance the organization places on IT governance, risk management, and auditing; and the maturity of its internal processes including the audit function. With some or all of these factors in mind, organizations may structure their own audit programs in a way that tries to align available audit processes, standards, and guidance with the organization's specific audit needs.

While some organizations may prefer to focus on a single auditing framework and corresponding set of audit standards and procedures, others find it more effective to distinguish different audit needs and areas of emphasis and choose specialized auditing approaches for each subject area. For organizations that have standardized on a particular governance, IT management, or service delivery framework—such as COSO, COBIT, ITIL, or other models described in the previous chapter—it often makes most sense to structure their auditing in a way that closely aligns to the framework to which they have committed. The alternative strategy of using multiple audit approaches can result in a single organization employing many different standards and approaches to cover the full scope of its audit universe. Numerous organizations provide standards, assessment frameworks, and audit guidance relevant to different types of IT auditing, so the development of an organizational audit strategy should involve some level of research or investigation into available materials and methods that organizations can apply to their own audit programs.

The flexibility to tailor audit performance in this manner is typically greater for internal auditing than it is for external auditing, as the policies, rules, regulations, or standards underlying external audit requirements often dictate the standards and processes to be employed. Any organization seeking to be successful with its internal audit program needs to understand very well the nature of the IT assets, functional processes, technical characteristics, and other aspects of its operations that need to be evaluated so that it can determine the appropriate manner in which to conduct audits. Organizational strategic goals, governance objectives, risk tolerance, and compliance needs also motivate IT auditing and influence the prioritization of audit subjects. Organizational choices for selecting audit procedures, protocols, and methodologies to use for performing internal audits, including specifying their own audit standards and criteria and audit processes instead of adopting externally defined alternatives. External auditors hired by or assigned to evaluate different types of organizations typically follow specific regulatory or organization-adopted standards and use audit personnel with certifications corresponding to those standards.

Similarly, when selecting personnel to perform internal audits—either assigning employees or choosing individuals or firms outside the organization—organizations try to ensure that the people conducting audits have the necessary knowledge, skills, and qualifications to do the job correctly. If a given standard or formal approach applies to an audit, then the auditors should be able to demonstrate familiarity with the standard to be used, either through prior experience, through a relevant certification or similar credential, or both. Certifications give those performing or undergoing audits confidence that the personnel doing the audits have sufficient expertise to accurately and efficiently complete the task. Certification alone is no guarantee of competency, as organizations issuing certifications or other credentials have varying certification requirements and levels of rigor in the process through which they award professional credentials. Most of the best-regarded certifications relevant to IT auditing are conferred by organizations that require demonstrated relevant work experience and education in addition to passing a certification exam against an explicit body of knowledge. Whether hiring new employees to perform audits, training existing staff to develop auditing skills, or evaluating proposed contractors or audit firm personnel, organizations need to be aware of professional certifications to assess their value in determining auditor qualifications and to decide whether to mandate specific credentials as a prerequisite for individuals who will perform audits on an organization's behalf.

This chapter identifies and briefly describes the major organizations responsible for producing IT audit standards and related guidance and for offering certification programs for individuals who might perform audits. Earlier chapters of this book make frequent reference to many of the organizations mentioned in this chapter, particularly those responsible for producing or maintaining commonly used IT management, governance, risk management, and audit frameworks. The focus of the material presented in this chapter is on standards and guidance relevant to various aspects of IT auditing that can be incorporated into more than one auditing process or framework, and on certifications and corresponding skill sets for auditors that may be valuable when conducting specific types of audits.

National and international perspectives

There are organizations that publish standards and offer certifications intended to apply internationally; organizations whose focus is on regional or national applicability but that conform to international principles or standards; and organizations that operate with a more explicitly limited geographic or industry scope. Many IT-focused management frameworks and standards, such as Information Systems Audit and Control Association (ISACA)'s COBIT, are intended to be used globally, typically with little local adaptation in different countries. Other international audit standards, such as the Generally Accepted Auditing Standards (GAAS) promulgated by the International Auditing and Assurance Standards Board (IAASB), are adapted for local use in different regions or countries by national standards organizations. International organizations also may choose to develop and disseminate standards, practices, and guidance or produce such information by incorporating, aggregating, or aligning standards and practices developed by other organizations that have a narrower scope. For example, the International Organization of Supreme Audit Institutions (INTOSAI) comprises nearly 200 national-level audit institutions responsible for external government audits and authorizes, endorses, and disseminates audit standards and best practices guidance developed in national-level member organizations and in collaboration with other international auditing standards bodies. Similarly, the International Federation of Accountants (IFAC) comprises more than 165 organizations in over 125 countries develops and promotes international standards that its members commit to implement. There are also examples of what are now international standards that were originally created at a national level, such as the ISO 27001 and 27002 information security management standards that began as British Standards before being adopted and enhanced for international consumption. In general, IT auditing standards and practices and related guidance often have multinational or global applicability, while audit standards focused on ensuring legal or regulatory compliance tend to be country- or region-specific.

Generally Accepted Auditing Standards

Auditing in many countries adheres to broad standards and principles collectively known as GAAS, analogous conceptually to the Generally Accepted Accounting Principles (GAAP) used in financial accounting and auditing. Despite the names of these standards and the work of international organizations to achieve some level of cross-national consensus on the standards, the specifics of what constitutes "generally accepted" varies from jurisdiction to jurisdiction, with the result that there is no single authoritative agreed-upon source of audit standards. Instead, leading national standards organizations in many countries work to develop standards that embody GAAS and promulgate those standards in their own countries. Such organizations often contribute or make available their standards and guidance for use or adaptation by auditing organizations in other countries. Some international standards organizations develop standards for general availability, giving authorities and individual organizations in multiple countries the option to use or adapt those standards if they choose. For example, the IAASB, part of the IFAC, produces numerous International Standards on Auditing (ISAs) that audit organizations in different countries (or multinational jurisdictions such as the European Community) adopt and mandate for organizations conducting audits subject to their jurisdiction. In the United States, the Statements on Auditing Standards (SAS) issued by the American Institute of Certified Public Accountants (AICPA) serve as GAAS for audits (especially external audits) in US organizations.

Auditing for legal or regulatory compliance

International auditing standards are least likely to be found in contexts driven by statutory requirements, even in industries in which organizations from many countries participate, as the criteria for demonstrating regulatory or legal compliance are typically dictated by national (or state or provincial) laws that have no international jurisdiction. Some of the most significant legislation affecting the conduct of audits—such as the Sarbanes–Oxley Act of 2002 in the United States or the 2006 Directive on Statutory Audits in the European Community—only affects organizations operating within the countries covered by the laws. Despite sharing some common audit needs, operational characteristics, and types of infrastructure, organizations in the same industries operating in different countries are typically subject to national regulatory requirements instead of or in addition to international standards. This sort of national regulatory variation exists in many industries, including financial services, health care, petroleum production, nuclear energy, and manufacturing. For some multinational corporations, this means that facilities and operations in different geographic areas are likely subject to different audit requirements and relevant standards to achieve and maintain compliance in all locations.

Audit-focused standards and certification organizations

Not all standards and personnel certifications applicable to IT auditing come from auditing-specific disciplines but external and internal auditing in virtually all organizations is influenced to some degree by standards, principles, and guidance developed by audit-focused organizations or by more broadly focused standards development organizations that produce audit-specific standards and professional certification.

Having a certification or other credential alone is not reliable evidence of qualifications to perform an audit task or do a specific job effectively. A sort of informal hierarchy among different certifications and certifying organizations exists in the industry, but hiring or contract managers evaluating an individual's credentials may not have sufficient familiarity with all the certifications to determine their relative merit. To use possession of a credential to help assess a candidate's skills and qualifications, anyone evaluating the individual needs to understand the criteria for attaining the certification, including any education or prior work experience requirements.

American Institute of Certified Public Accountants

The AICPA is one of the most prominent US organizations focused on the accounting profession and is a leading authority of many types of audit guidance. Although its focus is setting professional and ethical standards for accountants working in the United States and developing and maintaining audit standards for use in external audits of US organizations, AICPA has nearly 400,000 members in more than 125 countries [1], and contributes best practices, expertise, and other information to several international bodies. AICPA is perhaps best known generally for its administration of the Certified Public Accountant (CPA) credential, a prerequisite for becoming licensed as an accountant in the United States. For more than 40 years, the AICPA also has issued numerous SAS, which for auditors working in the United States constitute authoritative guidance on generally accepted auditing standards (GAAS). It is also one of the sponsoring organizations of the Committee of Sponsoring Organizations of the Treadway Commission responsible for the COSO Enterprise Risk Management and Internal Control integrated frameworks.

Audit standards

The SAS published by the AICPA cover all aspects of auditing and the professional practice of auditors. As of January 2013, there were 127 statements issued by the

Auditing Standards Board of the AICPA, although the total set of useful standards is somewhat less because newly issued statements often update, amend, or replace previously issued ones so some of the earliest SAS guidance has been withdrawn. With IT auditing in mind, the most relevant SAS include those enumerated in Table 10.1.

Recognizing the importance of attestation in many types of audits, the AICPA also issues Statements on Standards for Attestation Engagements (SSAE). SSAE guidance is particularly relevant to IT auditing controls implemented by service organizations (addressed in SAS No. 70), including providers of IT outsourcing, system or application hosting, cloud computing, and data centers and related environments. In current practice, SSAE No. 16, *Reporting on Controls at a Service Organization*, and its three types of Service Organization Control (SOC) reports has largely superseded SAS No. 70 as the basis for service providing organizations to report on their internal controls. SOC reports can be used by organizations

Table 10.1 SAS Applicable to IT Audits [2]

SAS	Title	Published
1	Responsibilities and Functions of the Independent Auditor	1972
25	The Relationship of Generally Accepted Auditing Standards to Quality Control Standards	1979
39	Audit Sampling	1981
56	Analytical Procedures	1988
70	Service Organizations[a]	1992
73	Using the Work of a Specialist	1994
88	Service Organizations and Reporting on Consistency	1999
95	Generally Accepted Auditing Standards	2001
102	Defining Professional Requirements in Statements on Auditing Standards	2005
103	Audit Documentation	2005
105	Amendment to SAS No. 95: Generally Accepted Auditing Standards	2006
106	Audit Evidence	2006
108	Planning and Supervision	2006
109	Understanding the Entity and its Environment and Assessing the Risks of Material Misstatement	2006
110	Performing Audit Procedures in Response to Assessed Risks and Evaluating the Audit Evidence Obtained	2006
111	Amendment to SAS No. 39, Audit Sampling	2006
114	The Auditor's Communication with Those Charged with Governance	2006
117	Compliance Audits	2009

[a]SAS 70 was superseded by SSAE 16 in 2011 but remains familiar to many auditors.

seeking services from providers to evaluate the relative completeness or strength of the service providers' controls. SOC reports include [3]:

- SOC 1, Report on Controls at a Service Organization Relevant to User Entities' Internal Control over Financial Reporting
- SOC 2, Report on Controls at a Service Organization Relevant to Security, Availability, Processing Integrity, Confidentiality or Privacy
- SOC 3, Trust Services Report for Service Organizations

AICPA certifications

The CPA designation is both an indication that an individual has successfully passed the AICPA's Uniform CPA Examination and met other certification perquisites and a necessary qualification for individuals to be licensed to provide auditing opinions on financial statements of entities operating in the US states. The CPA credential requires formal education in accounting and successful completion of the four-part CPA exam. Specific education, work experience, and other requirements for CPAs to become licensed vary by state, but passing the CPA exam is required in all US jurisdictions [4]. The four CPA exam sections are auditing and attestation; business environment and concepts, financial accounting and reporting, and regulation.

The Certified Information Technology Professional (CITP) is a specialty credential offered by AICPA to already certified CPAs who possess and can demonstrate expertise in information technology management and information assurance [5]. The CITP program uses an explicit body of knowledge comprising risk assessment; fraud considerations; internal control and its general controls; evaluate, test and report, and information management and business intelligence. In addition to holding a current CPA license and successfully passing the CITP exam, the program requires a minimum of 1000 h of relevant work experience and at least 75 h of continuing professional education in the 5 years preceding a candidate's application for the certification.

Institute of Internal Auditors

The Institute of Internal Auditors (IIA) is, like the AICPA, a very large US-based professional association with thousands of active members globally and an authoritative source of standards, procedures, and guidance on internal auditing, risk management, governance, and IT audit. As its name implies, the IIA's focus is on internal audit practices, including advocating for the profession and its value to organizations; providing professional education and certification programs; researching and publishing internal auditing best practices and their effective application in governance, risk, compliance, and controls; and sponsoring conferences and other knowledge-sharing and collaborative opportunities for internal auditors worldwide [6].

Audit standards

The IIA develops and disseminates a broad range of internal auditing standards and guidance, organized through the International Professional Practice Framework (IPPF) described in Chapter 9. Mandatory guidance within the IPPF is treated as prescriptive for internal auditors—at least those who are members of IIA—and is complemented by additional recommended guidance in the form of position papers, practice advisories, and practice guides. The IIA's documented IT audit guidance is made available to members and for sale to nonmembers in the form of 16 Global Technology Audit Guides, covering topics from general information technology controls (GTAG 1) and management of IT auditing (GTAG 4) to more narrowly focused IT domains including identity and access management (GTAG 9), business continuity (GTAG 10), and IT outsourcing (GTAG 7).

Certifications

The IIA offers five IT audit-related certifications, including the prominent Certified Internal Auditor (CIA) credential first established in 1973. In addition to successfully passing a comprehensive certification exam, qualifications for the CIA include minimum postsecondary education of a 4-year degree or equivalent, a character reference from a current IIA credential holder, at least 2 years of work experience as an internal auditor (or 1 year for candidates with a master's degree), and a commitment to abide by the IIA's code of ethics and to satisfying continuing professional education requirements once certified [7]. In addition to the CIA, the IIA offers four more specialized certifications:

1. Certification in Control Self-Assessment (CCSA)
2. Certified Government Auditing Professional (CGAP)
3. Certified Financial Services Auditor (CFSA)
4. Certification in Risk Management Assurance (CRMA).

These credentials do not require candidates to attain the CIA, but have substantially the same eligibility requirements in terms of education, demonstrated prior work experience, character endorsement, successful exam completion, and adherence to the code of ethics and continuing education requirements.

International Organisation of Supreme Audit Institutions

The International Organisation of Supreme Audit Institutions (INTOSAI) is both an autonomous international body focusing on external audits of government institutions and an umbrella organization representing national-level government audit institutions in approximately 190 countries. Established in 1953, it offers a framework for "supreme" (meaning primary or authoritative) government audit institutions to develop and facilitate knowledge sharing and dissemination of best practices, improve the quality and effectiveness of government auditing activities, and promote the capacities, position, and influence of its member organizations. By way of example, in the United States, the Government Accountability Office (GAO) is considered the supreme audit institution, while European member organizations include the European Court of Auditors (representing the EC), the National Audit Office in the United Kingdom, the Court of Audit (Cour de Comptes) in France, the Federal Court of Auditors (Bundesrechnungshof) in Germany, and the Accounts Chamber (Schetnaya Palata) of the Russian Federation. The World Bank and IIA are INTOSAI associate members [8].

Audit standards

INTOSAI does not offer individual certifications for auditors, but it does produce a series of audit guidance known as the International Standards of Supreme Audit Institutions (ISSAI). Many of the guidance documents available as ISSAI are substantially the same as artifacts produced by other audit standards bodies, such as IFAC's ISAs and AICPA's SAS. With respect to IT auditing, the most relevant ISSAI guidance is ISSAI 5310, *Information System Security Review Methodology*[9], which INTOSAI characterizes as its only IT audit-specific guidelines.

International Federation of Accountants

The IFAC is a global organization focused on the accounting profession that develops, through several independent accounting standards boards, ISAs and assurance, public sector accounting, accounting education, and ethics [10]. With members in more than 125 countries, IFAC and the standards it approves and endorses influence accounting practices worldwide and its governance—at the organizational level and through the Public Interest Oversight Board (PIOB)—contribute to increased credibility of accounting practitioners and public confidence in auditing activities. Prominent national and regional accounting organizations with IFAC membership include the AICPA in the United States, the Confederation of Asian and Pacific Accountants, the Fédération des Experts Comptables Européens (FEE), the Interamerican Accounting Association, and the Pan African Federation of Accountants. In contrast to organizations like AICPA, IIA, and ISACA, IFAC members are professional accounting organizations, not individuals.

The independent standards-setting boards established by IFAC include the IAASB, the International Public Sector Accounting Standards Board, the International Accounting Education Standards Board, and the International Ethics Standards Board for Accountants. The work of the IAASB is most directly relevant to IT auditing, as the IAASB both sets international standards for auditing—incorporating or assimilating national standards where appropriate—and promotes audit quality and uniformity of practice among countries that adopt its standards. The IAASB follows a formal process for developing its standards and other published guidance, gathering input national auditing standards organizations, IFAC member organizations, regulatory and oversight bodies, accounting firms, government agencies, and the public. By following a transparent and repeatable process the IAASB seeks to maximize the relevance of its standards in a way that is consistent with the practice of accounting and auditing in the public interest [11].

Audit standards

The primary output of the IAASB is the ISAs, a set of documents issued by IFAC on a wide range of issues and subjects related to financial auditing. While none of the ISAs are focused specifically on IT auditing, many of the standards address aspects of audit practices that are directly relevant to IT audits as well as other types. ISAs are numbered according to seven subject area: responsibilities, audit planning, internal control, audit evidence, using the work of external experts, audit reports, and specialized areas. In an effort to make ISAs as understandable and therefore as usable as possible, the IAASB in engaged in a project from 2003 to 2008 to improve the clarity of its standards documentation, during which time it redrafted and reissued a majority of the ISAs [12]. The ISAs are required for use in some national and multinational jurisdictions, notably including the European Community, which in 2006 mandated the use of International Standards on Accounting for statutory audits in member countries [13].

Information Systems Audit and Control Association

ISACA is an independent global organization focused on developing and disseminating standards, practices, and domain knowledge about information systems, particularly including governance, risk management, security, audit, and assurance. Originally established in 1969 as the Electronic Data Processing Auditors Association (EDPAA) and currently officially known only by its acronym, ISACA is the most prominent professional association dedicated explicitly to managing and auditing information systems and related technology [14]. Although its activities and publications span a wide range of subjects, ISACA is best known globally for its Control Objectives for Information and Related Technology (COBIT) framework and for administering the certification program for the Certified Information Systems Auditor (CISA) credential, which is among the most respected and sought after qualification for individuals engaged to perform IT audits.

Audit standards

As described in more detail in Chapter 9, the COBIT framework is designed to help organizations effectively manage their information technology, by describing nearly three dozen core processes organized into the four domains of plan and organize, acquire and implement, deliver and support, and monitor and evaluate. This framework provides the structure against which organizational processes and controls can be evaluated, but it is not explicitly designed to support or facilitate auditing. ISACA's Professional Standards Committee publishes Standards for IT Audit and Assurance (listed in Table 10.2), completely updated and re-released in 2013, that offer explicit requirements for various aspects of auditing practice, and another 19 IT Audit and Assurance Guidelines. ISACA considers its standards to be mandatory, while its guidelines and supporting tools and techniques are recommended for consideration by auditors but not required.

Table 10.2 Standards for IT Audit and Assurance [15]

Standard	Title
1001	Audit Charter
1002	Organizational Independence
1003	Professional Independence
1004	Reasonable Expectation
1005	Due Professional Care
1006	Proficiency
1007	Assertions
1008	Criteria
1201	Engagement Planning
1202	Risk Assessment in Planning
1203	Performance and Supervision
1204	Materiality
1205	Evidence
1206	Using the Work of Other Experts
1207	Irregularity and Illegal Acts
1401	Reporting
1402	Follow-up Activities

Certifications

The CISA designation, first awarded by ISACA in 1978 and now held by more than 100,000 individuals, is intended for professionals engaged in auditing or assessing information systems and related technology. The credential applies to those conducting either internal or external audits in a variety of operating environments and IT management or governance contexts. The CISA is highly regarded as an auditor credential and is commonly stated as a required qualification for organizational employees or contractors hired to perform information systems audits [16]. To qualify for the CISA, candidates must pass a comprehensive examination assessing knowledge of five practice domains: Auditing Information Systems; Governance and Management of IT; Information Systems Acquisition, Development and Implementation; Information Systems Operations, Maintenance and Support; and Protection of Information Assets. Applicants for the CISA must also provide evidence of 5 years of relevant prior work experience (or a combination of work experience and completion of higher education in a related field) and commit to uphold ISACA's Code of Professional Ethics, comply with information systems auditing standards, and maintain the credential through continuing professional education. As an indication of ISACA's global scope for the CISA, exam preparation materials and the exam itself are available in 11 languages.

In addition to the CISA, ISACA offers three other certification programs: Certified Information Systems Manager (CISM), Certified in the Governance of Enterprise Information Technology (CGEIT), and Certified in Risk and Information Systems Control (CRISC). Each of these credentials requires relevant prior work experience in addition to the successful completion of a certification exam. Readers should note that ISACA offers a "grandfathering" program for its credentialing programs when newly established, in which some candidates are able to qualify for the credential without taking an exam by submitting evidence and attestation of significant relevant experience. Both the CISA and CISM are accredited under ISO/IEC 17024 [17], an international standard specifying criteria for individual certification programs. The CGEIT and CRISC are the most recently launched ISACA certifications, developed partly as a result of ISACA's increased focus on standards and practices for IT governance and risk management.

> Individuals certified by more than one organization may be obligated to follow different audit standards or requirements to meet the expectations of the credential-issuing body. For example, someone holding a CIA from IIA and a CISA from ISACA is ostensibly required to use both IIA's mandatory guidance within the IPPF and ISACA's IT Audit and Assurance Guidelines. Fortunately for such individuals, the audit standards and guidance published by many of the leading organizations overlap significantly and have more in common than in conflict, due in part to efforts of the standards development organizations to adhere to GAAS.

International Organization for Standardization

The International Organization for Standardization (ISO) is the largest standards development organization in the world, having published nearly 20,000 standards in its 65-year history covering a vast array of scientific, technical, and business subjects [18]. The ISO is an independent organization with membership composed of national standards bodies of more than 160 countries (including the American National Standards Institute, the British Standards Institute, the Standards Council of Canada, and Standards Australia). The full scope of the ISO's standards development activities is beyond the scope of this book, but it oversees over 250 technical committees organized by subject matter that work to develop, refine, and promote ISO standards. Joint Task Committee 1 focuses on standardization in information technology and is responsible for ISO standards relevant to IT auditing, information security, risk management, and quality management.

Audit standards

ISO's 27000 series of standards address various aspects of information security management, particularly including a comprehensive control framework used by organizations in a variety of industries and sectors and referenced in leading IT management frameworks such as COBIT and COSO. ISO/IEC 27001 specifies an information security management system (ISMS) in the form of 12 sets of categorized security requirements that organizations adopting the ISMS must implement [19]. The ISMS defined in ISO/IEC 27001 is a not a technical system at all, but an integrated set of management processes and a framework for developing security requirements and selecting security controls to satisfy those requirements. The information security management code of practice described in ISO/IEC 27002, which identifies 133 controls across organized into 11 clauses (categories) collectively define information security practices relevant to a system or an organization [20]. ISO/IEC 27007 provides guidelines for auditors evaluating organizations' ISMSs against ISO/IEC 27001 [21]. ISO publishes two separately numbered but substantially similar standards on risk management: ISO/IEC 27005, which explicitly addresses information security risk management [22], and ISO 31000, a group of standards representing a structure and associated processes and guidance for organization-wide risk management [23]. Many organizations follow ISO standards related to quality management, most familiarly including the ISO 9000 family of standards and particularly ISO 9001 for quality management systems [24] and ISO/IEC 20000 for service management systems [25]. ISO 19011 provides guidelines for auditing quality management systems such as those organizations implement following ISO 9001 [26].

Government Accountability Office

The US GAO is an independent, nonpartisan agency positioned within the legislative branch of government that serves as the authoritative American institution auditing government organizations. Its work focuses on reviewing government spending and the effectiveness (or lack thereof) of various government programs and agencies, including auditing agency operations to assess whether federal funding is being used properly, cost-effectively, and efficiently [27]. The GAO conducts reviews, investigations, audits, and other investigations at the request of Congress or to satisfy legal requirements. With specific respect to auditing government agencies, GAO develops and maintains authoritative Government Auditing Standards (GAS) [28]—familiarly known as the Yellow Book—as well as formal audit procedures for government information systems and their controls through the Federal Information System Control Audit Manual (FISCAM) [29].

Audit standards

The generally accepted government auditing standards described in the Yellow Book provide a structural framework and explicit standards for conducting financial or performance audits of government organizations and nongovernment entities that receive government awards. The general accounting standards include four general standards—independence, professional judgment, competence, and quality control and assurance—and specify additional standards for financial audits, performance audits, attestation engagements, audit field work, and reporting [28]. While these standards have much in common with practices and guidance produced by nongovernment-focused national and international standards bodies, the GAS are rarely applied outside government-focused audits.

Auditors' oversight bodies

The increased scrutiny associated with auditing and financial accounting related to public companies led to the creation of oversight bodies responsible for ensuring the integrity of audit and accounting practices in countries under their jurisdiction. The two most prominent examples of these bodies are the US Public Company Accounting Oversight Board (PCAOB) and the European Community's European Group of Auditors' Oversight Bodies (EGAOB). The EGAOB has responsibility for all member countries in the European Union and coordinates the oversight activities of statutory audit firms. It also provides input to the European Commission on implementation aspects of the 2006 Directive on Statutory Audits.

Created as a provision of the Sarbanes–Oxley Act of 2002, the PCAOB is a US nonprofit corporation that oversees auditing of public companies by monitoring auditing firms that perform public company audits and by promoting accurate and independent audit reports [30]. Consistent with the language in the Sarbanes–Oxley Act, the PCAOB emphasizes external oversight and insists on auditor independence. The PCAOB has five members, appointed by the Securities and Exchange Commission (under whose jurisdiction the PCAOB falls) in consultation with the Federal Reserve Board of Governors and the Treasury Secretary. In order to conduct audits of publicly traded firms, accounting firms must register with the PCAOB. The Board maintains a publicly accessible registry of accounting firms that have applied for registration.

Audit standards

The EGAOB endorsed the ISAs for use in statutory audits of companies within the European Community. The PCAOB adopted 16 auditing standards and a variety of interim standards for use in audit activities for which the Board has oversight authority. The auditing standards have been formally approved by the Securities and Exchange Commission (SEC), while the interim standards comprise a set of GAAS identify by the AICPA in its SAS No. 95. None of the auditing standards or interim standards specifically addresses information technology auditing, but in general these standards apply to all types of auditing conducted on public companies.

A significant proportion of prominent audit standards and guidance is freely available to individuals and organizations that want to use it. Organizations interested in adopting cohesive or comprehensive sets of audit standards for some standards organizations may find however that more recent publications must be purchased. Individual or corporate membership in many of these organizations offers access to a much wider array of standards and documentation, typically at no additional cost or at reduced rates for members.

Organizations offering standards, guidance, or certifications relevant to IT auditing

Consistent with the idea proposed in Chapter 1 that capable and effective IT auditors may come from a variety of functional and technical backgrounds, many IT standards, practices, and certifications not explicitly about auditing are nonetheless relevant to IT audits and may be useful to organizations considering different audit approaches or evaluating the qualifications of personnel to perform audits. The organizations listed below develop and disseminate various types of IT standards, practices, procedures, and guidelines and operate certification programs covering skills and subject areas applicable to different kinds of IT audits.

SANS Institute

The SANS Institute is an information security-focused (the name SANS stands for SysAdmin, Audit, Network, and Security) research and education organization that offers extensive training classes and a wide range of technical certifications, most organized under the Global Information Assurance Certification (GIAC) program. Its training programs include workshops and multiday courses targeted at professional education and two information security focused master's degree programs. The organization also conducts ongoing security research and operates an Internet monitoring program known as the Internet Storm Center. SANS also contributed to a collaborative effort with the US Department of Defense and National Security Agency and numerous public and private sector organizations to identify and prioritize the most effective security controls from among the hundreds defined in federal guidance and control frameworks. The result of this effort was a recommended list of 20 security controls, originally known as the Consensus Audit Guidelines and currently published as the Twenty Security Controls for Effective Cyber Defense [31]. The use of the term *audit* to describe these security controls stems from their applicability to formal security control assessments required for federal information systems. The 20 controls include:

1. Inventory of Authorized and Unauthorized Devices
2. Inventory of Authorized and Unauthorized Software
3. Secure Configurations for Hardware and Software on Mobile Devices, Laptops, Workstations, and Servers
4. Continuous Vulnerability Assessment and Remediation
5. Malware Defenses
6. Application Software Security
7. Wireless Device Control
8. Data Recovery Capability
9. Security Skills Assessment and Appropriate Training to Fill Gaps
10. Secure Configurations for Network Devices such as Firewalls, Routers, and Switches

11. Limitation and Control of Network Ports, Protocols, and Services
12. Controlled Use of Administrative Privileges
13. Boundary Defense
14. Maintenance, Monitoring, and Analysis of Audit Logs
15. Controlled Access Based on the Need to Know
16. Account Monitoring and Control
17. Data Loss Prevention
18. Incident Response and Management
19. Secure Network Engineering
20. Penetration Tests and Red Team Exercises

Certifications

SANS offers training and certification in subject areas including security administration, audit, forensics, management, software security, legal, and advanced security expertise. The certification most directly relevant to IT auditing is the GIAC Systems and Network Auditor (GSNA), which focuses on technical knowledge and procedural capabilities necessary to perform information system audits. GIAC credentials are also available in several specialized technical domains, including assessing and auditing wireless networks, penetration testing, computer forensics, and ISO 27000 implementation and compliance.

Software Engineering Institute

The Software Engineering Institute (SEI) is a research and development organization within Carnegie Mellon University that focuses on improving technical and procedural aspects of software engineering and information systems. The SEI's work spans a variety of technology, computing, performance, management, and infrastructure domains, producing solutions in acquisition, process management, risk management, security, software development, and system design [32]. Organizations seeking guidance related to risk management or technical process improvement or looking to have the maturity of their internal capabilities assessed may find SEI's work highly applicable, particularly its capability maturity model integration (CMMI). CMMI is a five-level model measuring the extent to which an organization's processes operate effectively or can be improved. The SEI performs CMMI appraisals that assign a maturity level ranging from 1 to 5, corresponding to ratings of "initial," "repeatable," "defined," "quantitatively managed," and "optimizing." SEI uses a standardized appraisal methodology to perform organizational assessments, known as the standard CMMI appraisal method for process improvement (SCAMPI). These appraisals constitute a form of external audit, where the focus of the audit can be a single project or an entire organization (CMMI maturity levels are typically assigned at the organization level). SEI also trains and certifies individuals to be CMMI instructors, team leads, and appraisers.

Table 10.3 IEEE Standards Applicable to IT Audits [33]

Standard	Title	Date
730	Standard for Software Quality Assurance Plans	2002
828	Standard for Configuration Management in Systems and Software	2012
829	Standard for Software and System Test Documentation	2008
1012	Standard for System and Software Verification and Validation	2012
1028	Standard for Software Reviews and Audits	2008
1074	Standard for Developing a Software Project Life Cycle Process	2006
1220	Standard for Application and Management of the Systems Engineering Process	2005
16085	Standard for Software Engineering—Software Life Cycle Processes—Risk Management	2006

Institute of Electrical and Electronics Engineers

The Institute of Electrical and Electronics Engineers (IEEE) is a global nonprofit professional organization focused on technological innovation that conducts research and disseminates research results and other information through journal and magazine publication and through conferences and other knowledge-sharing events. The IEEE also develops and publishes technical standards on a variety of topics through the IEEE Standards Association.

Table 10.3 lists IEEE standards applicable to different types of IT auditing or audit-related processes such as system engineering, configuration management, quality assurance, and independent verification and validation.

International Information Systems Security Certification Consortium

The International Information Systems Security Certification Consortium (ISC)^2 is a global, nonprofit professional association with more than 90,000 members focused on training and certifying information security professionals [34]. The consortium's focus is on information security education and information dissemination, centered around the (ISC)^2 Common Body of Knowledge and, especially, the 10 security domains serving as the foundation for the Certified Information Systems Security Professional (CISSP)—access control; telecommunications and network security; information security governance and risk management; software development security; cryptography; security architecture and design; operations security; business continuity and disaster recovery planning; legal, regulations, investigations and compliance; and physical and environmental security. Knowledge and experience in these subject areas provides substantial support for various aspects of IT auditing, particularly with respect to information systems security assessments.

even loss of the ability to process credit card transactions (and therefore to accept credit cards from customers) [39]. Organizations covered by PCI DSS are also subject to compliance assessments—a specialized type of external audit performed by qualified security assessors designated by the PCI Security Standards Council.

Computer forensics and penetration testing

The disciplines of computer forensics and penetration testing incorporate numerous systems, network, software, and technical evaluation tools and procedures that IT auditors can often use when evaluating information systems or other components in their organizations. Organizations offering training and certification in these areas include:

- The International Council of E-Commerce Consultants (EC-Council), which administers the Certified Ethical Hacker (CEH), one of the best-known penetration testing credentials, and the Computer Hacking Forensic Investigation (CHFI) credential.
- The Information Assurance Certification Review Board (IACRB), which offers several information security-related certifications including the Certified Penetration Tester (CPT), Certified Expert Penetration Tester (CEPT), Certified Application Security Specialist (CASS), and Certified Computer Forensics Examiner (CCFE).
- The International Society of Forensic Computer Examiners (ISFCE), which offers the Certified Computer Examiner (CCE) credential.
- The International Association of Computer Investigative Specialists (IACIS), which offers the Certified Forensic Computer Examiner (CFCE) credential.
- Offensive Security offers several security certifications, including the Offensive Security Certified Professional credential in penetration testing, that require candidates to successfully complete hands-on exercises in a live testing environment rather than the multiple-choice question format typical of most certification exams.

While penetration testing is increasingly used as part of periodic security assessments or continuous monitoring activities, forensic investigations typically occur only after some sort of security incident, intrusion, or compromise. Depending on the scope and level of rigor sought for system-level IT audits, the tools and techniques used in computer forensics and penetration testing may help auditors assess the effectiveness of security controls and identify weaknesses that would be reported in audit findings.

Relevant source material

The most easily accessible information on most standards development and certification organizations is the web sites of the respective organizations. To obtain standards and guidelines and related documentation for use in their own environments, organizations can typically find most or all of the information they need in electronic document form at little or no charge, although some organizations limit free distribution to members of their organizations and others, like the ISO, typically charge fees for their standards. The price to obtain standards documentation may be easy for organizations to justify when compared against the time, material, and resource costs for their IT audit activities. Leading sources of IT audit-related standards and guidance include:

- AICPA Statements on Auditing Standards [2].
- IIA International Standards for the Professional Practice of Internal Auditing [40].
- INTOSAI International Standards of Supreme Audit Institutions [41].
- IFAC/IAASB Accounting Standards [42].
- ISACA Standards for IT Audit and Assurance [15].

Summary

This chapter identified and summarized some of the major organizations engaged in standards development and audit guidance used in IT auditing and in offering professional or technical certifications in auditing and related domains. Recognizing that there is a wide variety of potential sources of standards, documentation, and personnel to perform IT auditing activities, the information presented in this chapter should help organizations determine the most applicable standards and personnel qualifications for their IT audit needs and should serve as a reference to helpful sources of guidance.

References

[1] About the AICPA [Internet]; Durham, NC: American Institute of Certified Public Auditors [cited 2013 May 4]. Available from: <http://www.aicpa.org/About/Pages/About.aspx>.

[2] Statements on Auditing Standards [Internet]; Durham, NC: American Institute of Certified Public Auditors [cited 2013 May 4]. Available from: <http://www.aicpa.org/Research/Standards/AuditAttest/Pages/SAS.aspx>.

[3] Service Organization Control (SOC) Reports [Internet]; Durham, NC: American Institute of Certified Public Auditors [cited 2013 May 4]. Available from: <http://www.aicpa.org/InterestAreas/FRC/AssuranceAdvisoryServices/Pages/SORHome.aspx>.

[4] Become a CPA [Internet]; Durham, NC: American Institute of Certified Public Auditors [cited 2013 May 4]. Available from: <http://www.aicpa.org/BecomeACPA/Pages/BecomeaCPA.aspx>.

[5] The CITP Credential [Internet]; Durham, NC: American Institute of Certified Public Auditors [cited 2013 May 4]. Available from: <http://www.aicpa.org/InterestAreas/InformationTechnology/Membership/Pages/CITPOverview.aspx>.

[6] About the Institute of Internal Auditors [Internet]; Altamonte Springs, FL: Institute of Internal Auditors [cited 2013 May 4]. Available from: <https://na.theiia.org/about-us/Pages/About-The-Institute-of-Internal-Auditors.aspx>.

[7]   CIA Eligibility Requirements [Internet]; Altamonte Springs, FL: Institute of Internal Auditors [cited 2013 May 4]. Available from: <https://na.theiia.org/certification/CIA-Certification/Pages/Eligibility-Requirements.aspx>.

[8]   INTOSAI.org: About Us [Internet]; Vienna: International Organization of Supreme Audit Institutions [cited 2013 May 4]. Available from: <http://www.intosai.org/about-us.html>.

[9]   International Organization of Supreme Audit Institutions. Information system security review methodology. Copenhagen, DK: INTOSAI Professional Standards Committee; 1995. ISSAI 5310.

[10] Organization Overview | IFAC [Internet]; New York, NY: International Federation of Accountants [cited 2013 May 4]. Available from: <http://www.ifac.org/about-ifac/organization-overview>.

[11] About IAASB [Internet]; New York, NY: International Federation of Accountants [cited 2013 May 4]. Available from: <http://www.ifac.org/auditing-assurance/about-iaasb>.

[12] Clarity of IAASB Standards [Internet]; New York, NY: International Federation of Accountants [cited 2013 May 4]. Available from: <http://www.ifac.org/auditing-assurance/projects/clarity-iaasb-standards-completed>.

[13] Directive of the European Parliament and of the Council on Statutory Audits of Annual Accounts and Consolidated Accounts, Directive 2006/43/EC; 2006 May.

[14] About ISACA [Internet]; Rolling Meadows, IL: ISACA [cited 2013 May 4]. Available from: <http://www.isaca.org/about-isaca/Pages/default.aspx>.

[15] Standards for IS Auditing [Internet]; Rolling Meadows, IL: ISACA [cited 2013 May 4]. Available from: <http://www.isaca.org/Knowledge-Center/Standards/Pages/Standards-for-IT-Audit-and-Assurance-English-.aspx>.

[16] ISACA Certification: IT Audit, Security, Governance and Risk [Internet]; Rolling Meadows, IL: ISACA [cited 2013 May 4]. Available from: <http://www.isaca.org/CERTIFICATION/Pages/default.aspx>.

[17] ISO/IEC 17024:2012. Conformity assessment—General requirements for bodies operating certification of persons.

[18] About ISO [Internet]; Geneva: International Organization for Standardization [cited 2013 May 4]. Available from: <http://www.iso.org/iso/home/about.htm>.

[19] ISO/IEC 27001:2005. Information—Security techniques—Information security management systems—Requirements.

[20] ISO/IEC 27002:2005. Information technology—Security techniques—Code of practice for information security management.

[21] ISO/IEC 27007:2011. Information—Security techniques—Guidelines for information security management systems auditing.

[22] ISO/IEC 27005:2011. Information technology—Security techniques—Information security risk management.

[23] ISO/IEC 31000:2009. Risk management—Principles and guidelines.

[24] ISO 9001:2008. Quality management systems—requirements.

[25] ISO/IEC 20000-1:2011. Information technology—Service management—Part 1: Service management system requirements.

[26] ISO 19011:2011. Guidelines for auditing management systems.

[27] About GAO [Internet]; Washington, DC: U.S. Government Accountability Office [cited 2013 May 4]. Available from: <http://www.gao.gov/about/index.html>.

[28] Government Auditing Standards. Washington, DC: Government Accountability Office; 2011 December.

[29]   Federal information system controls audit manual (FISCAM). Washington, DC: Government Accountability Office; 2009 February.

[30]   About the PCAOB [Internet]; Washington, DC: Public Company Accounting Oversight Board [cited 2013 May 4]. Available from: <http://pcaobus.org/About/Pages/default.aspx>.

[31]   CSIC: Twenty Critical Security Controls [Internet]; Bethesda, MD: SANS Institute [cited 2013 May 4]. Available from: <http://www.sans.org/critical-security-controls/>.

[32]   About Us | Overview [Internet]; Pittsburgh, PA: Carnegie Mellon University [cited 2013 May 4]. Available from: <http://www.sei.cmu.edu/about>.

[33]   The IEEE Standards Association [Internet]; Piscataway, NJ: Institute of Electrical and Electronics Engineers [cited 2013 May 4]. Available from http://standards.ieee.org

[34]   About (ISC)^2 [Internet]; Vienna, VA: International Information Systems Security Certification Consortium [cited 2013 May 4]. Available from: <https://www.isc2.org/aboutus/default.aspx>.

[35]   CISSP—Certified Information Systems Security Professional [Internet]; Vienna, VA: International Information Systems Security Certification Consortium [cited 2013 May 4]. Available from: <https://www.isc2.org/cissp/default.aspx>.

[36]   About ASQ [Internet]; Milwaukee, WI: American Society for Quality [cited 2013 May 4]. Available from: <http://asq.org/about-asq/who-we-are/index.html>.

[37]   Quality Certification [Internet]; Milwaukee, WI: American Society for Quality [cited 2013 May 4]. Available from: <http://prdweb.asq.org/certification/control/index>.

[38]   Category: OWASP Project [Internet]; Bel Air, MD: OWASP Foundation [cited 2013 May 4]. Available from: <https://www.owasp.org/index.php/Category:OWASP_Project>

[39]   PCI SSC Data Security Standards Overview [Internet]; Wakefield, MA: PCI Security Standards Council [cited 2013 May 4]. Available from: <https://www.pcisecurity-standards.org/security_standards/index.php>.

[40]   International standards for the professional practice of internal auditing. Altamonte Springs, FL: Institute of Internal Auditors; 2012 October.

[41]   International Standards of Supreme Audit Institutions (ISSAI) [Internet]; Vienna: International Organization of Supreme Audit Institutions [cited 2013 May 4]. Available from: <http://www.issai.org/composite-347.htm>.

[42]   Accounting Standards | Governance | Publications and Resources [Internet]; New York, NY: International Federation of Accountants [cited 2013 May 4]. Available from: <http://www.ifac.org/publications-resources>.

References

Legislation and Statutes

[1] American Recovery and Reinvestment Act of 2009, Pub. L. No. 111-5, 123 Stat. 115.

[2] California Security Breach Information Act, S.B. 1386; 2002.

[3] Computer Fraud and Abuse Act of 1986, Pub. L. No. 99-474, 100 Stat. 1213.

[4] Directive of the European Parliament and of the Council on the protection of individuals with regard to the processing of personal data and on the free movement of such data, Directive 95/46/EC; 1995 October.

[5] Directive of the European Parliament and of the Council on statutory audits of annual accounts and consolidated accounts, Directive 2006/43/EC; 2006 May.

[6] E-Government Act of 2002, Pub. L. No. 107-347, 116 Stat. 2899.

[7] Electronic Communications Privacy Act of 1986, Pub. L. No. 99-508, 100 Stat. 1848.

[8] Federal Information Security Management Act of 2002, Pub. L. No. 107-347, 116 Stat. 2946.

[9] Financial Services Modernization Act of 1999, Pub. L. No. 106-102, 113 Stat. 1338.

[10] Health Insurance Portability and Accountability Act of 1996, Pub. L. No. 104-191, 110 Stat. 1936.

[11] Health Information Technology for Economic and Clinical Health Act of 2009, Pub. L. No. 111-5, 123 Stat. 226.

[12] Information Technology Management Reform Act of 1996, Pub. L. No. 104-106, 110 Stat. 679.

[13] Inspector General Act of 1978, Pub. L. No. 95-452, 92 Stat. 1101.

[14] Personal Information Protection and Electronic Documents Act, S.C. 2000, c.5; 2000.

[15] Privacy Act of 1974, Pub. L. No. 93-579, 88 Stat. 1896.

[16] Proposal for a regulation of the European Parliament and of the Council on the protection of individuals with regard to the processing of personal data and on the free movement of such data (General Data Protection Regulation), COD 2012/0011; 2012 December.

[17] Sarbanes–Oxley Act of 2002, Pub. L. No. 107-204, 116 Stat. 745.

[18] Securities and Exchange Commission; Management's report on internal control over financial reporting and certification of disclosure in exchange act periodic reports; final rule. 68 Fed. Reg. 36636; 2003.

[19] Securities and Exchange Commission; Standards related to listed company audit committees; final rule. 68 Fed. Reg. 18788; 2003.

[20] Securities and Exchange Commission; Strengthening the Commission's requirements regarding auditor independence; final rule. 68 Fed. Reg. 6006; 2003.

[21] Securities Exchange Act of 1934, Pub. L. No. 73-291, 48 Stat. 881.

[22] Single Audit Act of 1984, Pub. L. No. 98-502, 98 Stat. 2327.

[23] Standards for the protection of personal information of residents of the commonwealth, 201 CMR 17.00; 2010.

[24] The T.J. Hooper (1932) 60F.2d 737.

[25] *United States v. Carroll Towing* (1947) 159F.2d 169.

Books, Articles, Instructions, and Guidance

[1] American Institute of Certified Public Accountants Reporting on controls at a service organization relevant to security, availability, processing integrity, confidentiality, or privacy. Durham, NC: American Institute of Certified Public Accountants; 2012.

[2] American Institute of Certified Public Accountants Service organizations: reporting on controls at a service organization relevant to user entities' internal control over financial reporting. Durham, NC: American Institute of Certified Public Accountants; 2013.

[3] Office of Management and Budget Audits of states, local governments, and non-profit organizations. Washington, DC: Office of Management and Budget; 2007. [OMB Circular A-133].

[4] Barney JB, Clark DN. Resource-based theory. Oxford, UK: Oxford University Press; 2007.

[5] Bazerman MH, Moore D. Judgment in managerial decision making. Hoboken, NJ: John Wiley & Sons; 2009.

[6] Board of the International Federation of Accountants Statement of membership obligations. New York, NY: International Federation of Accountants; 2012.

[7] Cartlidge A, Hanna A, Rudd C, Macfarlane I, Windebank J, Rance S. An introductory overview of ITIL® V3. Wokingham, UK: IT Service Management Forum, UK Chapter; 2007.

[8] Cascarino RE. Auditor's guide to IT auditing Hoboken, NJ, 2nd ed. : John Wiley & Sons; 2012.

[9] Chambers A, Rand G. The operational auditing handbook: auditing business and IT processes. West Sussex, UK: John Wiley & Sons; 2010.

[10] International Ethics Standards Board Code of ethics for professional accountants. New York, NY: International Ethics Standards Board; 2009.

[11] Committee of Sponsoring Organizations of the Treadway Commission Enterprise risk management—Integrated framework. New York, NY: Committee of Sponsoring Organizations of the Treadway Commission; 2004.

[12] Committee of Sponsoring Organizations of the Treadway Commission Internal control—Integrated framework. New York, NY: Committee of Sponsoring Organizations of the Treadway Commission; 2013.

[13] Crouhy M, Galai D, Mark R. The essentials of risk management. New York, NY: McGraw-Hill; 2006.

[14] Davis C, Schiller M. IT auditing: using controls to protect information assets, 2nd ed. New York, NY: McGraw-Hill; 2011.

[15] Deming WE. Out of the crisis. Cambridge, MA: MIT Center for Advanced Educational Services; 1986.

[16] Internal Revenue Service Examination of returns, appeal rights, and claims for refund. Washington, DC: Internal Revenue Service; 2008. IRS Publication 556.

[17] Office of Management and Budget FEA consolidated reference model version 2.3. Washington, DC: Office of Management and Budget; 2007.

[18] Government Accountability Office Federal information system controls audit manual (FISCAM). Washington, DC: Government Accountability Office; 2009.

[19] Government Accountability Office Government auditing standards. Washington, DC: Government Accountability Office; 2011.

[20] Office of Management and Budget Guidance on Exhibit 300—planning, budgeting, acquisition, and management of it capital assets. Washington, DC: Office of Management and Budget; 2011.

[21] National Institute of Standards and Technology Guide for assessing the security controls in federal information systems and organizations. Gaithersburg, MD: National Institute of Standards and Technology, Computer Security Division; 2010. [Special Publication 800-53A revision 1].

[22] National Institute of Standards and Technology Guide for conducting risk assessments. Gaithersburg, MD: National Institute of Standards and Technology, Computer Security Division; 2012. [Special Publication 800-30 revision 1].

[23] International Auditing and Assurance Standards Board Handbook of international quality control, auditing review, other assurance, and related services pronouncements. New York, NY: International Auditing and Assurance Standards Board; 2012.

[24] Institute of Internal Auditors International Professional Practices Framework (IPPF) 2013 Edition. Altamonte Springs, FL: Institute of Internal Auditors; 2013.

[25] ISACA. COBIT 5: a business framework for the governance and management of enterprise IT; Rolling Meadows, IL: ISACA; 2012.

[26] ISACA COBIT 5 for assurance. Rolling Meadows, IL: ISACA; 2013.

[27] ISACA ITAF: a professional practices framework for IS audit/assurance, 2nd ed. Rolling Meadows, IL: ISACA; 2013.

[28] Federal Financial Institutions Examination Council IT examination handbook. Arlington, VA: Federal Financial Institutions Examination Council; 2012.

[29] IT Governance Institute Board briefing on IT governance, 2nd ed. Rolling Meadows, IL: IT Governance Institute; 2003.

[30] IT Governance Institute COBIT 4.1. Rolling Meadows, IL: IT Governance Institute; 2007.

[31] Cabinet Office. ITIL glossary and abbreviations. London, UK: Cabinet Office; 2011.

[32] Kissel R., Stine K., Scholl M., Rossman H., Fahlsing J., Gulick J. Security considerations in the system development life cycle. Gaithersburg, MD: National Institute of Standards and Technology, Computer Security Division; 2008. [Special Publication 800-64 revision 2].

[33] National Institute of Standards and Technology Managing information security risk: organization, mission, and information system view. Gaithersburg, MD: National Institute of Standards and Technology, Computer Security Division; 2011. [Special Publication 800-39].

[34] Moeller R.R. IT audit, control, and security. Hoboken, NJ: John Wiley & sons; 2010.

[35] Organisation for Economic Cooperation and Development OECD guidelines on the protection of privacy and transborder flows of personal data. Paris, France: Organisation for Economic Cooperation and Development; 1980.

[36] Orr A.T. Introduction to the ITIL service lifecycle. London, UK: Cabinet Office; 2011.

[37] Parasuraman A, Zeithaml VA, Barry LL. SERVQUAL: a multiple-item scale for measuring consumer perceptions of service quality. J Retailing 1988;64(1):12–40.

[38] Project Management Institute A guide to the project management body of knowledge, 4th ed. Newtown Square, PA: Project Management Institute; 2008.

[39] National Institute of Standards and Technology. {tag as book}Recommended security controls for federal information systems and organizations. Gaithersburg, MD: National Institute of Standards and Technology, Computer Security Division; 2009. [Special Publication 800-53 revision 3].

[40] Russell JP, editor. The ASQ auditing handbook (4th ed.). Milwaukee, WI: ASQ Quality Press; 2013.

[41] National Institute of Standards and Technology Security and privacy controls for federal information systems and organizations. Gaithersburg, MD: National Institute of

Standards and Technology, Computer Security Division; 2013. [Special Publication 800-53 revision 4].

[42] Senft S, Gallegos F, Davis A. Information technology control and audit Boca Raton, FL, 4th ed. : CRC Press; 2013.

[43] Teece D. Dynamic capabilities and strategic management. New York, NY: Oxford University Press; 2009.

[44] VA Office of the Inspector General Audit of veteran-owned and service-disabled veteran-owned small business programs. Washington, DC: Department of Veterans Affairs; 2011. Available from: http://www.va.gov/oig/52/reports/2011/VAOIG-10-02436-234.pdf.

[45] Wrightson MT, Caldwell SL. Further refinements needed to assess risks and prioritize protective measures at ports and other critical infrastructure. Report to Congressional Requesters. Washington, DC: Government Accountability Office; 2005. GAO 06-91.

Standards

[1] American Institute of Certified Public Accountants A firm's system of quality control. Durham, NC: American Institute of Certified Public Accountants; 2012. [Statement on Quality Control Standards 8].

[2] International Auditing and Assurance Standards Board Assurance reports on controls at a service organization. New York, NY: International Auditing and Assurance Standards Board; 2011. [International Standards for Assurance Engagements 3402].

[3] International Federation of Accountants Audit considerations relating to an entity using a service organization. New York, NY: International Federation of Accountants; 2012. [International Standard on Auditing 402].

[4] Object Management Group Business process maturity model, version 1.0. Needham, MA: Object Management Group; 2008.

[5] Software Engineering Institute CERT resilience management model, version 1.0. Pittsburgh, PA: Software Engineering Institute; 2010.

[6] Software Engineering Institute CMMI for acquisition, version 1.3. Pittsburgh, PA: Software Engineering Institute; 2010.

[7] Software Engineering Institute CMMI for development, version 1.3. Pittsburgh, PA: Software Engineering Institute; 2010.

[8] Software Engineering Institute CMMI for services, version 1.3. Pittsburgh, PA: Software Engineering Institute; 2010.

[9] Cloud Security Alliance Cloud controls matrix version 1.4. Seattle, WA: Cloud Security Alliance; 2013.

[10] American Institute of Certified Public Accountants Compliance audits. Durham, NC: American Institute of Certified Public Accountants, Auditing Standards Board; 2009. [Statement on Auditing Standards 117].

[11] Electronic Industries Alliance Earned value management systems. Arlington, VA: Electronic Industries Alliance; 1998. [ANSI/EIA 748].

[12] General Services Administration FedRAMP security controls baseline version 1.1. Washington, DC: General Services Administration; 2012.

[13] American Institute of Certified Public Accountants Generally accepted auditing standards. Durham, NC: American Institute of Certified Public Accountants, Auditing Standards Board; 2001. [Statement on Auditing Standards No. 95].

[14] IEEE P730-2002 Standard for software quality assurance processes. New York, NY: Institute of Electrical and Electronics Engineers; 2002.

[15] International Organization of Supreme Audit Institutions Information system security review methodology. Copenhagen, DK: INTOSAI Professional Standards Committee; 1995. [ISSAI 5310].

[16] Institute of Internal Auditors International standards for the professional practice of internal auditing. Altamonte Springs, FL: Institute of Internal Auditors; 2012.

[17] ISA 62443/IEC 62443-1 Security for industrial automation and control systems. Research Triangle Park, NC: International Society for Automation; 2007.

[18] ISO Guide 73:2009. Risk management—Vocabulary.

[19] ISO 9000:2005. Quality management—Fundamentals and vocabulary.

[20] ISO 9001:2008. Quality management systems—requirements.

[21] ISO 9004:2009. Managing for the sustained success of an organization—A quality management approach.

[22] ISO 13485:2003. Medical devices—Quality management systems—Requirements for regulatory purposes.

[23] ISO 14001:2004. Environmental management systems—Requirements with guidance for use.

[24] ISO/IEC 7498-1:1994. Information technology—Open systems interconnection—Basic reference model: the basic model.

[25] ISO/IEC 12207:2008. Systems and software engineering—Software life cycle processes.

[26] ISO/IEC 15026:2011. Systems and software engineering—Systems and software assurance.

[27] ISO/IEC 15288:2008. Systems and software engineering—System life cycle processes.

[28] ISO/IEC 15408:2009. Information technology—Security techniques—Evaluation criteria for IT security.

[29] ISO/IEC 15504:2004. Information technology—Process assessment.

[30] ISO/IEC 17021:2011. Conformity assessment—Requirements for bodies providing audit and certification of management systems.

[31] ISO/IEC 17024:2012. Conformity assessment—General requirements for bodies operating certification of persons.

[32] ISO 19011:2011. Guidelines for auditing management systems.

[33] ISO/IEC 20000-1:2011. Information technology—Service management—Part 1: Service management system requirements.

[34] ISO/IEC 20000-4:2011. Information technology—Service management—Part 4: Process reference model.

[35] ISO/IEC 27000:2009. Information technology overview and vocabulary.

[36] ISO/IEC 27001:2005. Information—Security techniques—Information security management systems—Requirements.

[37] ISO/IEC 27002:2005. Information technology—Security techniques—Code of practice for information security management.

[38] ISO/IEC 27003:2010. Information technology—Security techniques—Information security management system implementation guidance.

[39] ISO/IEC 27004:2009. Information technology—Security techniques—Measurement.

[40] ISO/IEC 27005:2011. Information technology—Security techniques—Information security risk management.

[41] ISO/IEC 27006:2011. Information technology—Security techniques—Requirements for bodies providing audit and certification of information security management systems.

[42] ISO/IEC 27007:2011. Information—Security techniques—Guidelines for information security management systems auditing.

[43] ISO/IEC TR 27008:2011. Information technology—Security techniques—Guidelines for auditors on information security controls.

[44] ISO/IEC 27014:2013. Information technology—Security techniques—Governance of information security.

[45] ISO/IEC 31000:2009. Risk management—Principles and guidelines.

[46] ISO/IEC 31010:2009. Risk management—Risk assessment techniques.

[47] ISO/IEC 38500:2008. Corporate governance of information technology.

[48] ISO/IEC TR 24748-1:2010. Systems and software engineering—Life cycle management.

[49] ISO/IEC/IEEE 42010:2011. Systems and software engineering—Architecture description.

[50] ISO/TS 16949:2009. Quality management systems—Particular requirements for the application of ISO 9001:2008 for automotive production and relevant service part organizations.

[51] ISO/TS 29001:2010. Petroleum, petrochemical and natural gas industries—Sector-specific quality management systems—Requirements for product and service supply organizations.

[52] International Federation of Accountants Overall objectives of the independent auditor and the conduct of an audit in accordance with international standards on auditing. New York, NY: International Federation of Accountants; 2012. [International Standard on Auditing 200].

[53] American Institute of Certified Public Accountants Reporting on controls at a service organization. Durham, NC: American Institute of Certified Public Accountants; 2011. [Statement on Standards for Attestation Engagements No. 16].

Online Sources

[1] About ASQ [Internet]; Milwaukee, WI: American Society for Quality [cited 2013 May 4]. Available from: <http://asq.org/about-asq/who-we-are/index.html>.

[2] About GAO [Internet]; Washington, DC: U.S. Government Accountability Office [cited 2013 May 4]. Available from: <http://www.gao.gov/about/index.html>.

[3] About IAASB [Internet]; New York, NY: International Federation of Accountants [cited 2013 May 4]. Available from: <http://www.ifac.org/auditing-assurance/about-iaasb>.

[4] About ISACA [Internet]; Rolling Meadows, IL: ISACA [cited 2013 May 4]. Available from: <http://www.isaca.org/about-isaca/Pages/default.aspx>.

[5] About (ISC)2 [Internet]; Vienna, VA: International Information Systems Security Certification Consortium [cited 2013 May 4]. Available from: <https://www.isc2.org/aboutus/default.aspx>.

[6] About ISO [Internet]; Geneva: International Organization for Standardization [cited 2013 May 4]. Available from: <http://www.iso.org/iso/home/about.htm>.

[7] About the AICPA [Internet]; Durham, NC: American Institute of Certified Public Accountants [cited 2013 May 4]. Available from: <http://www.aicpa.org/About/Pages/About.aspx>.

[8] About the Institute of Internal Auditors [Internet]; Altamonte Springs, FL: Institute of Internal Auditors [cited 2013 May 4]. Available from: <https://na.theiia.org/about-us/Pages/About-The-Institute-of-Internal-Auditors.aspx>.

[9] About the PCAOB [Internet]; Washington, DC: Public Company Accounting Oversight Board [cited 2013 May 4]. Available from: <http://pcaobus.org/About/Pages/default.aspx>.

[10] About Us | Overview [Internet]; Pittsburgh, PA: Carnegie Mellon University [cited 2013 May 4]. Available from: <http://www.sei.cmu.edu/about>.

[11] Accounting Standards | Governance | Publications and Resources [Internet]; New York, NY: International Federation of Accountants [cited 2013 May 4]. Available from: <http://www.ifac.org/publications-resources>.

[12] Audit and Attest Standards, Including Clarified Standards [Internet]; Durham, NC: American Institute of Certified Public Accountants [cited 2013 June 14]. Available from: <http://www.aicpa.org/Research/Standards/AuditAttest/Pages/audit%20and%20attest%20standards.aspx>.

[13] Audit Program Protocol [Internet]. Washington, DC: Department of Health and Human Services, Office for Civil Rights [cited 2013 July 18]. Available from: <http://www.hhs.gov/ocr/privacy/hipaa/enforcement/audit/protocol.html>.

[14] Become a CPA [Internet]; Durham, NC: American Institute of Certified Public Accountants [cited 2013 May 4]. Available from: <http://www.aicpa.org/BecomeACPA/Pages/BecomeaCPA.aspx>.

[15] Category: OWASP Project [Internet]; Bel Air, MD: OWASP Foundation [cited 2013 May 4]. Available from: <https://www.owasp.org/index.php/Category:OWASP_Project>.

[16] Certification—ISO [Internet]; Geneva: International Organization for Standardization [cited 2013 June 7]. Available from: <http://www.iso.org/iso/home/standards/certification.htm>.

[17] Certification Body Directory [Internet]; London: Standards.org [cited 2013 Jul 14]. Available from: <http://www.standards.org/certification_bodies/>.

[18] CIA Eligibility Requirements [Internet]; Altamonte Springs, FL: Institute of Internal Auditors [cited 2013 May 4]. Available from: <https://na.theiia.org/certification/CIA-Certification/Pages/Eligibility-Requirements.aspx>.

[19] CISSP—Certified Information Systems Security Professional [Internet]; Vienna, VA: International Information Systems Security Certification Consortium [cited 2013 May 4]. Available from: <https://www.isc2.org/cissp/default.aspx>.

[20] The CITP Credential [Internet]; Durham, NC: American Institute of Certified Public Accountants [cited 2013 May 4]. Available from: <http://www.aicpa.org/InterestAreas/InformationTechnology/Membership/Pages/CITPOverview.aspx>.

[21] Clarity of IAASB Standards [Internet]; New York, NY: International Federation of Accountants [cited 2013 May 4]. Available from: <http://www.ifac.org/auditing-assurance/projects/clarity-iaasb-standards-completed>.

[22] COBIT 4.1: Framework for IT Governance and Control [Internet]; Rolling Meadows, IL: ISACA [cited 2013 May 4]. Available from: <http://www.isaca.org/Knowledge-Center/COBIT/Pages/Overview.aspx>.

[23] COBIT 5: A Business Framework for the Governance and Management of Enterprise IT [Internet]; Rolling Meadows, IL: ISACA [cited 2013 May 4]. Available from: <http://www.isaca.org/COBIT/Pages/Overview.aspx>.

[24] COBIT 5 Product Family [Internet]; Rolling Meadows, IL: ISACA [cited 2013 May 4]. Available from: <http://www.isaca.org/COBIT/Pages/Product-Family.aspx>.

[25] Code of Ethics [Internet]; Altamonte Springs, FL: Institute of Internal Auditors [cited 2013 May 4]. Available from: <https://na.theiia.org/standards-guidance/mandatory-guidance/Pages/Code-of-Ethics.aspx>.

[26] Code of Professional Ethics [Internet]; Rolling Meadows, IL: ISACA [cited 2013 May 4]. Available from: <http://www.isaca.org/Certification/Code-of-Professional-Ethics/Pages/default.aspx>

[27] CSIC: Twenty Critical Security Controls [Internet]; Bethesda, MD: SANS Institute [cited 2013 May 4]. Available from: <http://www.sans.org/critical-security-controls/>.

[28] Definition of Internal Auditing [Internet]; Altamonte Springs, FL: Institute of Internal Auditors [cited 2013 May 4]. Available from: <https://na.theiia.org/standards-guid-ance/mandatory-guidance/Pages/Definition-of-Internal-Auditing.aspx>.

[29] FIPS Publications [Internet]. Gaithersburg, MD: National Institute of Standards and Technology [created 2007 July 3; updated 2012 March 6; cited 2012 March 24]. Available from: <http://csrc.nist.gov/publications/PubsFIPS.html>.

[30] The IEEE Standards Association [Internet]; Piscataway, NJ: Institute of Electrical and Electronics Engineers [cited 2013 May 4]. Available from: <http://standards.ieee.org>.

[31] IIA Certification [Internet]; Altamonte Springs, FL: Institute of Internal Auditors [cited 2013 May 4]. Available from: <https://na.theiia.org/certification/Pages/Certification.aspx>.

[32] Department of Defense Information assurance workforce improvement program. Washington, DC: Department of Defense; 2005. [DoD Manual 8570.01-M].

[33] The Internal Audit Function [Internet]; Altamonte Springs, FL: Institute of Internal Auditors [cited 2013 Jun 14]. Available from: <https://na.theiia.org/standards-guid-ance/topics/pages/the-internal-audit-function.aspx>.

[34] International Association of Computer Investigative Specialists [Internet]; Leesburg, VA: IACIS [cited 2013 May 4]. Available from: <https://www.iacis.com/certification/default_cert>.

[35] International Professional Practices Framework [Internet]; Altamonte Springs, FL: Institute of Internal Auditors [cited 2013 May 4]. Available from: <https://na.theiia.org/standards-guidance/Pages/Standards-and-Guidance-IPPF.aspx>.

[36] International Standards of Supreme Audit Institutions (ISSAI) [Internet]; Vienna: International Organization of Supreme Audit Institutions [cited 2013 May 4]. Available from: <http://www.issai.org/composite-347.htm>.

[37] International Society of Forensic Computer Examiners [Internet]; Brentwood, TN: ISFCE [cited 2013 May 4]. Available from: <http://www.isfce.org>.

[38] INTOSAI.org: About Us [Internet]; Vienna: International Organization of Supreme Audit Institutions [cited 2013 May 4]. Available from: <http://www.intosai.org/about-us.html>.

[39] INTOSAI.org: Membership List [Internet]; Vienna: International Organization of Supreme Audit Institutions [cited 2013 May 4]. Available from: <http://www.intosai.org/ organisation/membership-list.html>.

[40] ISACA Certification: IT Audit, Security, Governance and Risk [Internet]; Rolling Meadows, IL: ISACA [cited 2013 May 4]. Available from: <http://www.isaca.org/CERTIFICATION/Pages/default.aspx>.

[41] Open Standards Compliance [Internet]; Palo Alto, CA: Open Source Initiative [cited 2013 Jul 14]. Available from: <http://opensource.org/osr-compliance>.

[42] Organization Overview | IFAC [Internet]; New York, NY: International Federation of Accountants [cited 2013 May 4]. Available from: <http://www.ifac.org/about-ifac/organization-overview>.

[43] PCI SSC Data Security Standards Overview [Internet]; Wakefield, MA: PCI Security Standards Council [cited 2013 May 4]. Available from: <https://www.pcisecurity-standards.org/security_standards/index.php>.

[44] Quality Certification [Internet]; Milwaukee, WI: American Society for Quality [cited 2013 May 4]. Available from: <http://prdweb.asq.org/certification/control/index>.

[45] Register of Statutory Auditors [Internet]; Edinburgh, UK: Institute of Chartered Accountants of Scotland [updated 2013 July 8; cited 2013 July 9]. Available from: <http://www.auditregister.org.uk/Forms/Default.aspx>.

[46] Registered Firms [Internet]; Washington, DC: Public Company Accounting Oversight Board [cited 2013 Jul 9]. Available from: <http://pcaobus.org/Registration/Firms/Pages/RegisteredFirms.aspx>.

[47] Security Technical Implementation Guides [Internet]. Defense Information Systems Agency, Information Assurance Support Environment [updated 2011 February 14; cited 2012 February 18]. Available from: <http://iase.disa.mil/stigs/index.html>.

[48] Service Organization Control (SOC) Reports [Internet]; Durham, NC: American Institute of Certified Public Accountants [cited 2013 May 4]. Available from: <http://www.aicpa.org/InterestAreas/FRC/AssuranceAdvisoryServices/Pages/SORHome.aspx>.

[49] Standards for IS Audit and Assurance [Internet]; Rolling Meadows, IL: ISACA [cited 2013 May 4]. Available from: <http://www.isaca.org/Knowledge-Center/Standards/Pages/Standards-for-IT-Audit-and-Assurance-English-.aspx>.

[50] State Security Breach Notification Laws [Internet]; Washington, DC: National Conference of State Legislatures [updated 2012 August 20; cited 2013 July 18]. Available from: <http://www.ncsl.org/issues-research/telecom/security-breach-notification-laws.aspx>.

[51] Statements on Auditing Standards [Internet]; Durham, NC: American Institute of Certified Public Accountants [cited 2013 May 4]. Available from: <http://www.aicpa.org/Research/Standards/AuditAttest/Pages/SAS.aspx>.

[52] Statements on Standards for Attestation Engagements [Internet]; Durham, NC: American Institute of Certified Public Accountants [cited 2013 May 4]. Available from: <http://www.aicpa.org/Research/Standards/AuditAttest/Pages/SSAE.aspx>.

[53] Systems and Network Auditor Certification: GSNA [Internet]; Bethesda, MD: SANS Institute [cited 2013 May 4]. Available from: <http://www.giac.org/{give link to full address}certification/systems-network-auditor-gsna>.

[54] U.S. Government Configuration Baseline (USGCG) [Internet]. Gaithersburg, MD: National Institute of Standards and Technology, Information Technology Laboratory [created 2010 February 19; updated 2013 June 3; cited 2013 June 7]. Available from: <http://usgcb.nist.gov>.

Acronyms

Acronyms and abbreviations

ADP	Automatic Data Processing
AICPA	American Institute of Certified Public Accountants
ANAB	American National Accreditation Board
ANSI	American National Standards Institute
APT	Advanced Persistent Threat
ASQ	American Society for Quality
ATO	Authority (or Approval or Authorization) to Operate
BCP	Business Continuity Plan
BPMM	Business Process Maturity Model
C&A	Certification and Accreditation
CAP	Certified Authorization Professional
CC	Common Criteria
CCA	Clinger–Cohen Act
CCE	Certified Computer Examiner
CCEVS	Common Criteria Evaluation and Validation Scheme
CCFE	Certified Computer Forensics Examiner
CCFP	Certified Cyber Forensics Professional
CCM	Cloud Controls Matrix
CCSA	Certification in Control Self-Assessment
CEH	Certified Ethical Hacker
CEPT	Certified Expert Penetration Tester
CERT	Computer Emergency Response Team
CESG	Communications-Electronics Security Group
CFPB	Consumer Finance and Protection Bureau
CFCE	Certified Forensic Computer Examiner
CFO	Chief Financial Officer
CFR	Code of Federal Regulations
CFSA	Certified Financial Services Auditor
CGAP	Certified Government Auditing Professional
CGEIT	Certified in the Governance of Enterprise Information Technology
CHFI	Certified Hacking Forensic Investigator
CIA	Certified Internal Auditor
CIA	Confidentiality, Integrity, Availability
CIO	Chief Information Officer
CISA	Certified Information Systems Auditor
CISM	Certified Information Systems Manager
CISO	Chief Information Security Officer

CISSP	Certified Information Systems Security Professional
CITP	Certified Information Technology Professional
CGAP	Certified Government Accounting Professional
CM	Configuration Management
CMMI	Capability Maturity Model Integration
CMMI-ACQ	Capability Maturity Model Integration for Acquisition
CMMI-DEV	Capability Maturity Model Integration for Development
CMMI-SVC	Capability Maturity Model Integration for Services
CMVP	Cryptologic Module Validation Program
COBIT	Control Objectives for Information and Related Technology
CONOPS	Concept of Operations
COOP	Continuity of Operations
COSO	Committee of Sponsoring Organizations of the Treadway Commission
COTS	Commercial Off-the-Shelf
CP	Contingency Plan
CPA	Certified Public Accountant
CRISC	Certified in Risk and Information Systems Control
CRMA	Certification in Risk Management Assurance
CSIRT	Computer Security Incident Response Team
CVE	Common Vulnerabilities and Exposures
DISA	Defense Information Systems Agency
DHS	Department of Homeland Security
DoD	Department of Defense
DR	Disaster Recovery
EA	Enterprise Architecture
EC	European Community
EC	European Council
ECPA	Electronic Communications Privacy Act
EDP	Electronic Data Processing
EGAOB	European Group of Auditors' Oversight Bodies
ERM	Enterprise Risk Management
EU	European Union
FDCC	Federal Desktop Core Configuration
FedRAMP	Federal Risk and Authorization Management Program
FERC	Federal Energy Regulatory Commission
FFIEC	Federal Financial Institutions Examination Council
FIPS	Federal Information Processing Standards
FISCAM	Federal Information System Controls Audit Manual
FISMA	Federal Information Security Management Act
GAAS	Generally Accepted Auditing Standards
GAO	Government Accountability Office
GAS	Government Auditing Standards
GCFA	GIAC Certified Forensic Analyst

GCFE	GIAC Certified Forensic Examiner
GIAC	Global Information Assurance Certification
GLBA	Graham–Leach–Bliley Act
GRC	Governance, Risk Management, and Compliance
GSA	General Services Administration
GSNA	GIAC Systems and Network Auditor
GTAG	Global Technology Audit Guide
HHS	Department of Health and Human Services
HIPAA	Health Insurance Portability and Accountability Act
HITECH	Health Information Technology for Economic and Clinical Health Act
IA	Information Assurance
IaaS	Infrastructure as a Service
IAASB	International Auditing and Assurance Standards Board
IACIS	International Association of Computer Investigative Specialists
IACRB	Information Assurance Certification Review Board
IAM	Infosec Assessment Methodology
IDEAL	Initiating, Diagnosing, Establishing, Acting, and Learning
IDS	Intrusion Detection System
IEC	International Electrotechnical Commission
IEEE	Institute of Electrical and Electronics Engineers
IFAC	International Federation of Accountants
IIA	Institute of Internal Auditors
INFOSEC	Information Security
INTOSAI	International Organization of Supreme Audit Institutions
IP	Internet Protocol
IPPF	International Professional Practices Framework
IPS	Intrusion Prevention System
IPv6	Internet Protocol Version 6
IR	Incident Response
IRM	Information Resources Management
IRS	Internal Revenue Service
ISA	International Society for Automation
ISA	International Standard on Auditing
ISACA	Information Systems Audit and Control Association
ISAE	International Standards for Assurance Engagements
(ISC)^2	International Information Systems Security Certification Consortium
ISFCE	International Society of Forensic Computer Examiners
ISMS	Information Security Management System
ISO	International Organization for Standardization
ISSAI	International Standards of Supreme Audit Institutions
IT	Information Technology
ITIL	Information Technology Infrastructure Library
ITSCM	IT Service Continuity Management

IV&V	Independent Verification and Validation
JAB	Japan Accreditation Board
MOF	Microsoft Operations Framework
NERC	North American Electricity Reliability Corporation
NRC	Nuclear Regulatory Commission
NIST	National Institute of Standards and Technology
NSA	National Security Agency
NVD	National Vulnerability Database
NVLAP	National Voluntary Laboratory Accreditation Program
OCR	Office for Civil Rights
OCSP	Offensive Security Certified Professional
OECD	Organisation for Economic Cooperation and Development
OMB	Office of Management and Budget
OMG	Object Management Group
OSCP	Offensive Security Certified Professional
OWASP	Open Web Application Security Project
PaaS	Platform as a Service
PCAOB	Public Company Accouting Oversight Board
PCI DSS	Payment Card Industry Data Security Standards
PDCA	Plan-Do-Check-Act
PHI	Protected Health Information
PIA	Privacy Impact Assessment
PII	Personally Identifiable Information
PIOB	Public Interest Oversight Board
PMBOK	Project Management Body of Knowledge
PMI	Project Management Institute
POA&M	Plan of Action and Milestones
PRA	Paperwork Reduction Act
RA	Risk Assessment
RMF	Risk Management Framework
RTM	Requirements Traceability Matrix
SaaS	Software as a Service
SACM	Service Asset and Configuration Management
SANS	SysAdmin, Audit, Networking, and Security
SAS	Statement on Auditing Standards
SCA	Security Control Assessment
SCAP	Security Content Automation Protocol
SDLC	System Development Life Cycle
SEI	Software Engineering Institute
SERVQUAL	Service Quality
SIEM	Security Information and Event Management
SOC	Service Organizational Controls
SOX	Sarbanes–Oxley Act

SP	Special Publication
SSAE	Statements on Standards for Attestation Engagements
SSCP	Systems Security Certified Practitioner
STIG	Security Technical Implementation Guide
TCSEC	Trusted Computer System Evaluation Criteria
TQM	Total Quality Management
UKAS	United Kingdom Accreditation Service
USC	United States Code
US-CERT	United States Computer Emergency Response Team
USGCB	United States Government Configuration Baseline
VPN	Virtual Private Network

Index

Note: Page numbers followed by "*f*", "*t*" and "*b*" refers to figures, tables and boxes respectively.